WYATT: THE CRITICAL HERITAGE

THE CRITICAL HERITAGE SERIES

GENERAL EDITOR: B. C. SOUTHAM, M.A., B.LITT.(OXON.)
Formerly Department of English, Westfield College, University of London

---

For a list of books in the series see the back end paper

WYATT

THE CRITICAL HERITAGE

Edited by
PATRICIA THOMSON
Reader in English University of London

ROUTLEDGE & KEGAN PAUL: LONDON AND BOSTON

First published in 1974
by Routledge & Kegan Paul Ltd
Broadway House, 68–74 Carter Lane,
London EC4V 5EL and
9 Park Street,
Boston, Mass. 02108, USA
© Patricia Thomson 1974
ISBN 0 7100 7907 9
Library of Congress Catalog Card No. 74–79362

Set in Bembo 11 pt 1 pt leaded
and printed in Great Britain
by W & J Mackay Limited, Chatham

General Editor's Preface

The reception given to a writer by his contemporaries and near-contemporaries is evidence of considerable value to the student of literature. On one side we learn a great deal about the state of criticism at large and in particular about the development of critical attitudes towards a single writer; at the same time, through private comments in letters, journals or marginalia, we gain an insight upon the tastes and literary thought of individual readers of the period. Evidence of this kind helps us to understand the writer's historical situation, the nature of his immediate reading-public, and his response to these pressures.

The separate volumes in the *Critical Heritage Series* present a record of this early criticism. Clearly, for many of the highly productive and lengthily reviewed nineteenth- and twentieth-century writers, there exists an enormous body of material; and in these cases the volume editors have made a selection of the most important views, significant for their intrinsic critical worth or for their representative quality—perhaps even registering incomprehension!

For earlier writers, notably pre-eighteenth century, the materials are much scarcer and the historical period has been extended, sometimes far beyond the writer's lifetime, in order to show the inception and growth of critical views which were initially slow to appear.

In each volume the documents are headed by an Introduction, discussing the material assembled and relating the early stages of the author's reception to what we have come to identify as the critical tradition. The volumes will make available much material which would otherwise be difficult of access and it is hoped that the modern reader will be thereby helped towards an informed understanding of the ways in which literature has been read and judged.

B.C.S.

Contents

Acknowledgments

I should like to thank the following copyright-holders and publishers for permission to quote from various works: the University of London Press for the extracts from A. K. Foxwell's *The Poems of Sir Thomas Wyatt* (1913); Mrs Pamela Rodgers Berdan and her sisters for the passage from J. M. Berdan's *Early Tudor Poetry* (1920); Mr Stephen Tillyard and Chatto & Windus for passages from the introduction to E. M. W. Tillyard's *Selected Poems of Sir Thomas Wyatt* (1929); *The Times Literary Supplement* for the long review of Tillyard's *Selected Poems of Sir Thomas Wyatt* (19 September 1929); the Clarendon Press for the passage on Wyatt from C. S. Lewis's *English Literature in the Sixteenth Century* (1954).

It is also a pleasure to thank the Principal and English Department of Queen Mary College, University of London, for a term's study leave in which to pursue work on this book, and the Principal and Senior Common Room of St Hugh's College, Oxford for generously providing me with an asylum in which to do it. Finally I thank the Thomson and Vickery families for encouragement as well as practical help.

Introduction

The majority of critics can be expected only to parrot the opinions of the last master of criticism; among more independent minds a period of destruction, of preposterous over-estimation, and of successive fashions takes place, until a new authority comes to introduce some order. And it is not merely the passage of time and accumulation of new artistic experience, nor the ineradicable tendency of the great majority of men to repeat the opinions of those few who have taken the trouble to think, nor the tendency of a nimble but myopic majority of men to progenerate heterodoxies, that makes new assessments necessary. It is that no generation is interested in Art in quite the same way as any other; each generation, like each individual, brings to the contemplation of art its own categories of appreciation, makes its own demands upon art, and has its own uses of art.

(T. S. Eliot, *The Use of Poetry and the Use of Criticism* (1933), p. 109)

There are no 'masters of criticism' in T. S. Eliot's sense in the lifetime (1503–42) of Sir Thomas Wyatt, nor indeed, perhaps excepting Sir Philip Sidney, before the Restoration. Notwithstanding that, there is plenty of 'parroting' about him amongst the early commentators.

John Leland, Henry VIII's antiquary, and Henry Howard, Earl of Surrey are elegists, not critics.[1] Theirs is epideictic rhetoric with prominent use of the 'outdoing' convention proper to panegyric. For the patriotic Leland, England's Wyatt outdoes Italy's Dante and Petrarch, uniting their eloquence (No. 2b):

> Bella suum merito iactet florentia Dantem.
> Regia Petrarchæ carmina Roma probet.
> His non inferior patrio sermone Viatus
> Eloquij secum qui decus omne tulit.

Leland gives more, though by no means exclusive, attention to the man of letters. Wyatt's poetry receives almost immediate attention (No. 2a):

> ab ore profluebant
> musarum numeri rotundiores.

That it was an influence on Surrey's is brought out in No. 2c. Wyatt's eloquence is again affirmed by Leland in Nos 2e and 2i, while his songs are praised in No. 2g. Leland is the first to bring out Wyatt's importance as a refiner of the 'vulgar' tongue, a theme to be taken up in the next generation by Puttenham (1589), and thereafter parroted for a number of years.

For Surrey, more the man of public affairs than Leland, Wyatt's poetry was only part of his total achievement, and particularly his achievement, politically, in advancing England's interests, and also of setting a high example of wisdom and morality. In praising the poetry he, too, uses the 'outdoing' convention, hardly offering a critical estimate. Wyatt had (No. 3d):

> A hand, that taught what might be said in ryme,
> That reft Chaucer the glorie of his wytte,
> A marke the which, (vnperfytyd for tyme)
> Some may approche but neuer none shall hytte.

The idea that Wyatt's poetry marked a new era, in some ways superseding the Chaucerian, was soon to catch on.[2] But Leland was right about the relation between Wyatt and Surrey. And the truest sign that Surrey's elegiac praise of Wyatt's work is founded on a real knowledge and proper appraisal of it is shown by the fact that he also honours it by imitation. As commander at Boulogne in 1545–6 he recalled Wyatt's frustration as ambassador in Spain in 1537–9. 'At Mountzon thus I restles rest in Spayne' (LXXI) is expanded in Surrey's lines:[3]

> amiddes the hylles in base Bullayne;
> Where I am now, as restlesse to remayne,
> Against my will, full pleased with my payn.

Again, in the epitaph (No. 3c) he speaks of those who 'yeld Cesars teres uppon Pompeius hedd', following Wyatt's use of this classical topic in the sonnet, 'Caesar, when that the traytour of Egipt' (III).

Before the estimates of Leland and Surrey could be generally endorsed, obviously Wyatt's work had to reach a wider circle than theirs and other courtiers'. *The Quyete of Mynde*, printed in 1528, was the only publication of his lifetime. And this prose translation from Budé's Latin version of Plutarch's *De Tranquillitate* has contributed little to his reputation. Until its republication in 1931 it seems to have been forgotten. It may be noted in passing, however, that the preface (No. 1) characterizes Wyatt's prose style, his 'shorte maner of speche', fairly adequately.

Meanwhile, the poems gradually penetrated beyond the court circle. In about 1545, Thomas Whythorne, the musician, was engaged in copying out for his master, John Heywood, poems by Wyatt, Surrey, and William More. Afterwards giving himself to 'imitate and follow their trades and devices in writing,'[4] he becomes the first known pupil of the early Tudor poets. He knew the lyrics and satires well. For instance he quotes, obviously from memory, fom Wyatt's first satire,[5] while his 'Misdeem me not without cause why'[6] imitates Wyatt's lyric 'Disdain me not without desert' (CCLXVI).

But at this early stage it was, almost certainly, Wyatt's longest and most ambitious poem, the translation of the Penitential Psalms, that received most acclaim. Leland, in 'Viatus psaltes' (No. 2h) and Surrey (No. 3a) had distinguished them by special tributes. Later, in a manuscript version of part of *A Mirror for Magistrates*, an anonymous poet praises the 'sacred psalmes' by 'worthy wiat, worthiest of them all' (No. 5). In 1549 *Certayn Psalmes* came out under their author's name, the first of his poems to appear in print. The popularity and early publication of the Psalms fits in well with the immediately posthumous image of Wyatt as sage rather than as trivial songster or satirist. It also brings the important reminder that religious poetry held its own with secular right through the sixteenth century. Possibly Surrey's translations from the Bible were held in similar high esteem, while much later, in the 1580s, Sir Philip Sidney was to remind readers of his *Apologie for Poetrie* of the poetic and aesthetic appeal of the Bible.

What was later to be regarded as the most valuable part of Wyatt's work brought up the rear on 5 June 1557. Then the 'vngentle horders vp' of early Tudor lyrics, that is, those who clung to manuscript versions, or wrote them out in their commonplace books, at last met defeat with the publication of Richard Tottel's 'Miscellany' of *Songes and Sonettes written by the ryght honorable Lorde Henry Haward late Earle of Surrey and other*. The most prominent 'other' is Wyatt. From this point his name becomes inextricably linked with, and even subordinate to, Surrey's. Surrey's rank and the publication of his *Aeneid*, also in 1557, helped to give him precedence. Furthermore, he not only figures in splendid isolation on Tottel's title-page, but also introduces the anthology with thirty-six poems. Wyatt follows up with ninety pieces, the largest single contribution, and Nicholas Grimald with forty, while the ninety-five by 'uncertain authors' bring the volume to a close. Tottel's Preface reveals the novelty and importance of Wyatt and Surrey, and of the remoteness of these courtiers' 'statelinesse' from the 'rude skill of common eares', an antithesis which rapidly became the sixteenth-century critics' stock-in-trade. Tottel is also in tune with his age when, anticipating Sidney, Spenser and others, he boasts that English can equal Latin and Italian lyric (No. 4):

That to haue wel written in verse, yea & in small parcelles, deserueth great praise the workes of diuers Latines, Italians, and other, doe proue sufficiently. That our tong is able in that kynde to do as praiseworthely as ye rest, the honorable stile of the noble earle of Surrey, and the weightinesse of the depe-witted sir Thomas Wyatt the elders work, with seuerall graces in sondry good English writers, doe show abundantly.

Though sixteenth-century critical comments are, generally, too vague to last, Tottel's on Wyatt's weightiness and depth of thought weathers exceptionally well. The Preface is also of interest in that it touches on the proud theme that England can challenge other languages and litera-tures, a patriotism voiced increasingly as the century proceeds. The part played in it by Wyatt and Surrey is a favourite theme of Puttenham (No. 6), and is not dead till at least Nott's day, as his reference to 'these two great reformers of our language' shows (No. 9).

Tottel's fear that only the learned would appreciate his 'treasure' is proved groundless by the ignorant Slender's wistful acknowledgment that it would assist his wooing: 'I had rather than forty shillings I had my book of Songs and Sonnets here.'[7] The 'Miscellany', in fact, caught on quickly. It was republished, with additions, on 31 July 1557, and retained its popularity until superseded by more modern anthologies such as the Sidneian *Phoenix Nest* (1593). Editions appeared in 1559, 1565, 1567, 1585, and 1587, after which 'Tottel', and with him Wyatt and Surrey, practically fell silent for one hundred and thirty years. Before that happened, however, there was room for comment more learned than Slender's.

Roger Ascham, though ardently at one with Tottel in the wish to proclaim a national literature, was, in fact, *too* learned to get much out of the 'Miscellany'. It does not reach his neo-classical standard. Apart from two pieces by Grimald, which he overlooked, it contains no unrhymed verse. In *The Scholemaster*, written between 1563 and 1568 and published in 1570, Ascham praises Surrey as 'the first of all English men, in translating the fourthe book of *Virgill*', in which he 'auoyded the fault of Ryming'.[8] Wyatt is obviously the lesser poet in this point of view, for blank verse is the only important new early Tudor form with which he does not experiment. Nevertheless, Ascham gives him brief mention, with Chaucer, Surrey, Norton and other gentlemen, who, 'to their praise', have gone far in imitating the ancients, only erring in following 'rather the *Gothes* in Ryming, than the Greekes in trew versifying'.[9] Blank verse, though flourishing in Elizabethan drama, was never seriously to challenge rhyme, particularly in English lyric poetry. Apart from the few experiments with quantitative verse made in the late 1570s and early 1580s by Sidney and his friends,[10] Ascham's lead was followed only spasmodically, as, for example, by Thomas Campion.

Though the 1560s and 1570s yield little critical comment on Wyatt's lyrical or other gifts, knowledge of his work is shown in both imitation and parody. During these decades he is not superseded as one of the leading poets of the century. George Turbervile (1540–95?) is a blatant plagiarist. Wyatt's sonnet 'You that in love finde lucke and habundance' (XCII) is imitated in Turbervile's 'You that in May haue bathde in blis'.[11] His 'You hollow hilles and vallies wide'[12] is a long and free version of Wyatt's 'Resound my voyse, ye woodes that here me plain' (XXII). Turbervile's choice and imitation of Petrarch's poems often follow Wyatt's precedent: he, too, renders 'Ite caldi sospiri',[13] for example. Wyatt encouraged the sixteenth-century taste for proverbial sayings. His 'Sauf that a clogg doeth hang yet at my hele' (CV, 86) reappears in Turbervile's work as 'Though at my heele a cruell clogge they tye'.[14]

No account of sixteenth-century lyric is complete without some reference to puritanical condemnation of the vain amatorious stuff it so often contains. John Hall's *The Courte of Vertu* is a religious counterblast to such secular anthologies as 'Tottel'. Why, as George Herbert was later to complain, should no ink be used to praise God rather than women? Accordingly Hall makes religious parodies of well-known lyrics by Wyatt. 'Blame not my lute' (CCV) reappears in pious dress:[15]

> Blame not my lute though it doe sounde
> The rebuke of your wicked sinne,
> But rather seke as ye are bound
> To know what case that ye are in,

and 'My lute awake' (LXVI) as follows:[16]

> My lute awake and prayse the lord,
> My heart and handes thereto accord:
> Agreing as we haue begon,
> To synge out of Gods holy worde.
> And so procede tyll we haue done.

One of Wyatt's contemporaries, Sir Brian Tuke, introducing William Thynne's edition of *The Workes of Geffray Chaucer* (1532), declares that 'it is moche to be marueyled/howe in his tyme/whan doutless all good letters were layd a slepe throughout the worlde . . . soche an excellent poet in our tonge/shulde as it were (nature repugnyng) sprynge and aryse.'[17] But Chaucer was in fact the anchor by which the sixteenth century hung on to all that was best in the native tradition. Wyatt himself, in the first satire (CV, 50-1), clearly recognizes his classic status. From the point of view of his own poetry, it is clearly an advantage that no Ascham prompted him into reaction against the 'barbarous' Middle Ages: many of his lyrics relate more closely to the immediate English past than to the Latins, Italians and other foreign influences stressed by Tottel.

Nevertheless, in criticism following Ascham, Chaucer, though given recognition is not given *appropriate* recognition. Spenser, in lowering his bucket into that 'well', is deliberately archaizing, cultivating the neo-medieval. For Sidney, Chaucer is of 'reuerent antiquity', one who did miraculously well, considering that he wrote 'in that mistie time'.[18] His view is consequently much the same as Tuke's. Though at heart no Ascham, Sidney shares the neo-classical view of a barbarous Middle Ages, which produced such 'rude' items as the ballad 'Chevy Chase', which 'being so euill apparrelled in the dust and cobwebbes of that vnciuill age, what would it worke trymmed in the gorgeous eloquence of *Pindar*?'[19] He trembles on the edge of the recognition that the medieval poems that so strangely moved him could yield criteria as valid as the classical or Italian. But he is too much a man of his age to trust fully to his instinct here. Whatever modern scholars find, those of the sixteenth century believed that a Renaissance had occurred. The Middle Ages seemed as far behind them as the Victorian Age seems behind us. They lived, in Sidney's words, in a comparatively 'cleare age', and that age had dawned in the reign of Henry VIII. Chaucer apart, this considerably limits Sidney's search for English poems having 'poeticall sinnewes'. Writing *An Apologie for Poetrie* in about 1583, he can find only Surrey's lyrics, Sackville's *Mirror for Magistrates*, and Spenser's *Shepheardes Calender*. He omits Wyatt's poems, either because he thinks them less valuable than Surrey's, or, more likely, because Wyatt was not socially on an equal with his partner, who uttered 'many things tasting of a noble birth'.[20] His *Apologie* was, of course, influential. Even so, it is difficult to account for William Webbe's failure to mention Wyatt in the much longer list of sixteenth-century poets, (including such names as Lord Vaux and Thomas Churchyard) given in *A Discourse of English Poetrie* (1586).[21]

A few years later, in 1589, George Puttenham in *The Arte of English Poesie* (No. 6) agrees on the need to polish rude English, finding the means not only in ancient Greece and Rome, but in modern Italy. For him, too, reform is essentially an affair for well-educated Englishmen, and it has now become abundantly clear that Wyatt and Surrey owe their sixteenth-century authority partly to their rank. Puttenham's treatise, which is on a larger scale than Sidney's and displays confidence in a larger group than his or Webbe's, attempts something new—a durimentary history of the national literature. 'Of the first age' were Chaucer, Gower, Lydgate, Langland and Skelton. John Skelton (d. 1529), though the elder contemporary of Wyatt and Surrey, is never, here, mentioned in the same breath. Rightly, from the neo-classical and Italianate viewpoint of later sixteenth-century critics, he is grouped with the medieval poets. Furthermore his 'vulgarity' cuts him off from the approval afforded to either the venerable antiquity of Chaucer or the modern refinement of Wyatt and Surrey. Puttenham, unfavourably impressed by Skelton's 'rayling', 'scofferry', 'Scurrilities and other ridiculous matters' could not conceive what worthiness entitled him to be poet laureate.[22] He creates, in fact, Pope's image of 'beastly Skelton'. Forgetting Skelton's reputation for learning, Puttenham, like his immediate predecessor among critics, found 'reform' the affair of modernistic gentlemen; and his eloquence seems to arise according to the enthusiasm he felt for what happened at the latter end of Henry VIII's reign.

sprong vp a new company of courtly makers, of whom Sir *Thomas Wyat* th'elder & *Henry* Earl of Surrey were the two chieftaines, who, hauing trauailed into Italie, and there tasted the sweete and stately measures and stile of the Italian Poesie, as nouices newly crept out of the schooles of *Dante Arioste* and *Petrarch*, they greatly pollished our rude & homely maner of vulgar Poesie from that it had bene before, and for that cause may iustly be sayed the first reformers of our English meetre and stile.

Puttenham takes up loudly and frequently the notion adumbrated by Leland, Surrey and Tottel, the improvement of the rough, rude vernacular. Wyatt and Surrey remain his only landmark. They were, he repeats, 'the first reformers & polishers of our vulgar Poesie' (No. 6e), and, again, 'the two chief lanternes of light to all others that haue since employed their pennes vpon English Poesie' (No. 6b). And, yet again, 'They were the most excellent makers of their time' (No. 6h). Puttenham uses them frequently to illustrate metrical and tropical devices, noting, for example, that alexandrines were not used by 'auncient makers . . . before Sir *Thomas Wyats* time' (No. 6c). There can be little doubt that Puttenham was largely responsible for establishing the historical importance of Wyatt and Surrey. He also fed the Elizabethan ambition, strong in such poets as Spenser, to 'overgo' the great Italians. He also recognizes their intrinsic merits. His critical terms, though not very sophisticated according to twentieth-century standards, are adequate for their time: 'sweet', 'stately', 'proper', 'natural'.

At the same time Puttenham blurs the historical picture. Though he always names Wyatt first, he does not distinguish him as Surrey's predecessor, and, by erroneously making Surrey too, 'travel into Italy', (No. 6a) he robs Wyatt of his unique claim to have been the first to Italianize English poetry.[23] Hence spring the unfounded beliefs, characteristic of later literary historians, that Wyatt and Surrey co-operated, and, even, that Wyatt was Surrey's pupil. Puttenham, who confesses to 'finde little difference' (No. 6b) between them, makes 'Wyatt and Surrey' into the single entity of the school textbook, as indivisible as 'Dryden and Pope' or 'Keats and Shelley'.

The continued influence of Wyatt, even in the 1590s, when new poetic voices were loud, is illustrated by the imitation of the effective phrasing from Wyatt's first satire (CV). The 'I cannot' sequence reaches its climax in line 76, 'I cannot, I; no, no, it will not be.' And this obviously lies behind John Marston's even more ferocious attacks on false values:[24]

> I cannot hold, I cannot I indure
> To view a big womb'd foggie clowde immure
> The radiant tresses of the quickning sunne.

Nevertheless, at about this time the impact of Wyatt—and, of course Surrey—begins to lose force. 'The Earle of Surrey and *Sir Thomas Wiat*, that are yet called the first refiners of the English tong':[25] Sir John Harington's appreciation, in the Preface to *Orlando Furiosi* (1591), though appreciative, has gained an air of cliché.

Francis Meres's *Palladis Tamia* (1598), being neither critical nor historical, is worth little mention. He bundles everything and everyone in. However, it is worth remark that, in an attempt to divide English poetry by kind and theme, he lists Wyatt and Surrey and Wyatt's friend Sir Francis Brian with the Elizabethans Sidney, Raleigh, Spenser, Daniel, Drayton etc. 'as the most passionate among vs to bewaile and bemoane the perplexities of loue'.[26]

Ben Jonson, whose sense of literary period is good, threw off, at an

uncertain date, the remark that Wyatt and Surrey, with Sir Thomas
More and other early Tudors 'were for their times admirable: and the
more because they began Eloquence with us.'[27] Perhaps he had picked
the idea up from William Camden, his schoolmaster, who, mentioning
by name Surrey only, used the by now outworn phrase: he was one
who 'first refined our homely English Poesie'.[28]

Michael Drayton's account 'Of Poets and Posie' (1627) differs little
from Puttenham's except that it is briefer and in verse. Having dwelt on
noble Chaucer and given 'honest Gower' a quick nod, he passes on to
the reign of Henry VIII and 'those small poems, which the title beare/Of
songs and sonnets' (No. 7). 'That times best makers', he lists as 'Princely
Surrey', Wyatt and Brian.

If at the beginning of the seventeenth century Wyatt is still a revered
father of English poetry, by the end he has become merely a historical
curiosity. Thomas Fuller[29] and David Lloyd[30] who give no evidence of
having read a line of his poetry, put him on record as an English
'worthy'. Such oblivion is natural in view of the notion of refinement
and wit first of the Cavalier, then of the Restoration poets and critics.
John Dryden, searching the past, Puttenham-like, for our first refiners,
picked upon Edmund Waller and Sir John Denham.[31] Surrey did not
fare much better than Wyatt. True, his pen is called 'matchless' in
Windsor Forest (1713), but Pope's interest is really in the 'noble hero' of
Windsor and lover of Geraldine, and he finds it necessary to append a
note on him as 'one of the first refiners of the English poetry; who
flourished in the time of Henry VIII'.[32]

In 1717, however, Tottel's 'Miscellany' was reprinted for the first
time since 1587, and a few eighteenth-century historians of literature
therefore notice Wyatt and Surrey. They are given short measure in
The Lives of the Poets (1753) by Theophilus Cibber, who considers
Surrey comparatively 'well-polished', while Wyatt is 'laboured' and
'artificial'.[33] This judgment, which was to prevail for over a century,
owes its authority not to Cibber, but to Thomas Warton whose
History of English Poetry (1774–81) contains a much more thorough investigation, and criticism not to be despised even today (No. 8). Apart
from his failure to realize that Surrey was Wyatt's junior, Warton is
factually accurate. To their poems he applies Johnsonian standards:
harmony of numbers, perspicuity, elegance, simplicity, imagination,
good sense and, above all 'Nature'. The 'natural' of one age tends to
become the 'artificial' of the next. Wyatt, accordingly, shares in the
eighteenth century's disapproval of Renaissance artifice and affectation,

9

such as was also found in Donne and the metaphysicals. 'His compliments', says Warton, 'like the modes of behaviour in that age, are
ceremonious and strained'. In recognizing the historical reasons for his
subject's artificiality, Warton rises superior to the Johnson of 'The Life
of Cowley'. His eye for sources and contemporary influences is also
more acute. 'It was from the capricious and over-strained invention of
the Italian poets that Wyatt was taught to torture the passion of love by
prolix and intricate comparisons and unnatural allusions.' Puttenham's
opinion is thus, within two centuries, totally reversed. The distinction
between Warton's position and, on the one hand, that of the sixteenth
century and, on the other, that of the twentieth, is revealed in the use of
'Italian' and 'metaphysical' as pejoratives. 'Nothing of the metaphysical
craft which marks the Italian poets' is found, to his pleasurable surprise,
in Surrey's sonnets. On the contrary, they have much 'tenderness,
simplicity and nature'. Warton is traditional in his preference of Surrey
to Wyatt, but compared with any preceding critic, gives more literary
reasons for it. He is the first genuinely to identify convincing qualitative
differences. 'Wyatt, although sufficiently distinguishable from the
common versifiers of his age, is confessedly inferior to Surrey in harmony of numbers, perspicuity of expression, and facility of phraseology.' Yet Warton is as fair as he can honestly be to Wyatt. Surrey's
'Give place ye ladies', which has 'almost the ease and gallantry of
Waller, is correct, polished, musical, elegant'. Wherever Wyatt, as in
'My lute awake' (LXVI) or 'Tagus farewell' (XCIV), follows suit he,
too, earns praise for simplicity, propriety etc. Warton's sound sense has
led him here to what were to become two perennial favourites. Finally,
his recognition of the historical and intrinsic value of Wyatt's satires
fully earns him his place as the first modern critic of early Tudor poetry.
Wyatt's 'genius was of the moral and didactic species; and his poems
abound more in good sense, satire and observations on life, than in
pathos or imagination.' 'Wyatt may justly be deemed the first polished
English satirist', while 'Myne owne John Poynz' (CV) contains 'spirited
and manly reflections'. Though Wyatt's supposed lack of imagination
has long since been called in question, no later critic has bettered the
comment on his satiric 'manliness'. Warton's chief critical deficiency is,
perhaps, the one noted by Nott (No. 9). He is too perfunctory as well
as misleading in his declaration that Wyatt 'co-operated with Surrey,
in having corrected the roughness of our poetic style'. In places he just
parrots his predecessors.

    Scholarship now takes over possession of Wyatt. Bishop Percy and

Thomas Stevens produced an edition of 'Tottel' (1795–1807). The Rev.
George Frederick Nott worked upon another which was accidentally
destroyed in 1812. His great industry was, however, even better applied
to the monumental editions of Surrey's and Wyatt's works, which
appeared respectively in 1815 and 1816 (No. 9). Knowledge of Wyatt's
poetry was hitherto based on Tottel's smoothed and corrected text.
Nott first used the Egerton (mainly Wyatt's manuscript) and Devonshire manuscripts. Though he remained vague on the relationship between Wyatt and Surrey, he made the first thorough investigation of
their foreign sources and their lives. He explored the State Papers, and
because they contain Wyatt's correspondence as diplomatist, he was led
to admire Wyatt's vigorous prose style. Otherwise, as, for example, in
his preference for the satires, Nott treads in Warton's footsteps, if with
greater firmness of tread. At the time (1816), it must be admitted, his
edition was more important in providing the material for criticism, than
criticism itself. The response was slow. In 1816 the *Edinburgh Review*,
tackling Nott's two volumes, dismissed Wyatt as 'a man of wit . . .
but in no true sense of the word . . . a poet', and turned attention
exclusively to Surrey. Another scholar of the period, John Payne
Collier, compares Wyatt and Surrey with their contemporary, Henry
Parker, Lord Morley, the translator of Petrarch's *Trionfi*—as if the three
translators of Petrarch did not leave Morley well in the rear.[34] But to
return to Nott, unfortunately none of the great Romantic critics,
Coleridge, Hazlitt, or Lamb seems to have taken up Nott's hefty
volumes. Furthermore, the 'Tottel' text continued to be used in all later
nineteenth-century editions, such as the Aldine (1831), Robert Bell's
(1854), and George Gilfillan's (1858) and, of course, in Edward Arber's
reprint of the 'Miscellany' (1870).

Robert Bell's contribution of 1854 to the Annotated Editions of the
English Poets (No. 10) marks a new stage in the historical and qualitative assessment of Wyatt, and as this sold for only half-a-crown, it may
be presumed to have reached a fairly wide audience. While Bell still
takes it for granted that Surrey is 'the better poet', he insists that 'Wyatt's
claims have never been adequately recognized.' Noting that Wyatt was
the elder and did not mix much with Surrey, he corrects Nott's assumption that he took over the iambic metre from Surrey. Likewise he en-
dorses his two great predecessors' high opinion of Wyatt's 'manliness'.
But owing to his historical understanding, he parts company with them
again, on the matter of his artificiality: 'He is said to be overcharged
with conceits; but, taking into account the sources from which he

borrowed, and the age in which he wrote, it would be more just to say that he is singularly free from conceits.' Bell also has a better understanding than any previous scholar of the principles of Wyatt's scansion, finding him generally 'regular and sonorous', especially if French and Italian accentuation be adopted. His insight gives him a glimpse of the contemporary view—say, Tottel's—of Wyatt's depth. Surrey, he admits, was 'more impassioned, and had a finer sensibility and a more exact taste. But Wyatt possesses high merits of another kind. His verse is more thoughtful than Surrey's, more compressed and weighty.'

Neither the Rev. George Gilfillan's edition of Wyatt's *Poetical Works* (1858) nor Edward Arber's reprint of 'Tottel' (1870) contains much critical comment. But Gilfillan's brief note on the purity of Wyatt's love lyrics, 'subduedly sensual', yet 'never contaminated by corruption'[35] is more balanced than many longer disquisitions. Arber finds space to exclaim at the 'many beautiful poems' he had found, only wondering that 'such Literary Treasures should have for so long been hid from the world at large'.[36] Meanwhile F. W. Palgrave includes two lyrics by Wyatt (and none by Surrey) in *The Golden Treasury* (1861), though his annotated copy of the Aldine Wyatt, in the British Museum, shows that the anthologist had not been converted by Bell. 'In all these pieces W. has very little sign of renaissance style—he is direct, English, wanting in truth ideals (or idealism?) whether of phrase or sentiment. His lover is sentimental only for himself.'[37] Though evidently not in this context so intended, the comment on Wyatt's direct Englishness is a compliment, and a matter of which too little has been said up to this date. But generally Palgrave, lacking Gilfillan's sanity, suspects that Wyatt is up to no good. His passion is not 'disinterested'.[38] The 'pretty', 'elegant', 'good' poems, the 'isolated note of true feeling' that Palgrave painstakingly notes are needles in a haystack, and more often the 'vulgar' or 'very poor' reward his search.[39] The universal favourite 'They fle from me' (XXXVII) is, for him, 'natural, a little too natural.'[40] Even sympathetic critics, such as Bell, found Wyatt's translation of Petrarch's 'Amor che nel pensier mio vive e regna' less 'poetical' than Surrey's: for Palgrave it is 'very inferior'.[41] His judgment, when not limited by notions of moral refinement, must be respected; but he is a reactionary critic of Wyatt.

Suspicion of the 'Tottel' text and the realization that smoothness is not a criterion with the 'early' Wyatt give importance to W. E. Simonds's researches. Chiefly interested in Wyatt's development from 'laborious awkwardness' to 'easy fluency',[42] he stops short of the modern faith in his deliberate roughness of style, and his thesis *Sir Thomas Wyatt and his Poems* (published in 1889) is otherwise in the nature of an academic curiosity. For Simonds attempts what, in the absence of sufficient external evidence is an impossibility, a complete chronology of Wyatt's poems. Periods of Entreaty, Attainment, Disappointment, and Recovery succeed each other with an emotional logic reminiscent of that which brings Dowden's Shakespeare at last to his 'Epoch of Reposeful Contemplation'.

Contrary to the general belief, however, Wyatt studies in the nineteenth century are, taken as a whole, neither unsympathetic nor perfunctory. They reach their culmination in W. J. Courthope's *History of English Poetry* (1897) (No. 11), which gives Wyatt full recognition, placing him, as it were, on the English literature syllabus. Furthermore, Wyatt, for Courthope, is no longer merely an important representative early Tudor figure and innovator, meet to be used as a foil to Surrey. The 'individual energy of his thought' marks him out as a poet in his own right. Even the uninspired translations reveal an 'energetic mind'. While in handling the sonnet Surrey's 'advance beyond Wyatt is remarkable', Courthope constantly topples on the edge of declaring a preference for Wyatt. For at the outset he admits that Surrey's poems 'have none of the vehement individuality and character' of his predecessor's.

Hence A. K. Foxwell (No. 12) could express satisfaction that the criticism of the last fifty years had been 'steadily increasing in appreciation of Wiat'. Her own appreciation, no doubt, carries her off her feet: '*Wiat's life and work* is a song of harmony. The "music of the spheres" is here.' (Her italics). Many of her ecstasies, as well as her dating of the poems by their order in the Egerton manuscript, are questionable. But both in her *Study of Wiat* (1911) and, even more, in her edition (1913), she has put all students in her debt by establishing the importance of the Egerton MS; in (if not with full success) trying to trace the history of the Devonshire; and, above all, in providing the best text since Nott's.

J. M. Berdan, whose *Early Tudor Poetry* (1920) (No. 13) remains a standard work, was not won over. This is not surprising, for he mocks most eulogies of Wyatt, and, indeed, of early Tudor Poetry as a whole. He praises a few anthology pieces, but finds Wyatt generally cold: 'This lack of emotion is apparently one of the reasons why critics call him "virile".' Surrey wins a chapter to himself, the last in a book 545 pages long, and ominously concluding 'Early Tudor literature is primarily interesting, therefore, because it is prentice work.'[43]

At this point the balance of approval and disapproval was fairly evenly held. H. E. Rollins, editor of the definitive Harvard edition of 'Tottel' (1928–9), himself of the opinion that Miss Foxwell had been 'over-enthusiastic about Wyatt's merits',[44] felt that there was no present danger of Wyatt's being underestimated. E. M. W. Tillyard (No. 14), on the other hand, called in 1929 'attention to an author, who, though sometimes appreciated justly, has never really received his due'. 'It is time', he adds, 'someone spoke up in Wyatt's praise.' Rather strangely, he declares that 'Wyatt's critics have gone wrong from the beginning.' But he has his reasons: he himself reverses the opinion, which lasted from Nott to Courthope, that the 'manly' satires are preferable to the lyrics. The lyrics, he explains, are traditional, English, dramatic, and, often Donne-like in their roughness.

Evidently, here, the twentieth century can no longer see the Renaissance through Ascham's, Sidney's or Puttenham's eyes. It has, rather, a vision of continuity, of the extension of the medieval tradition, both social and literary, into the sixteenth century. Hence if Wyatt wrought change it was within this medieval tradition, and the critical emphasis begins to fall on his medieval background.

Here, Tillyard also gives Wyatt his twentieth-century new look by making him answer some of the same needs as T. S. Eliot, or those which H. J. C. Grierson, and Eliot himself, did so much to revive. Tillyard himself probably owes something to E. K. Chambers, who, commenting in *Early English Lyrics* (1907) had remarked, incidentally, that 'the deeper accents of emotion, with much else that is the soul of literature, come back with Wyatt.'[45] Chambers, in turn, resuming the subject of Wyatt in 1933, seems to echo Tillyard: 'Wyatt's real affinities, if with any, are with John Donne.'[46] Neither critic has, however, a limitless approval, and the ghost of Berdan remains, at this stage, unexorcized. 'Most of the poems' are still, with Tillyard, 'apprentice work', and Wyatt was 'not at home', especially in the rondeau, sonnet, and epigram.[47] These constitute the 'exotic' writing, which Chambers thinks 'of little account'.

If that is, as Chambers claims, a 'sane estimate', the ensuing years produce more than one instance of critical insanity. In a notable essay[48] of 1946, Hallett Smith, for the first time, compares Wyatt's traditionally clumsy version of 'Amor che nel pensier mio vive e regna' *favourably* (my italics) with Surrey's. The sonnets are still only 'of minor importance' for Kenneth Muir in 1949. But the idea that they are more than 'mere exercises' is warmly espoused by J. W. Lever in 1956.[49] But the whole matter of 'clumsiness' is also connected with early Tudor metre; and here, Wyatt studies have benefited from the improved understanding promoted by C. S. Lewis's 'The Fifteenth-Century Heroic Line'.[50] Even Nott seems to have an inkling that there existed the so-called 'pausing' line, for he remarks on the 'old Rythmical line' to which Wyatt had been accustomed, and which he opposes to the regular iambic line introduced, he believed, by Surrey and influencing Wyatt's later work. However, work on metrics has been largely the achievement of the twentieth century. D. W. Harding[51] shows a particularly sensitive response to rhythm, and Sergio Baldi[52] has gone into the subject in great detail.

Nevertheless, Wyatt's metre and, indeed, his whole achievement—particularly, perhaps, his introduction of Italian forms into England—remain something of a mystery. 'The mystery of Wyatt is whether he knew what he was doing or whether he did not' (No. 15). In this much-quoted passage, the anonymous reviewer of Tillyard's *A Selection and a Study* (1929) is much to the point. It has to be remembered that he left no statement of his poetic purpose, and though, almost at the outset he was declared a 'reformer', he never, in his extant writings, claims to be one. So, *The Times Literary Supplement*'s reviewer is rightly cautious. But he goes so far as to call Wyatt 'a laborious worker for poetic technique', gives an excellent account of 'I fynde no peace' (XXV), and notes his 'extraordinary faculty for convincing the reader that he means what he says'.

For all his reservations Kenneth Muir's authority has done more than any other to establish Wyatt, since he believes that he is 'not flattered by selections in anthologies'.[53] So he has produced a series of editions, starting with *The Collected Poems* (1949), proceeding to *Sir Thomas Wyatt and his Circle*, (Liverpool, 1961) (the valuable Blage manuscript collection), *The Life and Letters of Sir Thomas Wyatt* (Liverpool, 1963)[54] and, finally, (in collaboration with Patricia Thomson), *Collected Poems of Sir Thomas Wyatt* (Liverpool, 1969).[55]

The response to Wyatt, in studies too numerous to be named separately, has been mainly but not wholly favourable, during the past few decades. Sergio Baldi (1953),[56] D. W. Harding (1954),[57] and Maurice Evans[58] are all modern enthusiasts, as is the present writer.[59] H. A. Mason[60] sharpens favour and disfavour. For the first time since the sixteenth century, Wyatt's Psalms are highly rated, and Mason also maintains the old admiration for the satires. At the same time he aims a staggering blow at the popular English love lyrics, in which, with few exceptions, 'there is not the slightest trace of poetic activity'. As yet it is impossible to judge whether his most original study is a sport or a new growing-point in Wyatt criticism. John Stevens,[61] for one, has acknowledged a debt to Mason's account of the love poems. Again, the reader comes fresh from Muir's edition of the *Unpublished Poems*, many of which he claims, 'are worthy to stand by Wyatt's whether he wrote them or not; and there are at least seven which will . . . be ranked with his masterpieces'.[62] He is at once brought up short by Ralph Lawrence's review: 'The collection is more of historical than literary interest. Wyatt writes below his best throughout, and his poems are pervaded by a somewhat artificial pathos which never succeeds in touching the reader's heart'.[63]

From this work of the last few decades it has been difficult to make a fair selection. Were it not for large copyright fees more of the twentieth-century critics would have been included. As it is, I hope I have made a fair choice, of C. S. Lewis (No. 16), who represents moderation in his view of Wyatt: he at least is not one of T. S. Eliot's 'parrots'. Wyatt appears in a chapter called 'Drab Age Verse'. As Lewis is at pains to point out, 'drab' is not intended as a pejorative, but as a means of distinguishing the unornate from what he calls the 'golden' poetry of the sixteenth century. Perhaps the terms 'plain' and 'aureate', commonly used of fifteenth-century poets—and it should not be forgotten that Wyatt is their immediate successor—would have appeared less loaded. Lewis is well aware, as was Tillyard, of the native tradition, and the first point he makes is, in fact, that in early sixteenth-century lyric there is a direct continuity with the medieval lyric, whose 'tune' had never been lost. He gives emphasis to the musical accompaniments for which (though the point has not, I believe, been proved) the lyrics, he presumes, have been written.

Lewis is as just as Tillyard in his balancing of the native and the Italianate in Wyatt. He perceives that even some of the translations from Petrarch are in medieval English vein. An obvious example is 'Myne Olde dere En'mye' (VIII), a rendering of a canzone of Petrarch's in the form of rhyme royal, one of the most popular English stanzas since Chaucer. He also rightly perceives great variability in Wyatt's Petrarchan sonnets, generally thinking them remote from Petrarch himself (a questionable point, of course). Lewis condemns—as who cannot?—'the terrible poulter's measure' which seems to have been Wyatt's invention. In considering Wyatt's rhythms generally he comes down in favour of the view that he is floundering, while at the same time he takes full and fair account of their many subtleties. This is a vexed question which will never, I think, be settled to everyone's satisfaction.

Again, Lewis, with typical fairness, gives both praise and blame to different passages from the Psalms. He is also just to the satires. He is not impressed by the terza rima introduced from Italy by Wyatt, and used, probably for the first time, in the first satire (CV). But clearly he responds, as so many have done, to the originality and vigour of this version of Luigi Alamanni's tenth Provençal satire.

Like Tillyard, Lewis gives pride of place to the lyrics. He cites an example of a bad one (CXXVII) and, to balance it, an ample selection of good ones. He is again showing the rather patchy and variable quality of Wyatt; and, finally, he effaces himself with the casual, noncommittal, 'His fame is in the ascendant.'

So it is. Surrey's status has not been improved, in the twentieth century, in a manner similar to Wyatt's. The praise conferred on him by his editor F. M. Padelford,[64] in 1920 and 1928, is, if anything, likely to be considered excessive. More recently, however, the balance has been redressed by Emrys Jones, who gives an excellent appreciative account of Surrey in his (unfortunately) incomplete edition.[65] For once we meet a writer who does not use Surrey as a stick with which to beat Wyatt—or *vice versa*.

'One of the most curious delusions in English literary history', said Muir in 1949, 'has been the assumption that Surrey is a better poet than Wyatt.'[66] But surely the assumptions of all periods have been, in their day, perfectly natural, and delusion (or enlightenment) relative to current tastes? As Eliot says, 'No generation is interested in Art in quite the same way as any other.' Surrey answers the eighteenth-century need for harmony of numbers no less than Wyatt does for our own taste for 'harsh verse', as much like Donne's as possible (if I may draw on my experience of undergraduates studying English literature). The assessments over the centuries, in the following pages will have done all they can if they are merely each 'wrong in some new way'.

NOTES

1 Other of Wyatt's elegists at the time of his death are Sir Antony St Leger, John Mason, Thomas Challoner and John Parkhurst.

2 Leland shares Surrey's view, while John Bale considers that Wyatt equals Chaucer in enriching native literature; 'in illustratione patrij sermonis,

Chaucerum plane adæquabant' (*Illustrium Maioris Britanniæ Scriptorum* . . . *Summarium*, 1548, f. 233ᵛ).

3 Henry Howard, Earl of Surrey, *Poems*, ed. Emrys Jones (164), no. 10.

4 *Autobiography of Thomas Whythorne*, ed. James M. Osborn (1961), p. 14.

5 Ibid., p. 45.

6 Ibid., p. 40.

7 Shakespeare, *The Merry Wives of Windsor* (*c.* 1599), I. i. 192.

8 Roger Ascham, *The Scholemaster* (1570), ed. Edward Arber (English reprints, 1920), p. 147.

9 Ibid., p. 145.

10 The keenest of Sidney's group, Gabriel Harvey, mentions Surrey as the first to write quantitative or blank verse (verses 'that stand vppon the number') in his 'Letter Book' (1573–80): see *Elizabethan Critical Essays*, ed. G. Gregory Smith (Oxford, 1904), I, p. 126. Richard Carew, in *The Excellency of the English Tongue* (1595–6), an endeavour to show that English has the graces of all other languages, exclaims 'Will you reade *Virgille*? take the Earll of Surrey' (ibid., II, p. 293). Francis Meres follows Ascham in praising Surrey for avoiding 'the faulte of ryming' (*Palladis Tamia*, ibid., II, p. 315).

11 *Epitaphes, Epigrams, Songs, and Sonets* (1567). Fascimile reprint by J. P. Collier (n.d.? 1870), pp. 195–8.

12 *Tragical Tales* (*c.* 1574), quoted from the edition of 1587, f. 158ʳ⁻ᵛ.

13 Ibid., f. 149ʳ, Cp. Wyatt, XX.

14 Ibid., f. 147ᵛ.

15 *The Courte of Vertu* (1565), ff. 74ʳ–76ᵛ.

16 Ibid., ff. 76ᵛ–78ʳ.

17 Op. cit., Aiiᵛ.

18 *An Apologie for Poetrie* (1595 ed.), in *Elizabethan Critical Essays*, ed. G. Gregory Smith (Oxford, 1904), I, p. 196.

19 Ibid., loc. cit.

20 Ibid., I, p. 196.

21 Smith, op. cit., I, p. 242.

22 *The Arte of English Poesie* (1569), ed. G. D. Wilcock and A. Walker (Cambridge, 1936), pp. 60, 62.

23 An idea to which currency was given by Thomas Nashe's delightful fiction of Surrey in Italy, in *The Vnfortunate Traveller* (1594).

24 *The Scovrge of Villanie* (1598), II, 1–3: see Marston, *The Poems*, ed. Arnold Davenport (Liverpool, 1961).

25 Smith, ed. cit., II, p. 219.

26 Ibid., II, p. 320.

27 Printed posthumously in *Timber: or Discoveries* (1640): see Ben Jonson, *Works*, ed. C. H. Herford and Percy Simpson (1947), VIII, p. 591.

28 *Remaines Concerning Britaine* (1605), quoted from the edition of 1614, p. 37.

29 *The History of the Worthies of England* (1662), ed. J. Nichols (1811), I.

30 *State-Worthies* (2nd ed., 1760), p. 80.

31 'A discourse concerning the Original and Progress of Satire' (1693), prefixed to *The Satires of Decimus Junius Juvenalis*, ed. George Watson (London and New York, 1962), II, p. 150.

32 Op. cit., in Pope's *Poetical Works*, ed. A. W. Ward (Globe edition, 1911), II, pp. 291-8, and p. 37 n.

33 Op. cit., I, pp. 53-5.

34 *The Poetical Decameron* (Edinburgh, 1820), I, pp. 77f.

35 *Poetical Works with Memoir and Critical Dissertation*, ed. by George Gilfillan (Edinburgh, 1858), p. xv.

36 *Tottel's Miscellany*, ed. Edward Arber (1870), p. xvi.

37 Wyatt, *The Poetical Works* (Aldine edition, 1831), British Museum copy 'with copious notes by F. W. Palgrave'. The back fly-leaf.

38 Ibid., p. 29.

39 Ibid., pp. 24, 29, 98, 83, 76.

40 Ibid., p. 32.

41 Ibid., p. 1.

42 Op. cit. (Boston, 1889), p. 89.

43 Op. cit., p. 545.

44 *Tottel's Miscellany*, ed. H. E. Rollins (Cambridge, Mass., 1928-9), II, p. 62.

45 'Some Aspects of Medieval Lyric', in *Early English Lyrics* (1907), ed. E. K. Chambers and F. Sidgewick, p. 282.

46 *Sir Thomas Wyatt and some Collected Studies* (1933), p. 130.

47 Chambers, op. cit., p. 130.

48 'The Art of Sir Thomas Wyatt', *Huntington Library Quarterly* IX (1946), pp. 323-55.

49 *The Elizabethan Love Sonnet* (1956), p. 14.

50 In *Essays and Studies of the English Association* XXIV (1938), pp. 28-41.

51 'The Rhythmical Intention in Wyatt's Poetry', *Scrutiny* XIV (1946), pp. 90-102 and 'The Poetry of Wyatt' in *The Age of Chaucer*, ed. Boris Ford (1954), pp. 197-212.

52 *La Poesia di Sir Thomas Wyatt* (Florence, 1953).

53 *Collected Poems*, ed. cit. (1949), p. xvii.

54 Nott, because he searched so thoroughly through the State Papers, was the first to comment on Wyatt's prose style: 'he is the first English writer to have aimed at anything like a legitimate style in prose' (No. 9).

55 This includes the prose translation of Plutarch's *Quyete of Mynde*, of which a facsimile edition had earlier (1931) been published by Charles Read Baskerville (Cambridge, Mass.).

56 Op. cit.

57 Op. cit.

58 *English Poetry in the Sixteenth Century* (1955), ch. V.

59 Patricia Thomson, *Sir Thomas Wyatt and his Background* (1964).

60 *Humanism and the Early Tudor Court* (1959).

61 *Music and Poetry at the Early Tudor Court* (1961).

62 Op. cit., introduction, p. xviii.

63 *English* XIII (1961), p. 237.

64 *The Poems of Henry Howard, Earl of Surrey*, ed. F. M. Padelford (Seattle, 1920 and (revised) 1928).

65 Henry Howard, Earl of Surrey, *Poems,* ed. Emrys Jones (Oxford, 1964).

66 Ed. cit., p. xvii.

Note on the Text

The materials in this volume follow the original manuscripts or printed texts in most important respects. Some light punctuation has been added to Nos 3 and 5, and contractions expanded and omitted where they appear elsewhere in the volume (e.g. Surrey's elegies on Wyatt). Some antiquated footnotes in the originals (e.g. some of Nott's) and references to old editions, have been excised. I have appended, following every quotation from Wyatt, a reference to its number in the most recent edition, *Collected Poems of Sir Thomas Wyatt*, ed. Kenneth Muir and Patricia Thomson (Liverpool University Press, 1969). The prose translation of Leland's elegies is as literal as possible, making no pretensions to literary style. The place of publication, unless otherwise stated, is London. Original footnotes are marked with asterisk, dagger, etc., the present editor's footnotes are numbered. My additions to original footnotes are contained in square brackets.

1. Unsigned preface to *The Quyete of Mynde*

1527–8

This address 'To the reder' of Wyatt's translation of Guillaume Budé's Latin version, *De Tranquillitate et Securitate Animi*, of Plutarch's περὶ εὐθυμίας is the work either of Wyatt himself or of his printer, Richard Pynson. Wyatt presented his book, probably in manuscript form, to Queen Katherine of Aragon, dating his dedicatory epistle 31 December 1527. It was presumably published in 1528. Not listed in S.T.C.

A 1ᵛ It shall seme harde vnto the parauenture gentyll reder, this translation, what for shorte maner of speche, and what for dyuers straunge names in the storyes. As for the shortnesse aduyse it wele and it shalbe the pleasaunter, whan thou vnderstandest it. As for the straunge names stycke nat in them, for who that can take no frute in it, without he knowe clerely euery tale that is here touched, I wolde he shulde nat rede this boke. Farewell.

2. Leland's Elegies on Wyatt

1542

Extracts from *Naeniae in mortem Thomæ Viati equitis incompara-bilis*, London 1542. British Museum, first edition, 1075. m. 16 (4). S.T.C. 15446.

John Leland (1506?–52), Henry VIII's antiquary, dedicated this series of elegies, published shortly after Wyatt's death, to Henry Howard, Earl of Surrey, as his literary heir. Leland himself appears to have known Wyatt first at Cambridge, afterwards at court, and to have been his constant admirer. In another poem he celebrates his service, in his later years, to naval defence: this is *Cygnea cantio*, London, 1545. British Museum, 1075. m. 16 (2). S.T.C. 15444.

(a) A 2ᵛ   *Officium pietatis*
            Sint mœste Charites, lubentiæque,
            Et tristes sileant sales, leporesque.
            Extinctus iacet en Viatus ille,
            Ille inquam decus vnicum Britannæ
            Gentis, cuius ab ore profluebant
            Musarum numeri rotundiores.
            Vos cygni pia turba concinentes
            Sublimen medio locate cœlo
            Vestrum pro meritis suis poetam,
            Et famam date candidi perennem.

(*The service of piety*. Be sorrowful, beloved ones and those of goodwill, and tearful; and be silent wit and grace of language. Behold, Wyatt lies dead, he who was the ornament of the British people, from whom flowed elegant poetry. You swans, joining together in pious throng, for his merits lift to the midst of heaven your poet, and give him eternal and radiant fame.)

(b) A 3^v   *Anglus par Italis*
Bella suum merito iactet florentia Dantem.
Regia Petrarchæ carmina Roma probet.
His non inferior patrio sermone Viatus
Eloquij secum qui decus omne tulit.

(*The English the Italian's equal.* Beautiful Florence extols the merits of
Dante. Royal Rome approves the songs of Petrarch. No less inferior in
his own country, Wyatt bore the praise for eloquence and beauty of
language.)

(c) A 3^v   *Vnicus phœnix*
Vna dies geminos phœnices non dedit orbi.
Mors erit vnius vita sed alterius.
Rara auis in terris confectus morte Viatus
Houardum hæredem scripserat ante suum.

(*The one phoenix.* The world contains but one phoenix at a time. One
dead, another comes to life. When Wyatt, that rare bird, was snatched
away by death, Howard became his heir.)

(d) A 3^v   *Vita post cineres*
Dicere nemo potest recte perijsse Viatum
Ingenij cuius tot monimenta vigent.

(*Life beyond the grave.* None can justly claim that Wyatt has perished
when the monuments of his genius still thrive.)

(e) A 4^v   *Clades eloquentiæ*
Eloquij flumen, lumen, fulmenque Viatus
Concidit, argutum nunc silet omne melos.

(*The destruction of eloquence.* Wyatt, the stream, light and lightning of
eloquence is annihilated, and now all fine song is silent.)

(f) A 4^v   *Lima Viati*
Anglica lingua fuit rudis & sine nomine rhythmus:
Nunc limam agnoscit docte Viate tuam.

(*The file of Wyatt.* The English language was rough and its verses
worthless. Now, learned Wyatt, it has had the benefit of your file.)

(g) A 4^v   *Nobilitas debet Viato*
Nobilitas didicit te præceptore Britanna
Carmina per varios scribere posse modos.

(*Nobility indebted to Wyatt*. The nobles take you as Britain's instructor, who taught them to make songs of various kinds.)

(h) A 4ᵛ   *Viatus psaltes*
    Transtulit in nostram Dauidis carmina linguam,
    Et numeros magna reddidit [arte] pares.
    Non morietur opus tersum, spectabile, sacrum.
    Clarior hac fama parte Viatus erit.

(*Wyatt as psalmist*. He translated into our language the songs of David, and rendered them with great art, equal to his. This correct, admirable, sacred work will not die. It will become a yet more brilliant part of Wyatt's fame.)

(i) A 5ʳ   *Calculus Cæsaris*
    Carolus eximias vires laudare Viati
    Cæsar, & eloquium est solitus laudare Viati.
    Ingenuos mores Cæsar laudare Viati,
    Ingeniumque probum solitus laudare Viati.
    Cæsaris vnius multorum calculus instar.

(*The opinion of Caesar* (i.e., of the Emperor Charles V, to whose court Wyatt was ambassador). The Emperor Charles is wont to praise greatly Wyatt's powers, eloquence, sincere manners, genius, and honesty. Many share his opinion.)

(j) A 5ʳ   *Viatus aquila*
    Summa petit magni Iouis ales & ardua tentat.
    Talis naturæ dote Viatus erat.

(*Wyatt as eagle*. Wyatt, like Jupiter's bird, attempted the highest and most arduous. Such was his natural gift.)

(k) A 5ᵛ   *Corona Viati*
    Castalij fontis cum margine forte sederunt
    Ex hereda Musæ nuper texere corollam,
    Auro pingentes solito de more corymbos.
    Circulus & postquam iustum coijsset in orbem
    Quæstio Cyrrheas est inter oborta sorores
    Festa poetarum quis tandem præmia ferret.
    Virginei quæ prima chori sic ora resoluit
    Calliope: docto sunt munera digna Viato
    Dixerat, & placuit reliquis sententia nymphis.

Atropos has illi laudes inuidit acerba,
Infestaque manu vitalia stamina rupit.
Confectum Musæ crudeli vulnere mystam
Eluxere suum lachrimis, gemitusque dedere
Talia decentes: potuit mors tollere corpus
Viuet at ingenium nostri sine fine Viati.

(*The crown of Wyatt*. Sitting by the fountain of Castalia, as chance would have it, the Muses not long ago wove a crown of ivy, the cluster embellished with gold in the usual way. And afterwards they discussed who on earth should rightly bear it, who should have this prize at the feast of the poets. The first of the choir of virgins, Calliope, gave judgment. 'The learned Wyatt is worthy of the gift', she said, and this judgment pleased the other nymphs. Bitter Atropos envied these praises, and therefore cut the thread of his life. The Muses mourned the cruel blow with tears and groans, saying thus, 'Death can take his body, but the genius of our Wyatt will live for ever.')

3. Surrey on Wyatt and on his Penitential Psalms

c. 1542

Poems on Wyatt and his poetry by Henry Howard, Earl of Surrey (1517–47). Equal in importance as an early Tudor poet with Wyatt, he was also his imitator, admirer and, he claims, his friend.

(Some light punctuation has been added to the original texts.)

(a) This sonnet serves as an introduction to Wyatt's translation of the Penitential Psalms in British Museum Egerton MS 2711, from which the text has been taken. 'The great Macedon' is Alexander, who, having obtained a copy of Homer's poems after the defeat of Darius, carried it round in a 'riche arke' (f. 85ᵛ).

The great Macedon that out of Perse chasyd
Darius of whose huge power all Asy Rang,
In the riche arke if Homers rymes he placyd,
Who fayned gestes of hethen Prynces sang,

What holly grave, what wourthy sepulture,
To Wyates Psalmes shulde Christians purchace?
Wher he dothe paynte the lyvely faythe and pure,
The stedfast hoope, the swete returne to grace

Of iust Dauyd by parfite penytence,
Where Rewlers may se in a myrrour clere
The bitter frewte of false concupyscence,
How Jewry bought Vryas deathe full dere.

In Prynces hartes goddes scourge yprynted depe
Myght them awake out of their synfull slepe.

(b) Surrey refers again to Wyatt's Psalms. Text from British Museum Add. MS. 36529 (f. 56ᵛ).

> In the rude age when Science was not so rife,
> If Jove in crete and other where they taught
> Artes to reverte to profyte of our lyfe
> wan after deathe to have their temples sought,
> If vertue yet in no vnthankfull tyme
> fayled of some to blast her endles fame,
> a goodlie meane bothe to deter from cryme
> and to her steppes our sequell to enflame,
> In dayes of treuthe if wyattes frendes then waile
> (the only debte that ded of quycke may clayme)
> That rare wit spent employde to our avayle
> where Christe is tought deserve they monnis blame?
> his livelie face they brest how did it freate
> whose Cynders yet with envye doo the eate!

(c) Surrey's sonnet contains no comment on Wyatt's poetry, but is of interest for its claim that he was intimate with what 'harbourd' in his head, an intimacy which is also shown in his occasional imitation of Wyatt's poetry. Text from British Museum Add. MS. 36529 (f. 57ʳ).

> Dyvers thy death doo dyverslye bemone,
> Some that in presence of that livelye hedd
> Lurked, whose brestes envye with hate had sowne,
> yeld Cesars teres uppon Pompeius hedd.[1]
> Some that watched with the murdrers knyfe
> with egre thurst to drynke thy guyltles blood,
> whose practyse brake by happye end of lyfe,
> weape envyous teares to here thy fame so good.
> But I that knowe what harbourd in that hedd,
> what vertues rare were tempred in that brest,
> honour the place that such a iewell bredd

---

[1] Cp. Wyatt, III.

and kysse the ground where as thy coorse doth rest
with vaporde eyes from whence such streames avayle
As Pyramus did on Thisbes brest bewayle.

(d) The text of Surrey's epitaph on Wyatt is taken from British Museum
Harleian MS. 78. It was anonymously printed, probably late in 1542,
under the title *An excellent Epitaffe of syr Thomas Wyat.*

Epitaphim Tho wiat

Wyat resteth here that quicke cowlde neuer reste,
whose heavenly gyftes encresed by dysdayne
And vertue sanke the deper in his breste:
suche proffet he of enuye coulde optayne.

A heade wheare wysdome mysteries dyd frame,
whose hammers bete styll in that livelye brayne
As on a stythye wheare some worke of fame
was daylye wrought to turne to brytaynes gayne.

A visage sterne and mylde, whear bothe dyd groo
One to contemne, in vertues to reioyce,
Amyd great stormes, whome grace assured soo
To lyve vpright and smyle at fortunes choyse.

A hand that taught what myght by said in ryme,
That reft Chaucer the glorie of his wytte,
A marke the whiche, vnperfytyd for tyme,
Some may approche but neuer none shall hytte.

A tong that sarvyd in forayne realmes his kynge,
whose cortous talke to vertue dyd inflame
Eache noble harte, a worthy gyde to brynge
our englyshe youthe by travayle vnto fame.

A eye whose iudgment no effecte coulde blynde,
frendes to allure, and foes to reconcyle,
whose persinge looke dyd represent a mynde
wythe vertue fraught, reposed, voyde of gyle.

A harte wheare dreade yet neuer so opprest
To hyde the thought that myght the truthe avaunce,

In nether fortune lyfte nor so opprest,[1]
To swell at welthe, nor yelde vnto myschaunce.

A valiant corps wheare fors and bewtie mett;
happie, alas, to happie, but for foes,
lyvyd and ranne the race that nature sett,
of manodde shape wheare she the mould did lose.

But to the heavens that symple soule ys flede
which lefte with suche as covyt Chryst to knowe
wytnes of faythe that neuer shalbe dede,
sent for our welthe but not receavyd so.
Thus for our gylte this Juell have we lost
The yerthe his bones, the heavens possese his gost.

---

[1] Alternatively, the scribe possibly intended 'sore oppresst' or 'so represst'.

4. Tottel on English eloquence

1557

SONGES AND SONETTES, written by the ryght honorable Lorde Henry Haward late Earle of Surrey, and other. Printed by Richard Tottel, 5 June 1557, A iv.

This address from *The Printer to the Reader* is in the first edition of Tottel's famous 'Miscellany', one of the earliest sixteenth-century anthologies of printed poetry. The only known copy of the first edition is in the Bodleian library (Arch. G. f. 12 (1)): S.T.C. 13860.

Richard Tottel (d. 1594) was, from the reign of Edward VI, a stationer and printer, and advanced to high rank in the Stationers' Company.

That to haue wel written in verse, yea & in small parcelles, deserueth great praise, the workes of diuers Latines, Italians, and other, doe proue sufficiently. That our tong is able in that kynde to do as praiseworthely as the rest, the honorable stile of the noble earle of Surrey, and the weightinesse of the depewitted sir Thomas Wyat the elders verse, with seuerall graces in sondry good Englishe writers, doe show abundantly. It resteth nowe (gentle reder) that thou thinke it not euill doon, to publish, to the honor of the Englishe tong, and for profit of the studious of Englishe eloquence, those workes which the vngentle horders vp of such treasure haue hereto enuied thee. And for this point (good reder) thine own profit and pleasure, in these presently, and in moe hereafter, shal answere for my defence. If parhappes some mislike the statelinesse of stile remoued from the rude skill of common eares: I aske help of the learned to defend their learned frendes, the authors of this work: And I exhort the vnlearned, by reding to learne to be more skilful, and to purge that swinelike grossenesse, that maketh the swete maierome not to smell to their delight.

5. Sackville on Wyatt's Penitential Psalms

1563

Thomas Sackville, Earl of Dorset (1536–1608) was an Elizabethan courtier-poet, whose chief contribution to the non-dramatic literature is found in *A Myrroure for Magistrates* (1563). The following stanza is taken from a manuscript addition, not included in early printed versions of *The Mirror*, to Buckingham's complaint: St John's College, Cambridge MS. 364. It is printed in Lily B. Campbell's edition (Cambridge, 1938; Barnes & Noble, 1960), in Appendix C, p. 545. The addition expounds the idea that no poet—not 'Maro' (Virgil), Chaucer, Wyatt, Surrey, and 'lest of all' the author—has been able to express the 'houge dolours' of Richard III's victim, the Duke of Buckingham.

> not worthy wiat, worthiest of them all,
> whom Brittain hath in later yeres furthbrought,
> his sacred psalmes wherein he singes the fall
> of David dolling for the guilt he wrought,
> and Vries deth which he so dereli bought,[1]
> not his hault vers that tainted hath the skie,
> for mortall domes to hevenlie and to hie.

[1] Sackville refers to the narrative framework of Wyatt's translation of the Penitential Psalms, that is, to the story of David's penance for his love of Bathsheba and his responsibility for her husband Uriah's death (2 Samuel, 11–12).

6. Puttenham on Wyatt

1589

Extracts from *The Arte of English Poesie*, usually ascribed to George Puttenham (1529?–90), and printed by Richard Field in 1589. The text quoted is that of the first edition, owned by Ben Jonson, and the only known copy to contain four cancelled leaves between gatherings N and O. British Museum G. 11548. S.T.C. 20519.

(a) Book I, Chapter xxxi on *Who in any age haue bene the most commended writers in our English Poesie, and the Authors censure vpon them.* Puttenham is here, like Tottel, concerned to point out that the 'English tong . . . is in nothing inferiour to the French or Italian' for its beautiful poetry. He attempts a rudimentary history of English poetry starting at about the time of Edward III. To the 'first age' he assigns Chaucer, Gower, Langland, Lydgate, and, from amongst Wyatt's senior contemporaries, Skelton. He then goes on to describe the new dawn in the reign of Henry VIII (pp. 48–9).

In the latter end of the same kings raigne sprong vp a new company of courtly makers, of whom Sir *Thomas Wyatt* th'elder & *Henry* Earle of Surrey were the two chieftaines, who hauing trauailed into Italie, and there tasted the sweete and stately measures and stile of the Italian Poesie as nouices newly crept out of the schooles of *Dante Arioste* and *Petrarch*, they greatly pollished our rude & homely maner of vulgar Poesie, from that it had bene before, and for that cause may iustly be sayd the first reformers of our English meetre and stile.

(b) In the same chapter Puttenham continues to draw a sharp line of distinction between Skelton on the one hand and Wyatt and Surrey on the other (p. 50).

Skelton a sharpe satirist, but with more rayling and scoffery then became a Poet Lawreat, such among the Greekes were called *Pantomimi*, with vs Buffons, altogether applying their wits to Scurrillities & other ridiculous matters. *Henry* Earle of Surrey and Sir *Thomas Wyat*, betweene whom I finde very litle difference, I repute them (as before) for the two chief lanternes of light of all others that haue since employed their pennes vpon English Poesie, their conceits were loftie, their stiles stately, their conueyance cleanely, their terms proper, their meetre sweete and well proportioned, in all imitating very naturally and studiously their Maister *Francis Petrarcha*.

(c) Book II, Chapter iii on *How many sorts of measures we vse in our vulgar* (p. 60).

This meeter of twelue sillables the French man calleth a verse *Alexandrine*, and is with our moderne rimers most vsuall: with the auncient makers it was not so. For before Sir *Thomas Wiats* time they were not vsed in our vulgar, they be for graue and stately matters fitter than for any other ditty of pleasure.

(d) Book II, Chapter xiii on *A . . . declaration of the metricall feete of the ancient Poets Greeke and Latine*. Though he uses the classical metrical terms, Puttenham gives English examples, including the following of Wyatt's use of monosyllables in iambic pentameter verse (p. 120).

---

and ye shall find verses made all of *monosillables*, and do very well, but lightly they be *Iambickes*, bycause for the more part the accent falles sharpe vpon euery second word rather then contrariwise, as this of Sir *Thomas Wiats*.

> *I finde nŏ peăce ănd yēt mĭe wărre ĭs dōne,*
> *I feare and hope, and burne and freese like ise.*

(e) Book II, Chapter xiv *Of your feet of three times, and first of the Dactil*. Note that Puttenham, as in extracts (a) and (b), again mentions Petrarch's influence on his first English imitators (p. 105).

The same Earle of Surrey & Sir *Thomas Wyat* the first reformers & polishers of our vulgar Poesie much affecting the stile of the Italian *Petrarcha*, vsed the foote *dactil* very often but not many in one verse.

(f) Book II, Chapter xvi *Of your verses perfect and defectiue, and that which the Græcians called the halfe foote.* Puttenham seems to think Wyatt's poem a translation of Petrarch, though in fact it is from Sannazaro (pp. 107-8).

The Greeks and Latines vsed verses in the odde sillable of two sortes, which they called *Catalecticke* and *Acatalecticke*, that is odde vnder and odde ouer the iust measure of their verse, & we in our vulgar finde many of the like, and specially in the rimes of Sir Thomas Wiat, strained per-chaunce out of their originall, made first by *Francis Petrarcha*: as these

> *Like vnto these, unmeasurable mountaines,*
> *So is my painefull life the burden of ire:*
> *For hie be they, and hie is my desire*
> *And I of teares, and they are full of fountaines.* [XXXIII]

Where in your first second and fourth verse, ye may find a sillable super-fluous, and though in the first ye will seeme to help it, by drawing these three sillables, [*ĭm mĕ sŭ*] into a *dactil*, in the rest it can not be so excused, wherefore we must thinke he did it of purpose, by the odde sillable to giue greater grace to his meetre.

(g) Book II, Chapter xvii *Of the breaking your bissillables and poly-sillables and when it is to be vsed.* Puttenham stresses the need both to achieve a pleasant harmony and to retain the normal accen-tuation of English words (p. 110).

Sir *Thomas Wiat* song in a verse whoolly *trochaick*, because the wordes do best shape to that foote by their naturall accent, thus,

> *Fārewĕll lōue ănd āll thĭe lāwes fŏr ēuĕr.*

(h) Book III, Chapter xvi *Of . . . figures which because they serue chiefly to make the meeters tunable and melodious, and affect not the minde but very little, be placed among the auricular.* Here Puttenham voices his only criticism of Wyatt and Surrey, for using, like some other poets, imperfect rhymes 'neglecting the Poeticall harmonie and skill' (p. 145).

And th'Earle of *Surrey* with Syr *Thomas Wyat* the most excellent makers of their time, more peraduenture respecting the fitnesse and ponderositie of their wordes then the true cadence or simphonie, were very licencious in this point.

(i) In the same chapter Puttenham cites two examples of Wyatt's use of the figure of suspension (pp. 146–7).

Ye haue another maner of speach drawen out at length and going all after one tenure and with an imperfit sence till you come to the last word or verse which concludes the whole premisses with a perfit sence & full periode, the Greeks call it *Irmus*, I call him the [*long loose*] thus appearing in a dittie of Sir *Thomas Wyat* where he describes the diuers distempers of his bed.

> *The restlesse state renuer of my smart,*
> *The labours salue increasing my sorrow:*
> *The bodies ease and troubles of my hart,*
> *Quietor of mynde mine vnquiet foe:*
> *Forgetter of paine remembrer of my woe,*
> *The place of sleepe wherein I do but wake:*
> *Besprent with teares my bed I thee forsake.* (CLXXXVII]

Ye see here how ye can gather no perfection of sence in all this dittie till ye come to the last verse in these words *my bed I thee forsake.* And in another Sonet of *Petrarcha* which was thus Englished by the same Sir *Thomas Wyat.*

> *If waker care, if sodaine pale collour,*
> *If many sighes with little speach to plaine:*
> *Now ioy now woe, if they my ioyes distaine,*
> *For hope of small, if much to feare therefore,*
> *Be signe of loue then do I loue againe.* [XCVII]

Here all the whole sence of the dittie is suspended till ye come to the last three words, *then do I loue againe,* which finisheth the song with a full and perfit sence.

(j) Book III, Chapter xix *Of figures sententious, otherwise called Rhetoricall.* Puttenham's long list of figures of speech includes 'the figure of *Similitude*' as 'very necessary, by which we not only bewtifie our tale, but also much inforce & inlarge it', and he refers to Petrarch's 'Son animali al mondo' with Wyatt's translation, 'Som fowles there be' [XXIV], before proudly giving his own (pp. 202–3).

The *Tuskan* poet vseth this *Resemblance*, inuring as well by *Dissimilitude* as *Similitude*, likening himselfe (by *Implication*) to the flie, and neither to the eagle nor to the owle: very well Englished by Sir *Thomas Wiat* after his fashion, and by my selfe thus:

> *There be some fowles of sight so prowd and starke,*
> *As can behold the sunne, and neuer shrinke,*
> *Some so feeble, as they are faine to winke,*
> *Or neuer come abroad till it be darke:*
> *Others there be so simple, as they thinke,*
> *Because it shines, to sport them in the fire,*
> *And feele vnware, the wrong of their desire,*
> *Fluttring amidst the flame that doth them burne,*
> *Of this last ranke (alas) am I aright,*
> *For in my ladies lookes to stand or turne*
> *I haue no power, ne find place to retire,*
> *Where any darke may shade me from her sight*
> *But to her beames so bright whilst I aspire,*
> *I perish by the bane of my delight.*

7. Drayton on the 'Tottel' poets

1627

From Michael Drayton, 'To my most dearely loued friend
HENERY REYNOLDS Esquire, of *Poets and Poesie*', in the section of
'Elegies Vpon Svndry Occasions' in the collection of poems in-
cluding *The Battle of Agincourt* etc. (1627), p. 205, by the poet
Michael Drayton (1563–1631). S.T.C. 7190.

They with the Muses which conuersed, were
That Princely *Surrey*, early in the time
Of the Eight *Henry*, who was then the prime
Of *Englands* noble youth; with him there came
Wyat; with reuerence whom we still doe name
Amongst our Poets, *Brian*[1] had a share
With the two former, which accompted are
That times best makers, and the authors were
Of those small poems, which the title beare,
Of songs and sonnets, wherein oft they hit
On many dainty passages of wit.

[1] The contributions of Sir Francis Brian (d. 1550), the courtier and friend of Wyatt, to
Tottel's 'Miscellany' have not been identified.

8. Warton on Wyatt

1781

Thomas Warton, *The History of English Poetry* (1781), III, pp. 28–40. Warton (1728–90), the Oxford don and minor poet, is chiefly remembered for this work.

With Surrey's Poems, Tottel has joined, in his editions of 1557 and 1565, the SONGES and SONNETTES of Sir Thomas Wyat the elder, and of Uncertain Auctours.

Wyat was of Allington-castle in Kent, which he magnificently repaired, and educated in both our universities. But his chief and most splendid accomplishments were derived from his travels into various parts of Europe, which he frequently visited in the quality of an envoy. He was endeared to king Henry the eighth, who did not always act from caprice, for his fidelity and success in the execution of public business, his skill in arms, literature, familiarity with languages, and lively conversation. Wood, who degrades every thing by poverty of style and improper representations, says, that 'the king was in a high manner delighted with his *witty jests*.'* It is not perhaps improbable, that Henry was as much pleased with his repartees as his politics. He is reported to have occasioned the reformation by a joke, and to have planned the fall of cardinal Wolsey by a seasonable story.† But he had almost lost his popularity, either from an intimacy with queen Anne Boleyn, which was called a connection, or the gloomy cabals of bishop Bonner, who could not bear his political superiority. Yet his prudence and integrity, no less than the powers of his oratory, justified his innocence. He laments his severe and unjust imprisonment on that trying occasion, in a sonnet addressed to Sir Francis Bryan: insinuating his sollicitude, that although the wound would be healed, the scar would remain, and that to be acquitted of the accusation would avail but

* Ath. Oxon. i. 51.
† See Miscellaneous Antiquities.

40

little, while the thoughts of having been accused were still fresh in remembrance.[1] It is a common mistake, that he died abroad of the plague in an embassy to Charles the fifth. Being sent to conduct that emperor's embassador from Falmouth to London, from too eager and a needless desire of executing his commission with dispatch and punctuality, he caught a fever by riding in a hot day, and in his return died on the road at Shirburn, where he was buried in the great conventual church, in the year 1541.[2] The next year, Leland published a book of Latin verses on his death,[3] with a wooden print of his head prefixed, probably done by Holbein. It will be superfluous to transcribe the panegyrics of his cotemporaries, after the encomium of lord Surrey, in which his amiable character owes more to truth, than to the graces of poetry, or to the flattery of friendship.

We must agree with a critic above quoted, that Wyat co-operated with Surry, in having corrected the roughness of our poetic style. But Wyat, although sufficiently distinguished from the common versifiers of his age, is confessedly inferior to Surrey in harmony of numbers, perspicuity of expression, and facility of phraseology. Nor is he equal to Surrey in elegance of sentiment, in nature and sensibility. His feelings are disguised by affectation, and obscured by conceit. His declarations of passion are embarrassed by wit and fancy; and his style is not intelligible, in proportion as it is careless and unadorned. His compliments, like the modes of behaviour in that age, are ceremonious and strained. He has too much art as a lover, and too little as a poet. His gallantries are laboured, and his versification negligent. The truth is, his genius was of the moral and didactic species: and his poems abound more in good sense, satire, and observations on life, than in pathos or imagination. Yet there is a degree of lyric sweetness in the following lines to his lute, in which, *The lover complaineth of the unkindness of his love.*[4]

[Quotes the whole of 'My lute, awake!' (LXVI)]

Our author has more imitations, and even translations, from the Italian poets than Surrey: and he seems to have been more fond of their conceits. Petrarch has described the perplexities of a lover's mind, and his struggles betwixt hope and despair, a subject most fertile of sentimental complaint, by a combination of contrarieties, a species of wit

[1] CCXLIV.
[2] October 1542 is the correct date.
[3] See above, No. 2, published in 1542, the year of Wyatt's death.
[4] Tottel's title.

highly relished by the Italians. I am, says he, neither at peace nor war. I burn, and I freeze. I soar to heaven, and yet grovel on the earth. I can hold nothing, and yet grasp every thing. My prison is neither shut, nor is it opened. I see without eyes, and I complain without a voice. I laugh, and I weep. I live, and am dead. Laura, to what a condition am I reduced, by your cruelty!

> Pace non trovo, e non ho da far guerra;
>   E temo, e spero, ed ardo, e son en un ghiaccio:
>   E volo sopra'l cielo, e giaccio in terra:
>   E nulla stringo, e tutto l'mondo abraiccio.
> Tal m'ha in prigion, che non m'apre nè serra;
>   Nè per suo mi rittien, ne scioglie il laccio;
>   E non m'uccide Amor, e non mi sferra;
>   Nì mi vuol vivo, nì mi trae d'impaccio.
> Veggio senz' occhi, e non ho lingua, e grido;
>   E bramo di perir, e cheggio aita;
>   Ed ho in odio mesteffo, ed amo altrui:
> Pascomi di dolor, piangendo rido.
>   Egualmente mi spiace morte, e vita:
>   In questo stato son, Donna, per vui.*

Wyatt has thus copied this sonnet of epigrams.

> I finde no peace, and all my warre is done:
> I fear and hope, I burne and frese likewyse:
> I flye aloft, and yet cannot aryse;
> And nought I have, and at the world I season;
> That lockes nor loseth, [nor] holdeth me in prison.
> And holdes me not, yet can I scape no wise;
> Nor lettes me live, nor dye, at my devise,
> And yet of death it giveth me occasion.
> Without eye I se, without tong I playne:
> I wish to perish, yet I aske for helth;
> I love another, and I hate myselfe;
> I fede me in sorow, and laugh in all my paine.
> Lo thus displeaseth me both death and life
> And my delight is causer of this strife.   [XXVI]

It was from the capricious and over-strained invention of the Italian poets, that Wyat was taught to torture the passion of love by prolix

---

* Sonn. ciii. There is a Sonnet in imitation of this, among those of the Uncertain Auctours at the end of Surrey's Poems, fol. 107. And in Davison's Poems, B. ii. Canzon. viii. p. 108. 4th edit. Lond. 1621. 12mo.

and intricate comparisons, and unnatural allusions. At one time his love is a galley steered by cruelty through stormy seas and dangerous rocks; the sails torn by the blast of tempestuous sighs, and the cordage consumed by incessant showers of tears: a cloud of grief envelopes the stars, reason is drowned, and the haven is at a distance.[1] At another, it is a spring trickling from the summit of the Alps, which gathering force in its fall, at length overflows all the plain beneath.[2] Sometimes, it is a gun, which being overcharged, expands the flame within itself, and bursts in pieces.[3] Sometimes it is like a prodigious mountain, which is perpetually weeping in copious fountains, and sending forth sighs from its forests: which bears more leaves than fruits: which breeds wild-beasts, the proper emblems of rage, and harbours birds that are always singing.[4] In another of his sonnets, he says, that all nature sympathises with his passion. The woods resound his elegies, the rivers stop their course to hear him complain, and the grass weeps in dew. These thoughts are common and fantastic. But he adds an image which is new, and has much nature and sentiment, although not well expressed.

> The hugy okes have rored in the winde,
> Eche thing, methought, complaining in theyr kinde.

This is a touch of the pensive. And the apostrophe which follows is natural and simple.

> As stony hart, who hath thus framed thee
> So cruel, that art clothed with beautie![5]

And there is much strength in these lines of the lover to his bed.

> The place of slepe, wherein I do but wake,
> Besprent with tears, my bed, I thee forsake![6]

But such passages as these are not the general characteristics of Wyat's poetry. They strike us but seldom, amidst an impracticable mass of forced reflections, hyperbolical metaphors, and complaints that move no compassion.

But Wyat appears a much more pleasing writer, when he moralises on the felicities of retirement, and attacks the vanities and vices of a

[1] XXVIII, a translation of Petrarch's sonnet 'Passa la nave mia'.
[2] XCV, possibly a translation from an Italian source (see note in *The Collected Poems*, ed. Muir and Thomson).
[3] LXI, a translation of Serafino's strambolto, 'Se una bombarda'.
[4] XXXIII, a translation of Sannazaro's sonnet, 'Simile a questi smisurati monti'.
[5] XXII, possibly a free version of Serafino's 'Laer che sente'.
[6] CLXXXVII, a free version of Petrarch's sonnet 'O cameretta', or of an intermediate version of the latter.

court, with the honest indignation of an independent philosopher, and the freedom and pleasantry of Horace. Three of his poetical epistles are professedly written in this strain, two to John Poines, and the other to Sir Francis Bryan: and we must regret, that he has not left more pieces in a style of composition for which he seems to have been eminently qualified. In one of the epistles to Poines on the life of a courtier, are these spirited and manly reflections.

[Quotes 'Myne owne John Poyntz' (CV), 1–20[1]]

In pursuit of this argument, he declares his indisposition and inability to disguise the truth, and to flatter, by a variety of instances. Among others, he protests he cannot prefer Chaucer's TALE of SIR THOPAS to his PALAMON AND ARCITE:[2]

> Prayse SIR THOPAS for a noble tale,
> And scorne the STORY that the KNIGHT tolde;
> Praise him for counsell that is dronke of ale:
> Grinne when he laughes, that beareth all the sway;
> Frowne when he frownes, and grone when he is pale:
> On others lust to hang both night and day, &c. [CV, 50–5]

I mention this circumstance about Chaucer, to shew the esteem in which the KNIGHT'S TALE, that noble epic poem of the dark ages, was held in the reign of Henry eighth, by men of taste.

The poet's execration of flatterers and courtiers is contrasted with the following entertaining picture of his own private life and rural enjoyments at Allingham-castle in Kent.[3]

[Quotes CV, 76–103]

In another epistle to John Poines, on the security and happiness of a moderate fortune, he versifies the fable[4] of the City and Country Mouse with much humour.

> My mother's maids, when they do sowe and spinne,
> They sing a song made of the feldishe mouse, &c. [CVI, 1–2]

---

[1] A passage which, unknown to Warton, is largely translation of Luigi Alamanni's satire X in *Opere Toscane* (Lyons, 1532–3). This, therefore, offers evidence that, contrary to his general opinion, Italian sources were not always an injurious influence on Wyatt's poetry.

[2] Wyatt substitutes the references to Chaucer for Alamanni's to 'Maevius' (the poetaster), Homer, Virgil and Dante.

[3] Wyatt adapts Alamanni's references to his home in Provence to his own home, Allington Castle, 'in Kent and Christendome'.

[4] Told by Aesop, and repeated by Horace and Henryson in versions probably known to Wyatt.

This fable appositely suggests a train of sensible and pointed observations on the weakness of human conduct, and the delusive plans of life.

[Quotes CVI, 70–99]

These Platonic doctrines are closed with a beautiful application of
virtue personified, and introduced in her irresistible charms of visible
beauty. For those who deviate into vain and vicious pursuits,

> None other paine pray I for them to be,
> But when the rage doth leade them from the right,
> That, loking backwarde, VIRTUE they may se
> Even as she is, so goodly faire and bright! [CVI, 106–9]

With these disinterested strains we may join the following single
stanza, called THE COURTIERS LIFE.[1]

> In court to serve, decked with freshe aray,
> Of sugred meates feeling the swete repaste;
> The life in bankets, and sundry kindes of play,
> Amid the prease of wordly lookes to waste:
> Hath with it joinde oft times such bitter taste,
> That whoso joyes such kind of life to hold,
> In prison joyes, fettred with chaines of gold. [CCLIX]

Wyat may justly be deemed the first polished English satirist. I am
of opinion, that he mistook his talents when, in compliance with the
mode, be became a sonnetteer; and, if we may judge from a few
instances, that he was likely to have treated any other subject with more
success than that of love. His abilities were seduced and misapplied in
fabricating fine speeches to an obdurate mistress. In the following little
ode, or rather epigram, on a very different occasion, there is great
simplicity and propriety, together with a strain of poetic allusion. It is
on his return from Spain into England.

> Tagus farewel, that westward with thy stremes
> Turnes up the graines of gold al redy tride!
> For I with spurre and sayle go seke the Temes,
> Gainward the sunne that shewes her welthy pride:
> And to the town that Brutus sought by dremes,
> Like bended moone that leanes her lusty side;
> My king, my countrey I seke, for whom I live:
> O mighty Jove, the windes for this me give! [XCIV]

[1] Tottel's title.

Among Wyat's poems is an unfinished translation,[1] in Alexandrine verse,[2] of the Song of Iopas in the first book of Virgil's Eneid. Wyat's and Surrey's versions from Virgil are the first regular translations in English of an antient classic poet: and they are symptoms of the restoration of the study of the Roman writers, and of the revival of elegant literature. A version of David's Psalms by Wyat is highly extolled by lord Surrey and Leland.[3] But Wyat's version of the PENITENTIAL PSALMS seems to be a separate work from his translation of the whole Psaltery,[4] and probably that which is praised by Surrey, in an ode above quoted, and entitled, *Praise of certain Psalmes of David, translated by Sir T. Wyat the elder.* They were printed with this title, in 1549. 'Certaine Psalmes chosen out of the Psalmes of David commonly called vii penytentiall Psalmes, drawen into Englishe meter by Sir Thomas Wyat knyght, whereunto is added a prolog of the aucthore before every Psalme very pleasant and profettable to the godly reader. Imprinted at London in Paules Churchyarde at the sygne of the starre by Thomas Raynald and John Harryngton, cum previlegio ad imprimendum solum, MDXLIX.' Leland seems to speak of the larger version.

> Transtulit in nostram Davidis carmina linguam,
> Et numeros magna reddidit arte pares.
> Non morietur OPUS tersum, SPECTABILE, sacrum.

But this version, with that of Surrey mentioned above, is now lost: and the pious Thomas Sternhold and John Hopkins are the only immortal translators of David's Psalms.

A similarity, or rather sameness of studies, as it is a proof, so perhaps it was the chief cement, of that inviolable friendship which is said to have subsisted between Wyat and Surrey.[5] The principal subject of their poetry was the same: and they both treated the passion of love in the spirit of the Italian poets, and as professed disciples of Petrarch. They were alike devoted to the melioration of their native tongue, and an attainment of the elegancies of composition. They were both engaged in translating Virgil, and in rendering select portions of Scripture into English metre.

[1] It is hardly a translation, though obviously suggested by Virgil's description of Iopas' song about the cosmos in *Aeneid* I, 723–47. See Nott's correction of Warton (No. 9 p. 80 n).
[2] Properly, poulter's measure, that is, alternating lines of twelve and fourteen syllables.
[3] See Nos 2 and 3.
[4] Wyatt's translation of Psalm 37 (XCIV) provides the only surviving evidence that he intended to go beyond the Penitential group. Note Nott's scepticism, No. 9, p. 65 n.
[5] The claim largely rests on Surrey's assertions, as in No. 3c. He was, by about fourteen years, Wyatt's junior, and evidently his admirer, though opportunities for intimacy must have been relatively few.

9. Nott on Wyatt

1816

'An Essay on Wyatt's Poems', from *The Works of Henry Howard Earl of Surrey and of Sir Thomas Wyatt the Elder* (1815–16), ed. George Frederick Nott, II, cxv–clxviii. (A few of Nott's footnotes and his page references, which are to his own edition, are omitted).

Nott (1767–1841), a clergyman and a scholar, was noted for his enthusiasm for sixteenth-century literature and for the Italian language and literature.

What has been already observed concerning the Earl of Surrey, that though he was eminent for his virtues and personal accomplishments, yet his claim to celebrity rested principally upon his writings, applies equally to Sir Thomas Wyatt. It remains for us to inquire therefore what share of praise he likewise is entitled to in the same respect.

Of Sir Thomas Wyatt as a poet, Warton has drawn a character which is, like every thing that falls from that writer's pen, both lovely and elegant; it is just and satisfactory also, as far as it goes; but it is much too general.[1] We shall readily admit from Warton's observations that good composition began to dawn with Wyatt; but we do not collect from any thing he has said, what particular improvements were made by him in our language or style of writing; neither are we informed what the sources were from which he drew; or upon what authors he formed himself. These deficiencies I will endeavour to supply.

Wyatt, as a poet, can lay little claim to originality. It is true that his writings are diversified; far more so in fact than might have been expected at that early period of our literature. He wrote Sonnets, Rondeaus, Amatory Odes, both grave and gay, Epigrams, Poems of a moral and religious cast, and Satires upon common life. He employed also great diversity of measure, and supplies examples of almost every form of stanza that has since been used; still he was not an original

[1] See No. 8.

writer. He seems to have begun in every instance by translating from some other author; and as he was a good scholar, and a man of extensive reading, he took his models equally from the Greek,[1] the Latin, the French, the Italian, and the Spanish[2] writers. Having caught an author's style, he proceeded to write in his manner. His imitations are always good indeed; but still they are imitations; and are fewer in point of number than are his positive translations. When to this we add that many of the authors whom Wyatt was in the habit of reading have since fallen into obscurity, we may reasonably suspect that even of those pieces which we presume at present to be original, some might be found to be translations, had we the means of extending inquiry, or at best imitations only.

Of Wyatt's Sonnets, the greater part are translated from Petrarch; his Epigrams are borrowed chiefly from the Strambotti of Serafino D'Aquila, and his moral pieces are imitated from Seneca and Boethius. His Paraphrase of the Penitential Psalms seems to have been suggested by Dante's prior Paraphrase, or by that of Alamanni:* while the intro-ductory part is taken from a similar introduction by Beza.[3] Of his Satires, one is a free translation from Alamanni:[4] the other two are imitated from Horace and Persius.[5]

Of all Wyatt's compositions, those which can best lay claim to originality are his amatory odes. I mean his lesser odes, for the two

---

* Dante's Seven Penitential Psalms appear to have been first published by Spira at the end of the Comedia, in folio, at Venice in 1477, They were afterwards printed in 1478 at Milan, in folio likewise. Quadrio republished them in 8vo. at Milan in 1752, with notes. Which edition has been incorporated by Zatta into his complete edition of Dante's works in 4to. at Venice in 1758. Alamanni's Penitential Psalms were written in 1525, though they were not printed it should seem until 1532, when they appeared at the end of a volume of his Poems published that year at Lyons; and afterward, in the more complete edition of his works, printed in two volumes, at Venice, in 1542. They are to be found also in the 'Racolta di Salmi Penitenziali di diversi eccellenti Autori', published by Francesco da Trevigi at Venice in 1568, and again in 1572, and in the second book of Rime Spirituali printed at Venice, in 1550. Both Dante and Alamanni used the Terza Rima. Dante aims at being literal. Alamanni is paraphrastic. Wyatt's Paraphrase bears no marks of having been imitated from either. [Since Nott wrote the source of Wyatt's poems has been found, by Arundell Esdaile, in Aretino's prose Sette Salmi. It is probable however that he was also influenced by the terza rima of the Italian poets, particularly Alamanni, whom Nott mentions.]

[1] That Wyatt knew and imitated Greek is highly questionable. His prose translation of Plutarch came to him via the Latin of Budé, and no poem of his appears to be modelled on a Greek original.

[2] Though Wyatt was in Spain, and possibly influenced by Spanish Petrarchans, there is little direct evidence of a debt to any of them.

[3] Aretino supplies Wyatt's prologues.

[4] CV.

[5] CVI and CVII. Nott overestimates the influence of the two Latin satirists.

longest are taken from two Canzoni of Petrarch. But even of the lesser odes some are evidently borrowed from the French, some from Italian, and many I doubt not from Spanish writers: for it is not credible that Wyatt, with his love of poetry and knowledge of the language, should not have read and studied the Spanish poets during his residence in Spain.* Indeed, if we examine Wyatt's style with attention, we shall find it bearing a nearer resemblance to the style of the Spanish, than to that of either the French or the Italian poets.

There is a sort of gravity in the structure of Wyatt's periods, and a certain dignity in the flow of his versification, which is to be met with no where that I have ever remarked, but in the best Castilian writers. A single instance will suffice to explain my meaning.

Herrera thus begins one of his Elegies.

> Quién me daria, Amor, una voz fuerte,
> Y espíritu en mis lástimas osado,
> Para cantar las cuitas de mi suerte?[1]

What a striking resemblance does the turn of expression as well as thought in this passage bear to the following lines, with which Wyatt opens one of his odes.

> Where shall I have at mine own will
> Tears to complain? where shall I fet
> Such sighs, that I may sigh my fill,
> And then again my plaint repeat?   [LIII]

Had we not known that Wyatt wrote many years before Herrera was born, we might have supposed him to have studied and imitated the Castilian Poet.

If we examine particularly the several species of composition which Wyatt attempted, we shall find him to have failed most in his Sonnets. In these he has shewn great want of taste as well in the choice of his

---

* At the end of the Ode which begins,
> Where shall I have at mine own will, [LIII]
as it occurs in the Harington MS. p. 65, Wyatt has subjoined in his own hand-writing,
> Podra ser che no es.
It is probable that these words formed part of a Spanish piece which Wyatt had translated. Should this not have been the case, we may at least safely infer from the words that Wyatt wrote the poem in Spain.

[1] *Rimas de Fernando de Herrera* (Madrid), Vol. 1, p. 161. Nott's note (p. 347 in his edition) to Wyatt's poem shows that he realized the possibility that it derived from Giusto de' Conti's Italian *Rime* (1531). The Spanish, Italian and English poems all contain Petrarchan commonplaces, so that the matter of debts is difficult to estimate.

subjects, as in his manner of treating them. The Sonnets he has selected from Petrarch are for the most part the worst that Petrarch wrote. Instead of taking such as were true to nature, and expressive of simple feeling, he has fixed on those which abound with ingenious subtleties and conceits. Thus at one time he tells us that his heart is a ship steered by cruelty through stormy seas, and dangerous rocks.

> My galley charged with forgetfulness,
> Thorough sharp seas in winter nights doth pass
> 'Tween rock and rock, and eke mine enemy, alas!
> That is my Lord, steereth with cruelness. [XXVIII]

At another time he likens himself to an huge mountain covered with woods, and full of springs, birds, beasts, rocks, and fruit-trees.

> Like to these unmeasurable mountains
> Is my painful life the burthen of ire,
> For of great height be they, and high is my desire,
> And I of tears, and they be full of fountains.[1] [XXXIII]

And when he wishes to express the perplexities and conflicting hopes and fears that distract the Lover's mind, he tortures imagination to combine contrarieties. Thus he tells us that 'he burns and freezes at the same time; that he flies above the wind, yet cannot raise himself from the earth; that he sees without eyes, and utters lamentations without a tongue.'[2]

Nor are these the only defects remarkable in Wyatt's Sonnets. That species of composition requires an even and a simple flow of versification. But the versification of Wyatt's Sonnets is uniformly harsh and unmelodious. The lines are cumbered with heavy monosyllables, and are deformed with antiquated words and ungraceful contractions; so that though the thoughts may be pleasing in themselves, they are so expressed as to destroy the effect they might have otherwise produced; as in the following instance.

The lover seeing his mistress, as he thinks, with an expression of tenderness upon her countenance, fondly persuades himself that it proceeds from latent regard towards himself. Encouraged by this belief he resolves to address her; but finds so many thoughts press upon him for utterance, that he knows not how to begin. This perplexity is perfectly in nature, and is thus feelingly and elegantly described by Petrarch.

[1] The original is by Sannazaro, not by Petrarch.
[2] Nott refers to Wyatt's 'I fynde no peace' (XXVI), a translation of Petrarch's 'Pace non trovo'.

Ben s'io non erro, di pietate un raggio
Scorgo fra 'l nubiloso altero ciglio,
Che 'n parte rasserena il cor doglioso.
Allor raccolgo l' alma; e poi ch' i' aggio
Di scovririle il mio mal preso consiglio,
Tante le ho a dir, che incomminciar non oso.

Wyatt renders the thought thus.

Yet as I guess under disdainful brow
One beam of pity is in her cloudy look
That comforteth the mind that erst for fear shook.
And therewithal bolded I seek the way how
To utter the smart that I suffer within,
But such it is I 'not how to begin.   [LVI, 9–14]

It is in vain to seek in these lines for any of the grace or elegance of
the original. The sentiment itself thus expressed, loses all character of
tenderness; communicates no pleasure, and excites no interest.

The same want of taste is observable in most of Wyatt's Rondeaus;
of which, it should be observed, some are translations from Sonnets of
Petrarch.[1] Why Wyatt should have used that form in translating them,
it is difficult to say. The Rondeau is adapted to express thoughts of which
the character is artlessness and *Naïveté*, with a little turn of playfulness
and arch satire about them; and not studied sentiments of grave and
solemn complaint.*

---

* Boileau in his *Art Poetique* thus describes the Rondeau:

> Le Rondeau né Gaulois, a la naïveté.   *Chant. III. V.* 140.

On which his commentator observes; 'Ces petits Pöemes sont tout aussi difficiles à bien
faire que le Sonnet, et n'ont pas des regles moins génantes. Le Naïf en fait d'ailleurs le
caractere.' The following is considered to be, if I mistake not, an elegant specimen of the
amatory Rondeau.

> Le premier jour du mois de Mai,
> Fut le plus heureux de ma vie.
> Le beau projet que je formai,
>   Le premier jour du mois de Mai!
> Si ce dessein vous plut, Silvie,
> Le premier jour du mois de Mai,
> Fut le plus heureux de ma vie.

Wyatt must have read Marot's Rondeaus; they are almost all either playful, or satiric.

1 An example is 'Behold, love' (I). In view of 'If it be so' (XVIII) a translation from a
French rondeau, it is possible, even probable, that the substance of Petrarch reached Wyatt
through a French intermediate version. The rondeau form he uses is, at any rate, that of
French contemporaries such as Jean and Clément Marot.

Wyatt's two larger odes[1] from Petrarch,

> Mine old dear enemy, my froward master; [VIII]

and that which begins,

> So feeble is the thread" that doth the burthen stay, [XCVIII]

exhibit all the faults of style and language which we have already noted
in his Sonnets, and in his Rondeaus. Of these odes the second is the best.
It seems to have been written without effort, and therefore has in some
places the charm of simple feeling. In the first ode, however, there is a
total absence of ease and elegance; so that a person, unacquainted with
the original, will be at a loss to comprehend, upon what ground of taste
the Italians can consider it to be one of Petrarch's best compositions. A
single passage will suffice to confirm this remark, and shew Wyatt's
inferiority.

In Petrarch we find the following harmonious and feeling lines.

> Misero! a che, quel chiaro ingegno altero!
> E l'altre dote a me date dal cielo?
> Che vo cangiando 'l pelo,
> Nè cangiar posso l'ostinata voglia;
> Così in tutto mi spoglia
> De libertà, questo crudel ch'i accuso,
> Ch' amaro viver m' ha volto in dolce uso.

Wyatt renders them thus;

> But alas! where now had I ever wit,
>   Or else any other gift given me of Nature;
> That sooner shall change my wearied sprit,
>   Than the obstinate will that is my rulèr;
>   So robbeth my liberty with displeasùre
> This wicked traitor whom I thus accuse;
> That bitter life hath turned me in pleasant use. [VIII, 36–42]

But Wyatt is more fortunate in his lesser odes, which often afford
beautiful specimens as well of language, as of style, and turn of thought.
They were composed probably on the impulse of the moment, and
being written without effort are always natural, and frequently are
tender and pathetic. His ode to his Lute is a piece of singular beauty;
and has not been yet surpassed by any thing hitherto written in our

---

[1] Nott uses the term correctly, since the Italian canzone was considered the equivalent of
the 'larger' classical ode. It is not certain, however, that Wyatt himself recognized it as a
distinctive form.

language on a similar subject. The opening is dramatic, and em-passioned.

> Awake, my Lute! perform the last
> Labour, that thou and I shall waste,
> And end that I have now begun;
> And when this song is sung and past,
> My Lute be still! for I have done. [LXVI]

He then reproves his disdainful mistress for her cruelty; and having reminded her, that though in the pride of youth and beauty, she deemed herself secure from all reverse of fortune, the vengeance of offended Love still would overtake her, he proceeds to draw the following animated picture of her future mortifications.

> May chance thee lie wither'd and old,
> The winter nights that are so cold,
>   Plaining in vain into the moon.
> Thy wishes then dare not be told!
> But care who list, for I have done.
>
> And then may chance thee to repent,
> The time that thou hast lost and spent;
>   To cause thy Lovers sigh and swoon;
> Then shall thou know beauty but lent,
> And wish and want, as I have done.

The little ode on parting from his mistress is tender and simple. The picture drawn in the concluding stanza is natural, lively, and affecting.

> She wept and wrung her hands withall;
>   Her tears fell in my neck:
> She turn'd her face and let it fall,
>   And scarce therewith could speak.
>   Alas the while! [XXXVIII, 21-25]

In his ode entitled, 'An earnest suit to his unkind Mistress,' he gives a novel turn to amatory complaint:

> And wilt thou leave me thus?
> Say nay! say nay, for shame,
> To save thee from the blame
> Of all my grief and grame*

* _Grame_ means sorrow: it is derived from the Saxon, but it occurs with precisely the same meaning in the Italian. As in this passage from Dante;

> Ed una lupa, che di tutte brame
>   Sembrava carca, con la sua magrezzea,
>   E molte genti fè già viver grame. _Inferno. Can. I. V._ 49.

53

And wilt thou leave me thus?
Say nay! say nay! [CLXXXVI]

In the following lines he is pathetic, and writes with that air of truth, which ever distinguishes genuine from artificial passion.

Forget not yet the tried intent,
Of such a truth as I have meant;
My great travail so gladly spent,
Forget not yet!

Forget not yet the great assays,
The cruel wrong, the scornful ways,
The painful patience in delays,
Forget not yet!

Forget not! oh! forget not this,
How long ago hath been, and is,
The mind that never meant amiss!
Forget not this! [CCIII]

In the ensuing stanza we meet with expressions that are new, as well as beautiful.

And if an eye may save, or slay,
And strike more deep than weapon long;
And if a look by subtle play,
May move one more than any tongue;
How can ye say that I do wrong,
Thus to suspect without desert;
For the eye is traitor to the heart. [XCIII]

In the same ode we meet with another expression of still greater elegance and refinement.

But yet alas! *that look, all soul,*
That I do claim of right to have
Should not methink, &c.

The thought in the following passage is of a different nature; it is ingenious, but not overstrained, and is expressed with dignity.

My Love is like unto th' eternal fire
And I, as those that do therein remain;
Whose grievous pain is but their great desire,
To see the sight which they may not attain. [CC]

The following passage is adduced as affording a striking proof of

Wyatt's command of language. The thought is complicated, and laboured; yet it is expressed with ease, and precision. It is in the spirit of Cowley; and perhaps Cowley himself could not have rendered it better.

> For to the flame, wherewith ye burn
> My thought and my desire,
> When into ashes it should turn
> My heart, by fervent fire,
> Ye send a stormy rain,
> That doth it quench again,
> And make mine eyes express
> The tears, that do redress
> My life in wretchedness,
>
> Then, when these should have drown'd
> And overwhelm'd my heart;
> The heart doth them confound,
> Renewing all my smart.
> Then doth the flame increase;
> My torment cannot cease.
> My woe doth thus revive,
> And I remain alive,
> With death still for to strive.   [CXIV, 10–27][1]

But the style of thought and expression that is particularly characteristic of Wyatt's manner, is that of deep manly sorrow; which at the same time that it is descriptive of acute feeling, is free from querulousness. In the ode which begins

> Resound my voice, ye woods! that hear me playne,   [XXII]

though some expressions occur which we could wish altered, we meet with many passages in it of great strength. Thus, having said that all the surrounding objects in nature seemed to listen to his complaints and compassionate his sufferings, he adds,

> The hugy oaks have roared in the wind;
> Each thing methought complaining in their kind.

In the same elevated strain of manly sorrow are the following nervous lines

[1] The source of this poem, in Bembo's 'Voi mi poneste in foco' in *Gliasolani* (1505), was not discovered till 1954. The two stanzas Nott quotes are particularly close to the original, to which Wyatt owes the complicated thought and precision he notes.

> Heaven, and earth, and all that hear me playne,
>   Do well perceive what care doth make me cry;
> Save you alone, to whom I cry in vain
>   Mercy, Madam! alas! I die, I die!   [LXXIII, 1–4]

and thus afterwards, when he expostulates with his cruel mistress;

> It is not now, but long and long ago
>   I have you serv'd as to my power and might
> As faithfully as any man might do,
>   Claiming of you nothing of right, of right;
>
> Save of your grace only to stay my life,
>   That fleeth as fast as cloud before the wind;
> For since that first I entered in this strife
>   An inward death doth freat my mind, my mind.
>
> If I had suffered this to you unware,
>   Mine were the fault, and you nothing to blame;
> But since you know my woe, and all my care,
>   Why do I die, alas! for shame! for shame!   [Ibid., 17–28]

In these and many similar passages that might be adduced we observe a certain earnestness of expression, and a dignified simplicity of thought, which distinguishes Wyatt's amatory effusions from Surrey's, and I might add from those of every other writer in our language.

It will readily be granted that Wyatt's odes, as generally is the case with those who write much, are far from being all of equal beauty. In some, the thoughts are not expressed with sufficient care and precision; and in others, the thoughts themselves are not worth the labour bestowed upon them. Still the greater number possess considerable merit. Wyatt's feelings are those of no common mind; he knows how to complain, yet command respect; and excites pity without incurring humiliation.

In his Epigrams, for I know not by what other name to call his smaller poems, Wyatt formed himself on the Strambotti of Serafino D'Aquila, a poet now almost entirely forgotten, but once so famous, that it was deemed an honour to have even seen his tomb.*

> * Qui giace Serafin! Partirti or puoi.
>   Sol d'aver visto il sasso che lo serva,
>   Assai sei debitore agli occhi tuoi.

Serafino Cimino, generally known by the name of Serafino dell' Aquila, a town in Abruzzo, the place of his birth, was born in 1466. He died at Rome in 1500. Crescimbeni derives the word Strambotto from the Italian, '*strambo*', in the sense of fantastical: the Strambotto being used to express strange and fantastical thoughts, and subtle conceits. *Commentari, &c. Vol. I. Lib. III. Cap. iv.*

Serafino was a poet of a lively fancy, but no judgment: his works abound with extravagant conceits, and all the glitter of that false taste which distinguished the writers of his school. Wyatt therefore, in this respect, owed him no great obligation. The form of the Epigram, however, which he borrowed from him is pleasing, and may be often used with advantage. Wyatt availed himself of it to express those thoughts which are perpetually occurring to the poet's mind, but are not of sufficient importance to find place in laboured composition. Whenever he met therefore with any single idea or picturesque circumstance in the course of his reading, worthy notice, he moulded it into an epigram, such as we are now describing. Thus, one is taken from the account given by Josephus of the Hebrew Mother, who was driven by famine at the siege of Jerusalem to devour her own child.[1] Another, on the courtier's life, was suggested by a passage in Seneca's *Thyestes*;[2] and that of the man who hung himself for the loss of his treasure, by either the Greek of Plato, or the Latin of Ausonius.[3] The enigmatical epigram on a gun[4] is taken from a riddle in one of Pandulfo's Dialogues called Scopista: a work so little known that the reader will not be displeased to see transcribed from it the lines which Wyatt has translated.

> Vulcanus genuit; peperit Natura; Minerva
>   Edocuit; Nutrix Ars fuit, atque dies.
> Vis mea de Nihilo est; tria dant mili corpora pastum.
>   Sunt nati, Strages, Ira, Ruina, Fragor.
> Dic, Hospes, qui sum! Num terræ, an bellua ponti?
>   An neutrum! aut quo siun facta, vel orta modo.*

* The title of the work whence this Ænigma is taken, and that of the publication in which it is to be found are as follows: *Colloquia duo elegantissima, alterum Sensus et Paupertatis quibus viva humanæ vitæ imago exprimatur; Joanne Artopæo Spirensi auctore. Ejusdem, Arbor Eruditionis, et in eandem Oratio. Quibus propter elegantiam singularem et argumenti affinitatem adjunximus Pandulphi Collinutti Pisaurensis Apologos; Agenoriam; Misopeniam; Alethiam; Bombardam; Herculi Estensi Ferrarensi Duci dicatos.* Basiliæ; ex Officina Joannis Oporini Anno M.D.LXVII. Mense Maio.

In the Apologue, called Bombarda, from which Wyatt's Ænigma is taken, a person of the name of Phronimus is supposed to have built a city; and we are told, that being anxious to obtain for it the best means of defence possible, he went to consult on the subject with Heraclitus, called Scoteinos from the darkness of his answers. Heraclitus informs Phronimus that he would find what he wanted by looking into an egg. Unable to penetrate the meaning of this answer, Phronimus next goes to Diogenes the Cynic: who shews him a chesnut, and bids him take advice from that. This puzzles the poor man worse than ever, and makes

1 LXXX. The story originates in Josephus's *Jewish War*, but in 1956 Wyatt's immediate source was discovered, by J. G. Fucilla, in an anonymous Italian strambotto.
2 CCXL.
3 CCLVII.
4 CIII.

The best of Wyatt's epigrams are those which may be considered as original. Of these I will adduce two. They will be found to be as elegant and pleasing in their way as any thing to be met with in our best succeeding writers. The first was written when he was about to quit Spain on his return to London.

> Tagus, farewell! that westward with thy streams
> Turns up the grains of gold already tried:
> For I with spur, and sail go seek the Thames,
> Gainward the sun that shew'th her wealthy pride;
> And to the town, that Brutus sought with dreams,
> Like bended moon doth lend her lusty side.
> My King, my Country, alone for whom I live,
> Of mighty love for this the wings me give. [XCIV]

There is great tenderness of thought and richness of allusion in these lines; they prove Wyatt's mind to have been well stored with reading. But what constitutes their chief merit is a certain air of truth which shews them to have been the spontaneous effusion of feeling. They are

---

him resolve to apply at once to Pallas herself. The Goddess hears his story, and replies by giving him the riddle in question, telling him that when he should be able to solve it, he would obtain the information he wished for. Phronimus quits the Goddess, delighted with her condescension, but not much edified by her answer; for he finds himself utterly unable to understand it. To conquer this new difficulty, he goes about consulting all the wise men he could hear of; but they are all unequal to the task: so that having wandered fruitlessly half the world over he begins to despair, when suddenly it comes into his head to consult Hercules: who very goodnaturedly tells him that the riddle was the simplest thing to be understood imaginable; and bids him listen to the interpretation of it. 'In the beginning of time,' said Hercules, 'there was a mortal enmity between Nature and a certain person called Vacuum. Juno, Neptune and Æolus took part with Nature, which made the contest so unequal, that Vacuum was on the point of being overpowered. In his distress he applied', continued Hercules, 'to Vulcan for assistance, who advised him to build a brazen house, without any window in it, and present it humbly as a peace-offering to Juno; having first taken the precaution to lay in a store of three different sorts of food at the bottom of the house; and to close the opening with stones: this done, Vulcan said he would steal in at the backdoor of the house, and introducing Vacuum along with him, afford him an opportunity of suddenly expelling Juno. Vacuum, pleased with the project, made the present to Juno, who incautiously accepted it and thus gave Vulcan and Vacuum the means of driving her before them out of the brazen house. Nature, however, hastened to Juno's assistance, and rushing into the house again with a noise like thunder, put an end to the existence of Vacuum in a moment; and confined Vulcan, for a punishment, in a flint prison, from which,' said Hercules, 'he can never be extricated, but by stripes of iron.' Phronimus expresses his gratitude to Hercules for the trouble he had been at in explaining the riddle to him, but takes the liberty of suggesting, that he understood the explanation ten times less than the riddle itself. Hercules listens graciously to this modest representation on the part of Phronimus, and to remove all further difficulties gives him directions to make a gun, which not only explained to him the best mode of defending his town, but solved both Minerva's riddle and the prior answers of Heraclitus and Diogenes.

far superior on this account to some verses which the celebrated Naugerius wrote upon his return to Italy from Spain, whither he had been likewise sent as an ambassador from Venice, not long before Wyatt's appointment.

> Salve! cura Deum, mundi felicior ora!
> Formosæ Veneris dulces salvete recessus!
> Ut vos, post tantos animi mentisque labores,
> Aspicio, lustroque libens! ut munere vestro
> Sollicitas toto depello à pectore curas.
> Non aliis Charites perfundunt candida lymphis
> Corpora, non alios contexunt serta per agros.*

This is elegant and classical, but it is too general, particularly in the concluding lines, to excite much feeling.

The next Epigram I shall adduce is one of a different kind, but of singular beauty.

> A face that should content me wondrous well,
>   Should not be fair, but lovely to behold;
>   With gladsome chere all grief for to expel.
>   With sober looks so would I that it should
> Speak without words, such words as none can tell:
>   Her tress also should be of crisped gold.
> With wit and these might chance I might be tied,
> And knit again the knot that should not slide. [CXVIII]

Wyatt's Paraphrase of the Seven Penitential Psalms comes next to be considered. It seems to have been the work which his contemporaries, and he himself perhaps regarded as his highest effort. Surrey and Leland were sincere I doubt not in their commendations of it, when they both declared it to be a work worthy of eternal praise.[1] Posterity has judged otherwise. Of all Wyatt's compositions it is that which has sunk the earliest into oblivion; and now that it is reprinted will, I fear, notwithstanding its real merit, be the least read.

This is owing I apprehend not so much to want of skill in the writer, as to the nature of the subject which has occasioned failure, not in Wyatt's instance only, but in many others that might easily be cited. 'From poetry,' to use Johnson's words, 'the reader justly expects, and from good poetry always obtains the enlargement of his comprehension, and the elevation of his fancy: but this is rarely to be hoped for by Christians from metrical devotion. Whatever is great, desirable, or

---

* *Naugerii Opera.* Ed. Cominana, 4to. 1718. p. 221.
[1] See Nos 2h, 3a and 3b.

tremendous, is comprised in the name of the Supreme Being. Omnipotence, cannot be exalted; Infinity, cannot be amplified; Perfection, cannot be improved.' For this reason, Devotional Poetry is seldom found to please: indeed it cannot be, strictly speaking, poetical. 'Man admitted to implore the mercy of his Creator, and plead the merits of his Redeemer, is in an higher state than poetry can confer.' If Wyatt's Paraphrase, therefore, falls generally short of expectation, this cannot be a matter of wonder, and ought not to be one of blame.*

There are, however, some defects in the Paraphrase, with which, as they might have been avoided, Wyatt is justly chargeable.

Verse of every sort, as it is designed to affect the feelings, ought to delight the ear. This, which is a general principle, should have been particularly attended to in the composition before us; inasmuch as sentiments of sorrow and dejection require a versification of the simplest and most melodious kind. But Wyatt's versification in his Paraphrase is more crabbed and inharmonious than, perhaps, in any other part of his works. Its very structure is uncertain : it seems to fluctuate between the regular Iambic line, which Surrey had then introduced, and the old Rhythmical line to which Wyatt had been early accustomed; in consequence of which the even flow of metrical numbers is frequently interrupted by the occurrence of defective or redundant lines that cannot be reduced to measure but by means of the old cæsura and rhythmical cadence. The language also is unequal. Many words are distorted from

---

* That Wyatt's versification may not be thought more inharmonious than it really is, I must suggest that his lines ought to be read out loud. They would then be found to be constructed on regular principles, where they now seem altogether rude and licentious. The leading principles of Wyatt's versification, are three. I. He admits redundant syllables, which are to be disposed of in recitation, by forming them into feet, of which, either the first syllable is long and the two next short; like the dactyl of the Greeks and Romans; | — ‿ ‿ | or into feet, which may be called anapæsts; of which the first two syllables are short, and the third long. | ‿ ‿ — | II. He mixes feet, of which the first syllable is long, the second short; such as was the trochaic foot | — ‿ | with Iambic feet, or those of which the first syllable is short, the second long | ‿ — | III. He makes almost always a cæsura at the end of the fourth syllable. By attending to these rules, we shall not only read Wyatt's fluently, but feel them to possess an original and expressive flow of harmony. In the following lines the trochaic foot produces a fine effect.

> And rĕcŏncile ‖ thĕ grēat | hātrĕd | ănd strife.   [CVIII, 119]
> Mў strēngth | faīlĕth ‖ to reach it at the full.   [CVIII, 613]

The redundant short syllables produce often a fine effect.

> Sūddĕn | cōnfŭsiŏn ‖ as stroke without delay.   [CVIII, 181]

In the following line we find both the trochaic and the anapæstic foot; yet properly enounced, the verse is musical and pleasing;

> And found | mērcў ‖ at plen | tĭfŭl m̄er | cy's hand.   [CVIII, 299]

their natural pronunciation, and made to bear a strong accent on the last syllable for the sake of the rhyme; the old French mode of pronunciation, which Surrey succeeded in abolishing, is retained; and forced and inelegant contractions are used, as well as harsh and unpleasing licences. Thus '*quit*', is pronounced '*quite*', to rhyme with '*sprite*', [CVIII, 769, 771]; the noun '*assembly*', is made '*assemble*', to rhyme with '*tremble*', [CVIII, 202, 206]; and '*thirst*' is changed to '*thrist*', to rhyme with '*trust*', [CVIII, 688, 690]. In one place we find lines ending with '*redeemeth*', '*esteem'th*', and '*seem'th*', [CVIII, 593, 595, 597]; in another '*fever*' is made to rhyme with '*fervor*', [CVIII, 185, 187]; '*praiseth*' with '*poiseth*', and '*complisheth*', [CVIII, 518, 520, 522]; '*Son*', with '*salvation*', [CVIII, 712, 714]; and '*thing*', with '*bemoaning*' and '*deserving*', [CVIII, 77, 79, 81].

These are the defects of Wyatt's Paraphrase. Its merits are numerous, and such as shew its author to have been possessed of considerable learning and knowledge of his subject; to have had just and exalted views of the great mystery of Redemption; and to have been a pure, an humble, and a zealous Christian.

He sometimes in his Paraphrase gives a new and an ingenious turn to the original.[1] As in this passage.

> And when mine enemies did me most assail,
> My friends most sure, wherein I set most trust,
> *Mine own virtues*, soonest then did fail.
> And stand apart. Reason and Will unjust,
> As kin unkind, were furthest gone at need,
> So had they place their venom out to thrust
> That sought my death. [CVIII, 364–70]

I am not aware that any commentator has given his fanciful interpretation to the passage. It is not necessary to the sense, and probably was not the Psalmist's meaning; but to a pious and contemplative mind it opens a door to much useful meditation.

In the same strain of ingenious comment is the following passage.

> For like as smoke my days been pass'd away;
> My bones dried up as furnace in the fire;
> My heart, my mind, is wither'd up like hay,
> Because I have forgot to take my bread,
> *My bread of life, the word of Truth.*[2] [CVIII, 551–5]

---

[1] Nott was not, of course, able to take into account the variations on the Psalms suggested to Wyatt by Aretino's paraphrase, which accounts, for example, for the substance of the italicized phrase in line 366.

[2] The italicized phrase derives from Aretino's 'il vero pane de la vita nostra'.

The common translation is simply, 'my heart is smitten and withered like grass, so that I forget to eat my bread.'*

Wyatt sometimes introduces little distinctions of his own, which have a claim to an higher merit than that of mere ingenuity; they are those distinctions of which a heart, communing with itself, acknowledges at once both the force and the propriety.

> But thou O Lord how long after this sort
> Forbearest thou to see my misery!
> Suffer me yet in hope of some comfort
> *Fear, and not feel that thou forgettest me.* [CVIII, 112-15]

on which last line I would observe further, that it exhibits a fine instance of that compression by which one of the beneficial ends of poetry is effected. That of presenting truth to the mind on a form so precise, and in terms so chosen, that it is approved of by the judgment without the process of discussion, and retained without effort by the memory.

In some passages Wyatt is animated, as well as original.

> Thou of my health shall gladsome tidings bring,
> When from above remission shall be seen
> Descend on earth; then shall for joy upspring
> The bones, that were before consum'd to dust. [CVIII, 473-6]

Sometimes he approaches to the tenderness of a pathetic melancholy.

> ——then lift I up in haste
> My hands to Thee; my soul to Thee doth call,
> Like barren soil, for moisture of thy grace.
> Haste to my help, O Lord! before I fall;
> For sure I feel my spirit doth faint apace.
> Turn not thy face from me that I be laid
> In compt of them that headlong down do pass
> Into the pit; shew me by times thin aid,
> For on thy grace I wholly do depend. [CVIII, 750-8]

---

* Dante is as usual literal.

> Percosso io sono, come il fien ne' prati,
> Ed è già secco tutto lo mio core,
> Perchè li cibi miei non ho mangiati.

Bishop Fisher, however, in his 'treatise concerning the fruitful sayings of David on the Seven Penitential Psalms', gives the same turn to the thought, that Wyatt does. 'The soul in like manner is nourished with a certain meat; and if it refuse, and will not take that food, needs must it wax dry, and want good devotion. The proper meat for the soul is the word of God. Whosoever eateth not of his bread, shall wax lean in his soul, and at last wither, and come to nothing. Because, good Lord, I have not eaten this spiritual bread, I am blasted, and smitten with dryness like hay, having no devotion.' *p.* 192. *Ed.* 1714.

At other times he is solemn, full, and majestic.

> No place so far, that to Thee is not near.
> No depth so deep that thou ne may'st extend
> Thine ear thereto; hear Thou my woeful plaint.
> For, Lord, if thou observe what men offend,
> And put thy native mercy in restraint;
> If just exaction demand recompence,
> Who may endure, O Lord! who shall not faint
> At such account! dread and not reverence
> Should so reign large: but Thou seek'st rather love;
> For in thy hand is mercy's residence.   [CVIII, 672–81]

Wyatt's Paraphrase is accompanied with an introduction, describing the occasion on which the Penitential Psalms are supposed to have been written; and every psalm is preceded by a sort of prologue connecting each with the other, and marking, as it were, the progress of the Royal Penitent's contrition.[1] The introduction is fanciful and poetical.

> Love, to give laws unto his subject hearts,
> Stood in the eyes of Bersabee the bright;
> And in a look anon himself converts
> Cruelly pleasant before King David's sight:
> First daz'd his eyes, then further forth he starts.
> With venom'd breath as softly as he might,
> Touch'd his senses, and over-runs his bones
> With creeping fire, sparpled for the nones.   [CVIII, 1–8]

Thus fatally seduced by the allurement of his senses,

> And all forgot the wisdom and forecast,
> Which, woe to realms! when that their kings do lack,
>   [CVIII, 17–18]

David adopts the guilty measure which gives him possession of his mistress: but afterwards being admonished by the Prophet of the enormity of his offence, he is struck with horror at it, and casting his crown of gold, and his purple pall, and his sceptre to the ground, and renouncing all

> The pompous pride of state and dignity,   [CVIII, 49]

he retires to a dark and lonesome cave, taking nothing with him but his harp, to which he sings his several Penitential Psalms in succession.

---

[1] The source of the prologues and the narrative framework are supplied by Aretino. The following quotation of the opening lines is a translation of the beginning of his prologue to the first Penitential Psalm.

In the two opening lines of the prologue, we trace evident marks of imitation from Petrarch; but the whole contrivance seems to have been borrowed from a piece of Beza's, entitled, 'a Poetical Preface to David's Penitential Psalms.'[1] Wyatt has much abridged it; but all the leading circumstances are the same, as a few lines from the opening of Beza's Introduction will suffice to shew.

> Forte perreratis cœlo, terrâque, marique,
> Alex Amor, sacras Judææ callidus urbes
> Visebat, pharetrâque minas, flammataque gestans
> Tela manu. Jamque hospitium sedemque petebat
> Venturæ nocti; dumque acres undique versat
> Sæpe oculos, dubitatque etiam quâ sede moretur,
> Tandem ad Bersabes convertit lumina formam.

Then deeming Bersabe's eyes to be the place most fit for his abode;

> ———pharetrâque, arcuque relictis
> Aëreum sumit corpus, mirabile dictu!
> Sic indutus Amor, formosam hinc, inde, puellam
> Observat tacitus furtim, tandemque repertis
> Sese oculis infert claroque in lumine condit.*

In the prologues which connect the several Psalms, we find many passages well conceived and not inelegantly expressed. The prologue to the fifty-first Psalm opens with this simile.

> Like as the pilgrim that in a long way
> Fainting for heat, provoked by somewind,
> At some fresh shade lieth down at mid of day;
> So of David the wearied voice and mind
> Takes breath of sighs, when he had sung his lay
> Under such shade as sorrow had assigned:
> And as the one still minds his voyage end,
> So doth the other to mercy still pretend. [CVIII, 395-402][2]

In the prologue to the hundred and forty-third Psalm, having mentioned Redemption, Wyatt presents us with the following animated passage, of which the conception is noble throughout, though there are one or two expressions in it we could wish altered.

---

* Prefatio Poetica in Davidicos Psalmos quos pœnitentiales vocant. Theodori Bezæ Vezelii *Poemata, Sylva*, iv.

[1] Aretino again supplies the true source.

[2] Free translation from Aretino's prologue to the fourth Penitential Psalm.

This word 'Redeem', that in his mouth did sound,
    Did put David, it seemeth unto me,
As in a trance to stare upon the ground,
    And with his thought the height of heaven to see,
Where he beholds 'THE WORD' that should confound
    The word of death, by humble ear to be★
Of mortal maid, in mortal habit made;
Eternal life, in mortal veil to shade.

He seeth THAT WORD, when time full ripe should come,
    Do 'way that veil, by fervent affection,
Torn off with death (for death shall have her doom)
    And leap lighter from such corruption.   [CVIII, 695–706]

From all these passages it is evident that though Wyatt's Paraphrase has defects which will prevent it from being ever a popular performance, it bears marks of no common intellect and vigour of mind. It is the work of one who had read much and thought more; of one who loved virtue and aspired to heavenly things; a work that will be highly esteemed by all, who entertain a just sense of the misery of guilt, and, to borrow Surrey's expression, 'covet Christ to know.'†

★ Wyatt has borrowed this expression 'by humble ear', from the fortieth Psalm. 'Sacrifice and meat-offering thou wouldest not; but mine ears hast thou opened.' In which words allusion is made to the custom of passing a small sharp instrument through the ear of any one that became a voluntary servant; who by thus allowing himself to be fastened to the door post of the house, gave a pledge of his obedience to the master he had chosen. This was called to open the ear; 'aures fodere, forare'. The custom was prevalent in the East, and upon it was founded Cicero's well known sarcasm on Octavius. For Octavius one day in the Senate said he could not hear Cicero, upon which he instantly retorted, 'Certe solebas bene foratas habere aures'; intimating that he was, as Anthony reproached him with being, partly of African extraction. *Macrobii, Satur. Lib. VII. Cap. 3.* and *Suetonii Vita Octavii, cap.* 4. [For an alternative explanation, see *Collected Poems,* ed. Muir and Thomson, p. 388.]
† [See 3d above.] Warton tells us that Wyatt made a Version of the whole Psalter, and says it was a work distinct from the Paraphrase of the Penitential Psalms. [See No. 8, p. 46.] In proof of this, he speaks of the commendations bestowed upon that version by both Surrey and Leland. But Surrey never commended any other Version by Wyatt from the Psalter than that of the Penitential Psalms. That the Sonnet he wrote on the subject applies to the Paraphrase of the Penitential Psalms alone, is clear from the circumstance of its being found in Wyatt's own hand-writing prefixed to his manuscript copy of that Paraphrase. The assertion therefore rests on the sole authority of Leland. His words are;

    Transtulit in nostram Davidis carmina linguam.

This certainly might signify all David's Psalms, but it might also mean some of the Psalms only. In verse, people often are compelled to use general expressions, which, had they written in prose, they would have avoided. Certain it is, that if Leland in the passage above quoted alludes to a complete Version of the Psalms by Wyatt, distinct from the Paraphrase, then he has omitted to make any mention of the Paraphrase at all; which is hardly probable, seeing it was Wyatt's most laboured performance. It was 'opus tersum, spectabile': and one

The fate which has awaited Wyatt's Satires is somewhat remarkable, and deserves to be noticed. They are unquestionably his happiest and most finished productions. They may be ranked among the best satires in our language; and yet they never seem to have obtained either admirers or imitators; at least I do not recollect that any of our early writers have spoken of them in particular with commendation. This, I apprehend, may be easily accounted for. Wyatt had outstripped, as it were, his times. A taste for delicate satire cannot be general until refinement of manners is general likewise; and society is brought to that state which allows of the developement of foibles in character, and encourages philosophical inquiry into the motives and principles of human actions. As long as society is in a state of incipient refinement only, satire ever will be, and ever has been, coarse, personal, and indiscriminating; for the beauty of general allusions cannot then be felt; and few will be found enlightened enough to comprehend that the legitimate object of satiric poetry is not to humble an individual, but to improve the species.

What the prevailing notion of satire was in England in Wyatt's time may be ascertained by referring to the writings of Skelton, his contemporary. It is true indeed that Skelton's mode of writing has long been justly deemed almost a term of reproach; but when he wrote he was esteemed the best satiric poet of his age. I will adduce a few specimens of his style. In his satire on the Scots he thus speaks of the Duke of Albany.

> By your Duke of Albany,
> We set not a prane;
> By such a drunke Drane,
> We set not a mite,
> By such a coward Knight;
> Such a proud pailliard;
> Such a skyr-galliard;
> Such a stark coward;
> Such a proud poltron;

---

constructed 'magna arte', to use Leland's own words. [See No. 2h.] If Wyatt therefore really did make a Version of the whole Book of Psalms, and rendered it a finished, perfect, and admirable work, it seems surprising that there should be no traces of it discoverable; especially as we have so large a number of Wyatt's poems preserved in his own MS. and in the Harington, and in the Duke of Devonshire's MSS. That Wyatt made a Version of particular Psalms we know. A Version of the Thirty-seventh Psalm will be found printed from the Harington MS. (XCIV); and the lines printed at page lxxxvi. note 2, were, I doubt not, the Proem to a Version of some other Psalm. [The page references are to Nott's edition.] But that he made an entire Version of the whole Psalter, cannot, I think, without further proof be admitted.

Such a foul coystron;
Such a doughty dog-swain;
Send him to France again,
To bring with him more train.

In another place we have the following lines.

Sir Duke, nay, Sir Duck,
Sir Drake of the Lake, Sir Duck
Of the dunghill, for small luck
Ye have in feats of war,
Ye make not but ye mar:
Ye are a false entruster,
And a false abuser,
And an untrue knight;
Thou hast too little might
Against England to fight, &c.

In one of his latest poems he has these lines on Cardinal Wolsey.

Such a prelate I trow,
Were worthy to row,
Through the straights of Marock,
To the gibbet of Baldock:
For with us he so mells,
That within England dwells,
I would he were somewhere else;
For else by and bye,
He will drink us so dry,
And suck us so nigh,
That men shall scantly
Have penny or halfpenny.
God save his noble Grace,
And grant him a place,
Endless to dwell
With the devil of hell:
For an he were there
We need never fear
Of the fiend's black:
For I undertake,
He would so brag and cracke,
That he would then make
The devil to quake,
To shudder and to shake,
Like a fire-drake,

And with a coal rake,
Bruise them on a brake,
And bind them to a stake,
And set all hell on fire,
At his own desire,
He is such a grim sire.

All these passages are unquestionably below criticism. But that is not the conclusion we are aiming at. The age that could admire them may be well supposed incompetent to taste, or decide upon the merits of Wyatt's more classic satires. It is no wonder therefore that they should have been neglected at the time, and afterwards have become almost forgotten; so that when Hall published his own satires, more than fifty years after, he described himself to be the first who had attempted that branch of composition in England.

I first adventure, follow me who list,
And be the second English satirist.*

Hall's unblemished character leaves us no reason to doubt his word. We may conclude him therefore to have never heard of Wyatt's satires, or, from what he had heard, to have been deterred from reading them. A plain proof that their value had never been understood. In point of merit they are superior even to Hall's satires. Hall is too general and diffuse; he had evidently no deeper knowledge of mankind than the reading of the Classics supplied, or had been obtained from a partial view of human nature at the University, and during occasional visits to London; his learning, his piety, and sense of religion gave the rest. But Wyatt writes with a thorough insight into the human heart. His knowledge is his own, not gleaned from books, but actual observation. His remarks therefore are deep and penetrating, and will be found more and more just in proportion as they are studied.

The first [CV] of Wyatt's satires in point of time is, I apprehend, that

---

* See the Prologue to Hall's *Virgidemiarum, or Satires in Six Books.* In his Postscript, he tells us, that of modern satires he had never seen any he 'could use for his direction' save Ariosto's, and one other 'base French satire'. Hall honestly tells us that the motive which led him to write his satires was the hope of profit; and that he had given to them 'only the broken messes of his twelve o'clock hours'. This will sufficiently account for the generalities, in which he deals. Warton seems to have been particularly fond of Hall. He reprinted his satires in a neat form at Oxford, in 1753; and devoted no less than three sections in the fourth volume of his *History of English Poetry* to a particular consideration of them. Hall's satires are certainly entitled to much praise; they are the work of an elegant, a poetic, and a virtuous mind: they shew scholarship, and exhibit, moreover, in many places fine specimens of versification: still I think the opinion advanced in the text concerning them will be found to be correct. . . .

on the Courtier's Life. It is a translation, or rather a free and masterly imitation of Alamanni's tenth satire to Thomaso Sertini, which begins,

Io vi dirò poi che d' udir vi cale.[1]

From Alamanni, Wyatt took likewise his form of stanza, the Terza Rima, which he has employed in his two other satires; and, what was of greater importance, he borrowed from him his particular style likewise; a style which the Italian critics have censured as being somewhat more elevated than is, strictly speaking, suited to satiric poetry. Certainly on light occasions it is not sufficiently natural or playful: it wants that character of easy insinuation which has been so well described of old;

Omne vafer vitium ridenti Flaccus amico
Tangit, et admissus circum præcordia, ludit.

At the same time we must allow it to be well adapted to the expression of elevated sentiments, particularly in those passages which mark a generous contempt of vice and folly.

Wyatt's second Satire [CVI] on the 'Mean and sure Estate'[2] seems to have been suggested by Horace's story of the Town and Country Mouse, which Wyatt relates in a new and lively manner of his own; subjoining to it moral reflection, in a high strain of philosophic reasoning upon the beauty and dignity of virtue.*

* Among the fables of Robert Henryson, a Scottish poet of considerable merit who flourished in the 15th century, is one, 'Of the Uponlondis Mous, and the Burges Mous', to which it does not seem improbable but that Wyatt might have been indebted, if not for the idea of the story in this Satire, at least for the mode of telling it. . . . It is true that Henryson's *Fables* were not published until 1621. But Wyatt might have seen them in manuscript; in the same manner as Surrey must have seen Gawin Douglas' translation of the *Æneid* in manuscript; for we know that Gawin Douglas' translation was not printed till some years after Surrey's death. . . . Should Wyatt's Satire, on comparison, be thought to have been taken in any degree from Henryson's Fable, it must be considered a circumstance of no small credit to the Scottish poets that they were deemed worthy of being studied and imitated by the two great Reformers of our language: and a question will naturally arise, whether they may have been imitated by them in more instances than those two I have adduced. The question cannot well be decided until we have a good critical edition of all the early Scotch poets before us. This is a work which is loudly called for; but it is one which we hope no one but an able and impartial scholar will venture to undertake. The result would be highly honourable to Scottish literature. It has long since been remarked by Warton, and other writers, that several Scotch poets at the close of the 15th, and at the early part of the 16th century, had attained to a degree of elegance and richness in poetic composition and versification which our own native poets were then altogether strangers to.

1 Alamanni's satire is reprinted in *Collected Poems*, ed. Muir and Thomson, pp. 347–9.
2 Tottel's title.

The third Satire [CVII], 'How to use the Court',[1] is evidently an imitation of Horace's fifth Satire of the second book.

Hoc quoque Teresia præter narrata petenti, &c.

But it is one of those imitations which entitle to all the praise of originality, Wyatt is indebted to Horace for little more than general ideas. The particular subject to which the Satire is applied is different, and so likewise are the actors. In fact Wyatt cannot be said to have borrowed any one thought distinctly from Horace. His thoughts seem to have been rather excited by reading the Latin Satirist than taken from him. I will explain my meaning by an instance.

In Horace we meet with the following ironical direction. 'If,' says Tiresias, 'one of those who have been named in the same will with you, should happen to have a dangerous cough, offer to make over to him, provided he be older than yourself, at his own price, any part of your legacy he may wish to purchase.' This mode of flattery is not obvious: at all events the experiment would be a dangerous one; and few would be disposed to try it. Wyatt has caught the thought, but with incomparably greater shrewdness and penetration has given it another form.

> Some time also rich Age begin'th to dote.
> See thou, when there thy gain may be the more,
> Stay him by the arm whereso he walk or go.
> Be near alway, *and if he cough too sore,*
> *What he hath spit tread out, and please him so.*   [CVII, 51-5]

In what a lively dramatic manner does this last direction describe the mean servility of the parasite, in hiding from his feeble patron the near approach of death! and how forcibly does it put before us the childish pusillanimity of the rich old dotard, clinging to life with all its miseries, as the only state of existence he had ever thought of, or desired.

When we turn from this general view of Wyatt's Satires, to consider particular passages, we shall be struck with the opening to the Satire, 'Of the mean and sure estate.' It is very artificially contrived, as it immediately excites interest, by placing before us a circumstance of antient simple manners, highly descriptive of the tranquillity of domestic life; thus predisposing the mind to acquiesce in the moral reflections which were afterwards to be drawn from the story.

---

[1] Tottel's title.

> My mother's maids when they do sit and spin,
> They sing sometimes a song made of the Field Mouse;
> Who, for because her livelihood was but thin,
> Would needs go seek her townish sister's house. [CVI, 1–4]

The reflections themselves are conceived in the generous spirit of an exalted morality, and are expressed with force and dignity.

> Alas, my Poynz! how men do seek the best
> And find the worst, by error as they stray.
> And no marvel; when sight is so oppress'd,
> And blind the guide, anon out of the way
> Goeth guide and all——¹
> O! wretched minds! there is no gold that may
> Grant that ye seek; no war, no peace, no strife;
> No! no! although thy head were hoop'd with gold.
> Sergeant with mace, halberd, sword, nor knife
> Cannot repulse the care that follow should.   [CVI, 70–9]

The classical allusions in this passage are so obvious they need not be pointed out; but we may observe that they lose nothing by being accommodated to the circumstances of Wyatt's own times. The Lictor, and his fasces, would have presented but a trite allusion to commonplace learning, and could not have produced any great effect upon the mind: but the King surrounded by all the pomp and circumstance of power, his head, 'hooped with gold', and the serjeant of his guard, with the various insignia of his office, keeping watch over the entrance to the presence chamber, yet unable to exclude the intrusion of care and sorrow, and mental suffering, present a picture the truth and beauty of which cannot but be felt by every one.

The conclusion to the same Satire is in a strain of thought even still more solemn and dignified; imitated indeed, but enlarged and much improved from the philosophic Persius, who closes his third Satire with these spirited lines.

> Magne Pater divum, sævos punire tyrannos
> Haud aliâ ratione velim, cum dira libido
> Moverit ingenium ferventi tincta veneno,
> Virtutem videant intabescantique relictâ.

Wyatt thus expresses himself.

> Henceforth, my Poynz, this shall be all and sum:
> These wretched fools shall have nought else of me.

---

¹ The portion of the line omitted by Nott reads 'in seking quyete liff'.

> But to the great God, and to his high doom,
> None other pain pray I for them to be,
>> But that, when rage doth lead them from the right,
>> Then looking backward, Virtue they may see
> Even as she is, so goodly fair and bright.
>> And when they clasp their lusts in arms across,
>> Grant them, good Lord, as thou may'st of thy might,
>> To fret inward for losing such a loss.   [CVI, 103–12]

In the Satire on the Courtier's Life, Wyatt gives us the following natural and pleasing picture of himself. Having described his occupations at Allington Castle, and congratulated himself that he was neither in France or Flanders, where sensuality alone was studied; nor yet in Spain, where those who wish to thrive must incline themselves,

> Rather than to be, outwardly to seem;   [CV, 92]

Nor yet in Italy,

>> —where Christ is given in prey
> For money, poison, and trahison, at Rome
> A common practice, used night and day.   [CV, 97–9]

He adds;

> But here I am in Kent, and Christendom,
>> Among the Muses; where I read and rhyme.
> Where, if thou list, mine own John Poynz, to come,
> Thou shalt be judge how I do spend my time.   [CV, 100–3]

The conclusion to the last Satire 'How to use the Court', addressed to Sir Francis Bryan, is singularly happy. He points out to him in a strain of fine irony the different arts by which he might attain to wealth and power, and bids him above all things avoid Truth, as that was the most unprofitable thing imaginable, and tells him to use Virtue as it went then a-days,

> In word alone, to make his language sweet.   [CVII, 38]

This premised, he proceeds to give him more particular directions for the advancement of his fortunes, and suggests among other things, that if he should have a niece, a cousin, sister, or even a daughter, whom a great man should solicit, though dishonestly, he ought without any foolish scruple,

Advance his cause, and he shall help thy need:
It is but Love; turn thou it to a laughter. [CVII, 71-2]

Perceiving however that his friend, instead of listening to his advice, treats it with contempt, he suddenly interrupts himself, and asks in a lively dramatic manner,

Laugh'st thou at me? Why! do I speak in vain?
'No, not at thee, but at thy thrifty jest.
Wouldst thou I should for any loss or gain
Change that for gold, which I have ta'en for best?
Next godly things to have an honest name!
Should I leave that, then take me for a beast.'
Nay then farewell! an' if thou care for shame,
Content thee then with honest poverty;
With free tongue what thee mislikes to blame,
And for thy Truth some time adversity;
And therewithal, this gift I shall thee give,
In this world now little prosperity,
And coin to keep, as water in a sieve. [CVII, 79-91]

It was not possible for Wyatt to have paid his friend an higher or a more natural compliment, or at the same time to have marked more pointedly his own detestation of the arts by which he saw dishonest men rising into favour at Court.

From the consideration of Wyatt's merits thus generally, in point of composition, we turn next to consider his language and style of versification.

Wyatt's versification when he first began to write was evidently rhythmical, and differed in no essential point from that of either Hawes or Barclay, or the other writers, who preceded him. This will be evident from the following lines, as they occur in all the printed copies.

But death were deliverance " and life length of pain.
Of two ills lest see " now chuse the least.
This bird to deliver " you that hear her playne,
Your advice you Lovers " which shall be best!

And again;

Mine old dear enemy, " my froward màstèr,
Afore that Queen I caused " to be accited
Which holdeth the divine " part of natùre,
That like as gold in fire " he might be trièd. [VIII, 1-4]

But the conclusive proof of Wyatt's having had rhythmical verse in contemplation is to be drawn from his manuscript, where we find him marking the Cæsura in his own hand-writing; and sometimes the mode of disposing of the redundant syllable, so as to preserve the rhythm of the verse; as in the following instances.

I am in hold: if pity thee meveth: [I, 10]
Go bend thy bow: that stony hearts breaketh: [I, 11]
Right at her ease: and little thee dreadeth. [I, 5]
Weapon'd thou art: and she unarm'd sitteth: [I, 6]
So chanceth it oft: that every passion. [III, 9]
Disdainful doubleness × have I for my hire. [V, 6]
O cruel causer of undeserved change: [V, 13]

In the pieces that were written by him at a later period of his life, Wyatt seems to have adopted the Iambic form of verse, which Surrey's better taste had by that time introduced. We find him also paying a greater attention to the variety of his pauses; aiming likewise at studied involution of sentence, and borrowing particular idioms from the Italian, instead of the French writers, with whom he appears to have been at first most conversant.★ But his early habits were so strong, that in what he attempted he was not always successful. His versification to the last was disfigured by verses, which being formed on the old rhythmical system were either defective or redundant, and could not be reduced to harmony without the use of the Cæsura in the middle, and the pause at the end of the line. He retained likewise the use of the

★ This is evident, not only from some of his poems which bear evident marks of having been taken immediately from the French, such as is the ode which begins,

Though this the port, and I thy servant true. [LXXVIII]

of which the burden is 'En vogant la Galere'; but from the large number of words purely French, and idioms peculiar to that language used by Wyatt throughout all his writings. A striking instance of this occurs . . . where speaking of the Nuns at Barcelona, he says, that 'most were gentlewomen, which walk upon their horses'. This phrase, which is taken from the French, is one so foreign from our own language, that I thought the passage was corrupt, till I found that Lord Calthorpe's MS. agreed with the Harleian MS. in giving that reading. That Wyatt afterwards adopted the Italian idiom, as better suited to the purposes of poetry, is clear from the following passage:

Because I knew the wrath of thy favour
Provoked by right, *had of my pride disdain.*

Sometimes Wyatt adhered servilely to the Italian, as in this line,

That bitter life have turned me in pleasant use. [VIII, 42]

Which runs thus word for word in Petrarch,

Ch' amaro viver m' ha volto in dolce uso.

French pronunciation in those words which were derived originally from that language; and he flung a strong and heavy accent on final syllables, which renders it now difficult for us to read some passages of his poems with pleasure, or trace in them any of that beauty, which as they were once commended, we must suppose them to have once possessed. Such are the following lines:

> So chaunceth it oft that every passion`
> The mind hideth by colour contrary`
> With feigned visage now sad, now mery`,
> Whereby if I laugh any time or season`, &c. [III, 9–12]

This remark, however, applies to Wyatt's heroic verses rather than to those written in shorter measure; which being not so studied are often simple, fluent, and harmonious. Of his versification in the octo-syllabic measure the following passages may serve as specimens. The reader's taste and selection will readily supply more.

> Blame not my Lute, for it must sound
> Of this, or that, as pleaseth me.
> For lack of wit the Lute is bound
> To give such tunes as pleaseth me.
> Though my songs be somewhat strange,
> And speak such words as touch thy change,
>   Blame not my Lute.* [CCV, 1–7]

The following lines boast more merit than that of fluency alone.

> And when in mind I did consent
> To follow this, my fancy's will;
> And when my heart did first relent
> To taste such bait, my life to spill,
> I would my heart had been as thine,
> Or else thy heart had been as mine. [CCLII, 19–24]

Not that Wyatt's heroic verses are always wanting in either elegance or harmony. The following lines are musical and fluent.

> Wherefore, O Lord, as thou has done alway,
> Teach me the hidden wisdom of thy lore. [CVIII, 466–7]

---

* The Ode, of which this stanza forms the opening, is first printed in this volume from the Duke of Devonshire's MS. The whole piece is one of considerable merit, and must have been once very popular, as we find it was moralized by John Hall, who published some poems of a religious and serious nature under the title of *The Court of Virtue*, in 1565. [Nott refers to Hall's religious parody 'My lute awake and prayse the lord' (op. cit., f. 76ᵛ).]

So are these likewise, though they retain a certain character of gravity.

> Thou place of sleep, wherein I do but wake,
> Besprent with tears, my bed! I thee forsake. [CLXXXVII, 6–7]

Wyatt sometimes attains to that terseness and compression which reminds us of Dryden's happiest manner; as in the following line.

> Their tongues reproach, their wit did fraud supply. [CVIII, 371]

And again,

> He granteth most to them that most do crave. [CVIII, 719]

In which, and in many other similar lines, we find a good model of the heroic verse.

When he attempted involution, Wyatt was not always happy. In the following lines the sense is obscured and injured by it.

> O Lord! since my mouth thy mighty name
> Suff'reth itself my Lord to name and call. [CVIII, 73–4]

And again,

> The pompous pride of state and dignity
> Forthwith rebates repentant humbleness. [CVIII, 49–50]

In the use of his pauses he is more successful.

> I, Lord, am strayed; I, sick without recure,
> Feel all my limbs that have rebell'd, for fear
> Shake—in despair unless thou me assure. [CVIII, 97–9]

And thus in another place;

> Perceiving thus the tyranny of sin,
>   That with his weight hath humbled and depress'd
>   My pride; by grudging of the worm within
> That never dieth—I live withouten rest. [CVIII, 349–52]

From these passages, therefore, we are warranted in concluding that Wyatt when he wrote his latter pieces understood the principles of correct versification; and that, had he lived to revise what he had written, he probably would have corrected all the faults of his early style.

In point of language Wyatt does not seem to have done as much, or to have made as many improvements as might have been expected. A far greater number of antiquated words, and obsolete forms of speech are to be found in his writings, than in Surrey's; which is the more remarkable, as he enjoyed the same advantage which Surrey did, of living in the Court, and conversing continually with the great.* It was a circumstance indeed in favour of the latter, that he began to write a few years later than Wyatt did. The interval it is true was not greater than perhaps ten or fifteen years; but even that interval was of importance when the change had been once begun, and things were tending rapidly towards improvement. It operated much to Wyatt's disadvantage, that he translated early from several languages. This, unavoidably gave an uncertainty and a want of precision to his style, which might have been avoided had he proposed to himself only one author as his model. He seems also not to have studied with any definite view the writers in his own language. For though it is evident that he had read Chaucer, and admired him, his imitations are neither frequent, nor of a description to make us suppose that he took him as his master, or considered him to be 'the well-head of English undefiled.'† In both

* See the Dissertation, *Vol. I, p. ccxliv*. If the opinion there advanced should be deemed to want the support of authority, it might be supported by that of the best Italian writers, who called the language suited to the higher purposes of poetry, 'parlar Cortigiano'. Thus Ciampi, in his life of Cino da Pistoia, speaking of the attempt made by him and Dante to improve the poetic language of Italy, says; 'Sì l'uno che l' altro s' accorsene di non poter ben riuscire nell' impresa, se prima non avessero nobilitata, dirozzata, et arrichita la lingua che adoprare nei loro versi dovevano. Di qui è, che a niuno degli italiani dialetti data la preferenza, ma da tutti il meglio scegliendo, e specialmente dal parlar Cortigiano, cioè dal linguaggio usato dalle culte persone nelle corti dei Grandi, col quale i volgari di tutte le città d' Italia si hanno a misurare ponderare, et comparare.' In the xviiith chapter of the same book he goes on to explain why this 'Volgare Illustre' was to be 'aulico, e Cortigiano', that is the language used by polished persons in the courts of princes.

† I will illustrate my meaning in a single instance. In one of his serious odes, Wyatt uses the following expression;

> Alas the grief, and deadly woeful smert
> The careful chance, *shapen afore my shert.* V, [1–2[

It is taken from Chaucer.

> Y-sticked through my true careful hert,
> That shaped was my death *erst than my shert. Knight's Tale, v.* 1568.

Mr. Tyrwhitt, indeed, comparing this passage with another in *Troilus and Cressida,*

> O! fatal Sistren, *which or any cloth*
> *Me shapen was* my destiny me spun. *B. III. l.* 734.

conjectures that the word 'shirt', is not to be taken in a familiar sense, but that it meant generally the cloth in which the new born infant was wrapped. This is a very ingenious conjecture: but, supposing it were granted, still the word in Wyatt's time being used only in a familiar sense, ought, in good taste, to have been avoided.

77

these points Surrey acted with better taste, and obtained more successful results. He directed his attention to Chaucer and Petrarch exclusively, choosing the one as the model for his style in composition; the other as the ground-work of his language. It is to this cause principally, that the greater uniformity of Surrey's language is to be attributed. That the superiority should have been so great as it is, still remains a matter of surprise, because Wyatt and Surrey studied much together; and were in the habit of communicating their compositions to one another. They appear to have sometimes chosen purposely the same subject, for the sake probably of experiment, and friendly competition. Thus Surrey's sonnet,

> Love that liveth and reigneth in my breast,

and Wyatt's, which begins

> The long love that in my thought doth harbour,   [IV]

were written as a sort of exercise of style; as were also Surrey's little ode,

> As oft as I behold and see,

and Wyatt's ode, preserved among the Harleian MSS. which begins,

> Like as the wind with raging blast;   [CCXLV]

for there is in reality no difference between those two poems, except that which arises from the difference of style, peculiar to their respective writers.

A further proof of their community of study may be drawn from their frequent imitations of one another. The Paraphrase of the Seven Penitential Psalms alone supplies a sufficient number of parallel passages to establish the fact. Wyatt thus describes David immersed in thought.

> And whilst he ponder'd these things in his heart
> His knee his arm, his hand sustain'd his chin.   [CVIII, 661-2]

Surrey thus describes himself, when lost in contemplating the objects below him from his prison.

> When Windsor walls sustained my wearied arm
> My hand, my chin, to ease my restless head.

Surrey thus paints his grief for the loss of his friend;

> The tears berain my cheeks of deadly hue,
> The which as soon as sobbing sighs, alas!
> Upsupped have, thus I my plaint renew.

Wyatt thus represents David's sorrow,

> Else had the wind blown in all Israel's ears
> The woeful plaint, and of their King the tears;
> Of which some part when he upsupped had
>
> . . . .
>
> He turns his look, &c.   [CVIII, 417–19, 421]

Again; in one of Wyatt's smaller odes we meet with the following thought;

> Such hammers work within my head
> That sound nought else into my ears.

which thought Surrey has adopted when speaking of Wyatt himself;

> A head where wisdom mysteries did work,
> Whose hammers beat still in that lively brain.[1]

These instances make it clear that Wyatt and Surrey studied much together; and as we find that Wyatt's later pieces bear a nearer resemblance to Surrey's than those which were written by him at an early period, it is probable that their style would ultimately have been as nearly the same as the style of two poets of original genius ever can be. As they now stand, Wyatt's style, when compared with Surrey's, must be deemed rude and unformed. And, indeed, that Wyatt was generally considered inferior to Surrey as a writer, is evident from this, that though he is often highly commended, he is but little imitated; we find, therefore, that while the works of succeeding authors abound with passages either imitated from Surrey, or modelled upon his principles of composition, few comparatively speaking, occur borrowed from Wyatt.

And now, after what has been said of the particular merits of these two great reformers of our language, and fathers of modern English poetry, it will be easy to form a comparison between them.

They were men whose minds, may be said to have been cast in the same mould; for they differ only in those minuter shades of character which always must exist in human nature; shades of difference so infinitely varied, that there never were and never will be two persons in all respects alike. In their love of virtue, and their instinctive hatred and contempt of vice; in their freedom from personal jealousy; in their thirst after knowledge, and intellectual improvement; in nice observation in nature, promptitude to action, intrepidity, and fondness for romantic enterprise; in magnificence and liberality; in generous support of others, and high-spirited neglect of themselves; in constancy in

[1] See No. 3d.

friendship, and tender susceptibility of affections of a still warmer nature, and in every thing connected with sentiment and principle, they were one and the same; but when those qualities branch out into particulars, they will be found in some respects to differ.

Wyatt had a deeper and a more accurate penetration into the characters of men than Surrey had: hence arises the difference in their Satires. Surrey in his satire against the citizens of London, deals only in reproach; Wyatt, in his, abounds with irony, and those nice touches of ridicule which make us ashamed of our faults, and therefore often silently effect amendment.

Surrey's observation of nature was minute, but he directed it towards the works of nature in general, and the movements of the passions, rather than to the foibles and the characters of men; hence it is that he excels in the description of rural objects, and is always tender and pathetic. In Wyatt's complaints we hear a strain of manly grief which commands attention; and we listen to it with respect for the sake of him that suffers. Surrey's distress is painted in such natural terms, that we make it our own, and recognize in his sorrows, emotions which we are conscious of having felt ourselves.

In the point of taste, and perception of propriety in composition, Surrey is more accurate and just than Wyatt; he therefore seldom either offends with conceits, or wearies with repetition; and he imitates other poets, he is original as well as pleasing. In his numerous translations from Petrarch, he is seldom inferior to his master; and he sometimes improves upon him. Wyatt is almost always below the Italian, and frequently degrades a good thought by expressing it so, that it is hardly recognisable. Had Wyatt attempted a translation of Virgil as Surrey did, he would have exposed himself to unavoidable failure.*

---

* Warton twice mentions Wyatt as a translator from Virgil in the same terms with which he describes Surrey. 'Wyatt's and Surrey's versions from Virgil are the first regular translations in English of an antient classic poet.' *Vol. III.* p. 38; and again, 'They were both engaged in translating Virgil', *p.* 40. I wish Warton had been particular in his reference, and that he had cited Wyatt's translation by name. I am not aware that he attempted any thing of the kind. In his song of Iopas, indeed, which is a description of the sphere, Wyatt, to give an introduction to the poem, feigns that it was the song which Virgil, in the first Æneid, speaks of Iopas as having sung before Æneas, when received by Dido at a solemn banquet at Carthage.

> ———— citharâ crinitus Iopas
> Personat auratâ docuit quæ maximus Atlas.
> Hic canit errantem Lunam, Solisque labores;
> Unde hominum genus, et pecudes; unde imber et ignes;
> Arcturum, pluviasque Hyadas, geminosque Triones.

But though in all these points Wyatt confessedly ranks below Surrey, and though his works have not produced as general an effect upon our literature as Surrey's have done, still we owe him much. He was the first English writer who can be said to have aimed at any thing like legitimate style in prose. His two letters to his son, formed on the model of Seneca's Epistles, are grave and sententious, and often exhibit well constructed periods, and a graceful flow of language. In his Oration, his style is even still more varied and artificial. In some places it is grave and dignified; in others it is terse and pointed, and admirably well suited to sarcasm and satire;* when to this we add that Wyatt was the first in point of time to draw our attention to classic composition;† and reflect, that he taught succeeding writers to give refinement of thought to amatory strains, and that he led the way to genuine satire, though his own age was not refined enough to profit by the example; we must allow that he is entitled to an ample share of praise and admiration.‡

* Wyatt's merits as a prose writer will be best estimated by comparing him patiently and critically with the prose writers who immediately preceded him. To make the proof complete, therefore, of what has been asserted above, a series of specimens from their writings ought to be here adduced. But that would extend the notes to an inconvenient length; for if the quotations were not both long and numerous, I might be suspected of having selected such passages only, as suited my purpose. I shall refer the question therefore to the reader's own judgment, if he is disposed to pursue it. The only caution I will give is this, that he do not suffer himself to be misled by an happily expressed sentence that may now and then be found to occur in our prose writers at the period we are speaking of. Were those passages more numerous than they are, they could not be adduced as instances of style. They are happy accidents only, growing out of the genius of the language, and not the result of system on the part of the writers themselves.

† Leland expressly says of Wyatt,

> Nobilitas didicit, te præceptore, Britanna,
> Carmina per varios scribere posse modos. [See No. 2g.]

‡ What has been said above of Wyatt, that he led the way to the improvements made in our style of amatory composition, must not be so understood as to contradict any thing advanced respecting Surrey in the Dissertation prefixed to his poems at p. 229 [In Nott's edition of Surrey's works, 1815]. In point of time Wyatt certainly preceded Surrey;

> Quid tantum Oceano properent se tingere soles
> Hiberni, vel quæ tardis mora noctibus obstet.

[Cp. Warton on 'Iopus' Song' (No. 8, p. 46).]
Of these lines Wyatt can be said to have imitated only the first and second.

> That mighty Atlas did teach," the supper lasting long,
> With crisped locks, on golden harp" Iopas sang in his song. [CIV, 4–5]

Every thing else in Wyatt's piece is purely of his own invention, and has no place whatever in Virgil. I can hardly suppose Warton not to have been aware of this, and therefore am sorry that he did not specify what Wyatt's translations were to which he has alluded, or where they may be found.

I hope it will not be objected to these expressions, that they tend to give a greater importance to the writers of a few obscure Songs and Sonnets at the beginning of the sixteenth century, than can with any propriety, be claimed for them. That those writers have remained so long obscure is a sort of reproach upon our literature: that the general question connected with their works is of importance, what scholar, or what reflecting person will venture to deny?

There is no subject of inquiry connected with human learning, that can be presented to the mind more interesting than what concerns the progress of improvement in language. For as reason, next to the capacity of immortality, with which it is interwoven, is the most precious gift that has been bestowed on man; and as it is language that endows reason with efficacy, he who labours to improve, enlarge, and fix the language of any country; he who by adding to its graces and its harmony adapts it to the purposes of poetry; and by giving it strength and precision, makes it adequate to the higher purposes of science, is entitled to public gratitude, as well as commendation.

This the wisdom of antiquity discerned; and therefore conferred liberal honours upon all, who, by improving language, promoted the common interests of society. Surely if in Egypt, or in Greece, those who first invented, or afterwards increased the number of letters were ranked among the tutelary deities of nations; if statues were erected and public honours decreed to such as contrived new measures in poetic composition, or added to the compass of the lyre, it would be injustice no less than insensibility in us to deem it an idle speculation only, whether Surrey and Wyatt are entitled to the praise which is here claimed for them.

---

perhaps, however, not more than ten, or fifteen years at most. Could we ascertain the date of Wyatt's poems, it would be found, I doubt not, that his earliest productions did not differ in style from those of the writers who had preceded him. Wyatt's style was improved by Surrey. From him he learnt, in a great degree, elegance of expression and fluency of numbers, without which his poems would not have had any sensible effect at all upon our literature. Moreover, when it is said that Surrey was 'the first who gave us a model of the sonnet in our language', the observation applies to sonnets of original composition; and to those only is the reference made. See the *Dissertation ut sup*. It is probable that Wyatt must have translated some sonnets from Petrarch before Surrey began to write; but of Wyatt's sonnets which may be deemed original, not one can lay claim to the merit of being a model in that species of composition; which Surrey's sonnets are. The best of Wyatt's original sonnets, in point of conduct, is that which begins,

Divers do use, as I have heard and know. [CCXVII]

But even that is far inferior to Surrey's original sonnets, and bears evident marks of having been written by him at a late period of his life.

In the long interval that had elapsed between Chaucer and themselves, the English language had not advanced in elegance, perspicuity, copiousness, or strength. To this cause chiefly was it owing, that during the above period no works were written of any account in our native tongue, either in history, poetry, morals, or science. Genius was not extinct among us; but our language not seconding exertion, exertion was discontinued. What was written in one generation, was difficult to be understood in the next; and was therefore soon to be superseded by something more intelligible.

The inconveniences arising from this uncertain state of our language Surrey and Wyatt perceived, and applied themselves to remedy. That they did much towards fixing it, the most careless observer must allow. That they did not effect more, is no fault imputable to them. Had not an untimely death taken Wyatt away just as his taste and judgment were matured; and had not the unrelenting jealousy of political intrigue cut Surrey off in the vigor of his youth, there seems no reason to doubt but that they would have perfected their undertaking: and having revised and polished the works they had written, and undertaken others of a larger scope, and such as might have called forth all the powers of their mind, they probably would have fixed, even then, the standard of our language, and have placed it beyond the reach of those changes to which after their death it was exposed. For from the time the noble Surrey fell beneath the hand of oppression, until Spenser appeared, no poet arose equal to the task of finishing what he and Wyatt had begun; and even of Spenser himself it must be allowed, that he did less than might have been expected from his genius and his learning.*

* It was the opinion of Ben Jonson, an opinion often copied from him, though not always acknowledged, that 'Spenser, in affecting the ancients, writ no language. Yet,' continues that admirable writer, 'I would have him read for his matter, as Virgil read "Ennius".' See *Ben Jonson's Explorata, or Discoveries.* Having Jonson's work before me, I trust I shall be pardoned in extracting from it another passage, which I would strongly urge on the reader's attention. It is one that applies as well to some opinions advanced in the dissertation prefixed to Surrey's poems, respecting a vitiated taste in language and composition, as to what I shall have to remark at the close of the present essay. 'There cannot be one colour of the mind; another of the wit. If the mind be staid, grave, and composed, the wit is so; that vitiated, the other is blown and deflowered. Do we not see if the mind languish, the members are dull? Look upon an effeminate person! his very gait confesseth him. If a man be fiery, his motion is so; if angry, it is troubled and violent; so that we may conclude, WHERESOEVER MANNERS AND FASHIONS ARE CORRUPTED, LANGUAGE IS. It imitates the public riot. The excess of feasts and apparel are the notes of a sick state; and the wantonness of language, of a sick mind.' *Ibid. p.* 101. With great propriety therefore did that sterling old writer rank the observation just cited concerning corruption of language, under the head of 'Corruption of Manners.' For there ever has been a connection between the decay of national virtue, and the decay of national taste and language. The corruption

On this ground, therefore, our regret at the untimely fate of those two great reformers of our language cannot be deemed ill-founded; neither ought the praise bestowed upon them to be condemned as a blind prepossession in favour of antiquity.

Accustomed from infancy to hear our native tongue spoken as it now is finally settled, and adapted to all the purposes of learned as well as civil life; capable alike of expressing elevated ideas with dignity, and things familiar with elegance, we are hardly qualified to judge of the extent of the benefit conferred upon us by those who rescued it from its original rudeness and deformity. But, if we consider the case as it occurred in another country, we shall be able to appreciate the value of what was done in our own.

What was it that gave at the time, and still continues to give so much importance to the writings of Petrarch? It was not that he wrote feelingly and tenderly of love; though he himself seems to have considered that as the reason why he was so much honoured and admired;* but because he had taught Italy the use and the power of its native tongue. Before his time the common language of the country, the 'Volgare Lingua', was not thought competent of any of the higher purposes of learning or of business. It was deemed suited to domestic uses only. If ideas of more than ordinary refinement were to be expressed, or transactions of importance recorded, recourse was had to the Latin. This produced much inconvenience. The end proposed could not be answered but with labour and trouble; and after all, the lower and

---

* See particularly that sonnet of Petrarch which begins,

> S'io avessi pensato, che sì care
> Fossin le voci de' sospir mie' in rima! &c.

Towards the conclusion of the sonnet he adds with his usual elegance and feeling,

> Pianger cercai, non già del pianto honore.

The work upon which Petrarch meant to build his fame, was a long Latin poem, called *Africa*, on the subject of Scipio's wars. To the writing and correcting this poem, he devoted a great portion of his life; yet so entirely is it swallowed up in the superior merits of his compositions, in 'Volgare Lingua', that few of Petrarch's admirers have ever read it, and many perhaps have never heard its name.

---

of the Roman language first shewed itself in the captivating but meretricious graces of the style of Tacitus. How nearly connected with this, those more fatal corruptions were which about the same time took place in Roman manners; and how closely both kept pace together, until the mighty fabric of the Roman empire itself fell into utter ruin, I need not here stop to shew. Suffice it to remark, that we have seen in our own country an admiration bestowed upon the style of Gibbon, equal to that which the style of Tacitus, its prototype, obtained from the rising youth of Rome. Here may the parallel cease!

DII! MELIORA PIIS ERROREM QUE HOSTIBUS ILLUM!

the middle orders of society were excluded from a knowledge of things, in which, nevertheless, they had a common interest with persons of a more exalted rank. But when once Petrarch had shewn them that the 'Volgare Lingua' was capable of such improvement as would render it equal to any exertion that could be required of language; when the lover learnt that he could address his mistress in his own tongue with an elegance, to which the Poets of Provence alone were deemed capable of attaining; and when princes found that they could discuss all points of business with ease and precision, without the intervention of the dead languages, the astonishment of the nation at large was equal to its delight. The effect produced upon them was similar to that which music is said to have on savage nations the first time they hear the sweetness of modulated sounds. They seemed to awake as from sleep; they felt as if some new intellectual power had been discovered; and the faculty of reason itself became of greater importance to them; for they felt that from that period they had the means of perpetuating all the operations and conclusions of their minds, and by fixing past discoveries, proceed step by step to future;

Sì che 'l piè fermo sempre era 'l piè basso.

Under these circumstances, therefore, what wonder was it that a single sonnet addressed by Petrarch, in his harmonious and expressive language, to any of the princes of his times, should have been received as a present more precious than gold; and that kings and emperors should have united to court the favour of a man, whose writings were about to form an epoch in the history of their country.

It is true that the change effected by Wyatt and Surrey in our own country was not of equal magnitude; still they did much. Take the quaint and unharmonious periods of the prose writers who preceded Wyatt, and compare them with the terse and fluent style of his oration before the Privy Council: read the lifeless attempts to express passion in Hawes and Skelton, and contrast them with the elegance and pathos of Surrey's tender muse. If the comparison be fairly and impartially made, no one, I think, will censure me as claiming too much for Wyatt and Surrey when I say, that they are entitled to the same sort of respect among us, that Italy has long since bestowed upon Petrarch. Not that they are equal to him in point of beauty; but that they wrote with similar views, and went far to accomplish the same object.*

---

* I shall not be accused, I hope, of any desire to derogate from Petrarch's merits, when I suggest that, much as he did for the language and poetry of Italy, he possessed advantages

And let it not be objected either to Wyatt or Surrey, that they devoted so large a portion of their writings to describe the hopes and the

---

which few writers but himself enjoyed. He was placed early in a situation which enabled him to devote his whole time and thoughts to study and composition. He lived, moreover, to polish all his poems with the nicest care and attention; and when they were finished they were transcribed with scrupulous fidelity, and copies were multiplied to be placed in the libraries of the great, or to be publickly commented upon by the learned. Afterwards, when the art of printing was invented, his poems were among the first works to be published, and editions were repeated upon editions, for the most part with such religious exactness, that it might be said his very words were numbered. These advantages respect the text of Petrarch; he himself enjoyed that of studying the Provençal poets, in their own country, confessedly the most elegant and polite poets of the times: and from them he is supposed to have borrowed largely. He was preceded also in his own country by many writers of great genius and learning, who had gone a considerable way towards perfecting the Italian language before he began to write, and had left specimens in every branch of composition which he is found to have attempted. Not to mention Guido d' Arezzo, and Guido Cavalcanti, and Dante himself, of whose fame Petrarch was said to have been jealous (though he so studiously imitated him in his *Triumphs* that he has been styled in consequence 'il Dante ingentilito'), if we consider the works of Cino da Pistoia, those alone will be sufficient to prove that Petrarch was greatly indebted to the poets who preceded him. From Cino, Petrarch sometimes borrowed entire verses: as in his VIIth Canzone, where we meet with the following line;

La dolce vista e 'l bel guardo soave;

which forms the opening to Cino's XVIth Canzone. Sometimes Petrarch took thoughts from him with little change of expression. Thus in the first of his three celebrated odes to Laura's eyes, fancifully called 'Le tre Sorelle', he has the following passage.

Luci beate e liete,
Se non che 'l veder voi stesse v' è tolto;
Ma quante volte a me vi rivolgete,
Conoscete in altrui quel che voi sete.

But Cino had previously written an ode in praise of the eyes of Madonna Selvaggia, his mistress, in which he had said,

Poichè veder voi stessi non potete
Vedete in altri almen quel che voi sete.

In the following lines, which form the opening to Cino's second sonnet, we find so many expressions and turns of thought used by Petrarch, that we perceive at once he must have studied him attentively as his master.

Io son sì vago della bella luce
Degli occhi traditor che m' hanno ucciso,
Che là dov' io son vinto, e son deriso
La gran vaghezza pur mi riconduce.

Many other passages might be adduced, in which the same general resemblance of style is to be found. But the strongest proof of Petrarch's obligations to him may be found in the circumstance of his having formed his celebrated ode, which begins

Quell' antiquo mio dolce empio Signore,

on one of Cino's sonnets. I am aware that Muratori supposes that sonnet to have been written by one Gandolfo Porrino, in the 16th century, for the purpose of imposing on Castelvetro; but he assigns no other reason than that he thinks no one could have written so

fears, the enjoyments and the disappointments of love. It has ever been so in the history of all nations. Love the most universal, is the most importunate of all the affections of the mind; it will make itself felt; and when felt, will press forward for utterance, whilst every other passion is either unheard, or silent.* This, however, is not without benefit to the world at large. Men are for the most part won to intellectual pursuits by the early fascinations of pathetic and amatory poetry; having thus acquired a taste for letters, they are easily led afterwards step by step to the attainment of solid learning, which, had it been proposed to them at the commencement under the severe aspect of science, might have repressed the rising ardour of inquiry. It is the verdant meadow, and the gentle acclivity, studded with flowers, and watered with rivulets at the bottom of the mountain, that first induces us to undertake the laborious task of climbing to its

* Speaking of Laura's and Petrarch's romantic passion, the Italians say,

> Da lor' onesto, ardente, e vivo amore
> Naque uno stil, che mai non ebbe equale.

---

well, previous to Petrarch. As the sonnet occurs in MS. collections of Cino's poems, written before Porrino lived, Muratori's conjecture cannot be for a moment admitted. The sonnet in question is as follows.

> Mille dubbi in un di; mille querele,
> Al tribunal dell' alta Imperatrice
> Amor contra me forma irato, e dice;
> 'Giudica chi di noi sia più fidele!
> Questi, sol mia cagion, spiega le vele.
> Di fama al mondo, ove saria infelice.'
> 'Anzi d'ogni mio mal sei la radice'
> Dico, 'e provai già di tuo dolce il fele.'
> Ed egli; 'Ahi! falso servo fuggitivo!
> E questo il merto che mi rendi, ingrato,
> Dandoti una, a cui 'n terra egnal non era?'
> 'Che val,' seguo, 'se tosto me n' hai privo?'
> 'Io no,' risponde. Ed ella; 'A sì gran piato
> Convien più tempo a dar sentenza vera.'

What has been here said does not go to detract any thing essential from Petrarch's merits as a writer: but when the merits of Surrey and Wyatt are under consideration it is but common justice to remark, that had those two early restorers of English literature been possessed of equal advantages, they would have been able to have stood on the fair ground of competition with the proudest names of modern Italy. Cino da Pistoia was born 1270: he died in 1336 or 1337. Petrarch was born in 1304, and died in 1374. Quadrio thus describes the several poets that have been mentioned above. 'Dante è ne' suoi pensamenti, nerboruto, fantastico, e forte: il Cavalcanti, in luogo delle materiali idee le spirituali usando, filosofeggia con sentimenti maravigliosi, e ne' suoi concetti è sempre elevato; Cino è naturale, tenero e soave; Petrarca e maravigliosamente affectuosso, gentile e pulito.' *Storia d'ogni Poesia, Vol. III. p. 62.*

airy top: the outset is pleasurable, and the amusement we receive be-
guiles our toil; as we advance the ascent is more difficult, but by this
time habit has reconciled us to exertion: the air grows purer and fresher
the higher we proceed; the space we have already measured gives us
strength and spirits to encounter what remains, until at length we reach
the highest summit, and then looking down with complacency on the
difficulties surmounted, smile as we contemplate far below us the
flowery paths that first caught our attention.

Thus much may be urged in the defence of all those poets, who like
Surrey and Wyatt have made love the chief subject of their strains; but
then like them they must have described love under the form, in which
alone it can be recognized by good and honourable minds; as a passion
free alike from effeminacy and libertinism, moving under the controul
of reason, and making itself subservient to the real happiness and moral
improvement of our being.

There never have been wanting writers, indeed, who, abusing talents
bestowed upon them for better purposes, delight to describe passion in
its worst and most offensive form; who are either base enough to solicit
desire; or dwell with horrid complacency on characters in which love,
if such an abuse of the term can be allowed, is found coupled with
violence and rapine, and daring contempt of moral rectitude, and savage
promptitude to deeds of murder and revenge.

But Surrey and Wyatt were not writers of that description. Had they
been such, I should not have come forward to claim for them an
honourable place in the literature of their country; or the attempt, I
trust, would have proved abortive.

As for those writers who set at defiance all the sound and sober laws
of chaste composition, and in their affectation of singularity, and love
of popular applause, offend against the very principles of moral feeling;
of them we will indulge an hope, that calmer thoughts, and maturer
reflection may yet reclaim them to efforts more worthy of their talents
and themselves, and such as shall give them a fair claim to lasting
celebrity. Should we be disappointed in that hope, we will wait in
patience until the time come, for come it will (would! that it were
arrived already) when looking back dispassionately upon past illusions,
we shall be astonished to think that the seductions of fashion, and the
prevalence of a corrupt taste, had ever led us to tolerate writings of
pestilential example; shall tremble to reflect that we suffered the un-
suspecting ear of youth and female purity, to be assailed by strains
breathing sentiments which no sophistry can palliate, no plea of passion

excuse; and, with the burning blush of shame, erase the very names of such as wrote them from that bright list of authors, of whom alone the literature of any country can with justice be proud; of those, who have made Poetry the graceful handmaid and attendant upon Religion; who have engaged our feelings on the side of Virtue; and approved themselves to be, like the honoured Bard of old, the faithful guardians of domestic innocence, and the morals of the age.*

10. Bell on Wyatt

1854

Introduction to Wyatt, *The Poetical Works*, ed. Robert Bell, the Annotated Edition of English Poets (1854), pp. 53–60.

Bell (1800–67) was a journalist and minor author.

As a poet, Wyatt's claims have never been adequately recognized. While he has obtained the credit of having co-operated with Surrey in 'correcting the ruggedness' of English poetry, his share in the reform has not received the acknowledgment to which it appears to be entitled. Surrey, being the better poet, has carried off all the honours. Dr Nott says that at a late period Wyatt adopted the iambic form of verse which Surrey had *at that time* introduced.[1] Setting aside the doubtful hypothesis that Surrey was the first to introduce the iambic, the immediate question that arises out of this assertion is, At what time did he introduce it, and at what time was it adopted by Wyatt? The priority

---

* When Agamemnon went on his fatal expedition against Troy, he left his Bard behind him in his palace; and to him he entrusted the guardianship of Clytemnestra's virtue. The Son of Song was faithful to his charge; and Ægysthus was not able to prevail. He was removed. The fatal policy succeeded. Clytemnestra yielded to the arts of the seducer.

1 See No. 9, pp. 60 and 74 above.

is simply a matter of dates; and, as Dr Nott is specific and absolute in his statement, we have a right to expect that he is prepared to support it by the requisite proofs. But no such proofs are in existence. The dates when the poems were written are unknown. Wyatt's and Surrey's poems were published for the first time in Tottel's Miscellanies in 1557, ten years after the execution of Surrey, and fifteen years after the death of Wyatt. If we could even suppose, which for obvious reasons we cannot, that Tottel's editor had arranged the productions of each author in the order of their composition, it would afford us no assistance towards the determination of their relative dates. Here and there particular allusions may suggest a speculation as to the period when certain pieces were written; but that kind of evidence is not always to be relied upon, nor does it furnish sufficiently extensive data to warrant a general inference. In the absence, therefore, of more direct testimony, we must turn to such collateral circumstances as bear upon the inquiry; and here all particulars concur in proving that Wyatt was several years antecedent to Surrey. The confusion into which Dr Nott's tendency to substitute speculation for fact has thrown the circumstantial evidence is not a little remarkable.

Wyatt was fourteen years older than Surrey. The greater part of his poems—including the whole of his love poems—may be presumed to have been written in his youth. The subjects of these pieces can hardly be supposed to have engaged his attention after he went upon his embassy to Spain;[1] and, according to Dr Nott's theory, they must have been written before. Anne Boleyn became the King's mistress in 1530, when Wyatt was twenty-three years of age; and Dr Nott says that many of his sonnets were addressed to her before she formed that connection, and that from the time of her death, which took place in 1536, his writings assumed a more grave and moral tone. This assertion, like the former, is purely conjectural; but it is important as marking the period, previously to which the writer supposes Wyatt to have produced the principal portion of his poems. It is clear that Wyatt could not have followed the example of Surrey in any of these pieces, Surrey being only thirteen years old in 1530. In his memoir of Wyatt, Dr Nott allows that an interval of ten or perhaps fifteen years elapsed between them; but in his memoir of Surrey he makes the interval still greater, and completely disposes of the hypothesis concerning the iambics, by supposing that Surrey did not begin to write till 1541, only one year before the death of Wyatt.

[1] There is at least one exception, XCVIII, entitled *In Spayne*.

That Wyatt 'co-operated' with Surrey[1] is one of those pleasant traditions which must be taken on trust. It is said that they were devoted friends, and Surrey's lines on the death of Wyatt seem to indicate a close and intimate intercourse:—

> But I, that knew what harboured in that head,
> What virtues rare were tempered in that breast,
> Honour the place that such a jewel bred.[2]

Yet it is singular that not a solitary trace of their friendship has survived. We know, indeed, that Surrey was the companion of Wyatt's son, who was about four years his junior, as we find them both concerned in the frolic of breaking the citizens' windows, for which they were cited before the Privy Council, in 1543, the year after the death of Wyatt, the elder; but this is the only scrap of information respecting their connexion that has been preserved. It is on many accounts unlikely that Surrey and Wyatt held that poetical communion which has been attributed to them. It can, I think, be satisfactorily shown that no opportunities existed for its cultivation. When Wyatt wrote his early poems, Surrey had not yet begun to write. In 1537, Surrey being then about twenty years of age, Wyatt went abroad, and did not come back to England till the June or July of 1539. In the following November he was despatched on his second embassy, which detained him on the Continent till May, 1540. In the winter of that year, or the succeeding spring, he was arrested and sent to the Tower, and was not released till the ensuing June. And in the interval from that time till his death, in October, 1542, it is clear that little intercourse could have taken place between them, as early in July Surrey was committed to the Fleet, and soon after his liberation, in August, took a command under his father in the Scotch campaigns, from which he did not return till after Wyatt's death. Surrey's admiration of Wyatt's character, and the affection he felt for him, must, therefore, have been formed in his youth, and strengthened, not by personal intimacy, but by subsequent observation of his public and literary career. Under these circumstances, their literary pursuits must have been prosecuted independently of each other; and, although we may conclude that Surrey was stimulated by Wyatt's example, we cannot discover equally cogent grounds for transferring to Surrey the credit of having exerted any very material influence over Wyatt.

[1] Warton: see No. 8, p. 41.
[2] See No. 3c.

Dr Nott had overlooked these facts when he stated that 'Wyatt and Surrey studied much together, and were in the habit of communicating their compositions to one another';[1] which is, in reality, nothing more than a conjecture, founded on the existence of certain resemblances in their works. These resemblances sometimes arise out of the choice of subjects, as, for instance, when they both translated the same sonnet of Petrarch;[2] and sometimes from a similarity in the turn of expression and the use of a current phraseology. In neither case are we warranted in inferring that they must of necessity have written in concert. The selection of two or three prominent passages for translation, or imitation, from an original of which both were ardent students, cannot be reasonably assumed as an evidence of design; and the similarity in their style and diction may be traced to a more obvious source than that of the constant communication of their compositions to each other. The idioms and particular forms that abound in their poems, and in which the chief features of resemblance consist, are common to the poets of their time. The readers of Surrey and Wyatt must have observed the frequent recurrence of such expressions as 'to put in ure,' to 'bear in hand,' to 'take in worth,' and the like, drawn directly from colloquial usage; the practice of adapting the pronunciation and orthography to the rhyme and the measure; and the liberal employment of inversions and ellipses. These peculiarities impart a complexional resemblance to their productions, which might suggest a suspicion of imitation at one side or the other, if we had not proofs that this language and these forms were also the language and forms of other writers who flourished about the same period, and who were as close to Surrey as Surrey was to Wyatt. But if we are to suppose, with Dr Nott, that there was any imitation in the case, it must be charged upon the younger and later poet.

There were, undoubtedly, remarkable resemblances of another and a subtler kind between Wyatt and Surrey. They modelled their poetry upon the same originals; they cultivated the same class of subjects, and were the first to treat the passion of love in a refined and courtly spirit; their sympathies carried them in the same direction, and led them to prosecute the same ends; and in both there was a purity of taste and morals which rejected alike the corruptions, pedantries, and licentiousness of their age. To these sources may be referred that homogeneity of character which has linked their names together almost as inseparably

1 See No. 9, p. 78.
2 'Amor che nel pensier mio'.

as those of Beaumont and Fletcher. But a critical investigation of their poetry discovers differences which completely set aside the supposition that they formed or modified their style by communication with each other. Dr Nott, in a subsequent passage, admits the points of contrast and difference so fully as to annihilate his previous speculation. He says that 'Wyatt's style, when compared with Surrey's, must be deemed rude and unformed;' that 'Wyatt was generally considered inferior to Surrey;' and he adds, as a proof of the fact, that 'while succeeding authors abound with passages either imitated from Surrey, or modelled upon his principles of composition, few, comparatively speaking, occur borrowed from Wyatt.'[1] If their principles of composition were so widely different, there can be little reason to suppose that they held the literary intercourse attributed to them. It is extremely probable that occasional copies of some of their poems (which, it must be remembered were circulated only in MS.) may have fallen into each other's hands, or even been directly communicated, when opportunity, which rarely favoured such interchanges, happened to serve. But if they studied together, or were in the habit of mutually communicating their writings, incidental evidence of the fact must have crept out somewhere, either in allusions in the poems themselves, or in reliques of their correspondence. No such evidence, however, has been found.

That Wyatt, at an early period, did not adopt the regular iambic, said to have been then introduced by Surrey, is shown by the poems which belong to that period, and confirmed by Dr Nott's own judgment upon them. The Satires and the Psalms were his last pieces, written at Allington, with all the advantages of leisure, retirement, and experience. The Satires are highly finished; the Psalms are the worst specimens of metrical composition he produced. In fluency, ease, and melody of versification, both are excelled by some of his early poems. The versification of the Psalms, Dr Nott observes, 'is more crabbed and inharmonious than, perhaps, in any other part of his works; its very structure is uncertain; it seems to fluctuate between the regular iambic line, which Surrey had then introduced, and the old rhythmical line to which Wyatt had been early accustomed.'[2] Yet these Psalms are the principal tests of the accuracy of the assertion that Wyatt had adopted the iambic from Surrey. It might be proved, on the contrary, by a multitude of examples, that he had used it long before Surrey began to write.

1 See No. 9, p. 79.
2 See No. 9, p. 60.

The comparison between them on general grounds must unhesitatingly be admitted to be largely in favour of Surrey. He was more impassioned, and had a finer sensibility and a more exact taste. But Wyatt possesses high merits of another kind. His verse is more thoughtful than Surrey's; more compressed and weighty. He had not so graceful a way of making love; but his love, nevertheless, has an air of gallantry and self-possession that captivates the imagination by different approaches. His diction is less poetical than that of Surrey; but a careful examination of his poems must reverse the judgment which has pronounced it to be more antiquated. He uses, comparatively, few expressions that are not intelligible to the modern reader. His vocabulary is extensive, and imparts constant novelty to his descriptions. His versification, incidentally harsh and refractory, is, generally, regular and sonorous. In order, however, to obtain the full music of his lines, it is necessary to remember that he drew largely on French and Italian models, and that apparently deficient syllables must be occasionally supplied by adopting foreign accents.

The charge of want of originality is not so easily answered. Wyatt was largely indebted to the French and Italian poets; and reminiscences of many writers, classical and continental, may be detected flitting through his poems. But it was no slight merit in his day to have enriched English poetry with the fruits of extensive reading; and if it diminished his claim to originality, it enabled him to give greater scope and variety to his compositions than any of his contemporaries attained. His success in transplanting into our language the forms of the Spanish, French, and Italian writers, contributed in an important degree to the subsequent improvement of our poetry. He is said to be overcharged with conceits; but, taking into consideration the sources from which he borrowed, and the age in which he wrote, it would be more just to say that he is singularly free from conceits. After the manner of Petrarch, he persecutes an image, now and then, to extremity, and sometimes involves it in obscurity; and, after the fashion of the day, which he himself helped to bring into contempt, he occasionally condescends to indulge in alliteration. But these trifling blemishes are amply expiated by conspicuous excellences. His poems are never stained by indelicacies; and if his poetical taste is not always faultless, his moral taste is irreproachable. His satires are amongst the earliest, and most admirable specimens of that style—close in texture, elastic in expression, and displaying a profound knowledge of the world. In his tender and pensive passages, there is a vein of manliness that inspires them with dignity.

Nor is he deficient in grace and beauty. His Rondeaux are sparkling and animated; and he is particularly happy in the refrains with which, at the close of the verse, he returns to his subject, and gives back, as it were, the echo of the predominant sentiment.

11. Courthope on Wyatt

1897

W. J. Courthope, *A History of English Poetry* (1895–1905), II, pp. 49–66.

Courthope (1842–1917) was a civil servant and literary historian.

Two very marked and contrary features distinguish Wyatt's poetry, the individual energy of his thought, and his persistent imitation of foreign models. The former is what separates him sharply from the poets of the Middle Ages. Hitherto, with the exception of the *Canterbury Tales*, almost every English poem of importance had been didactic in intention, thereby denoting its clerical source; symbolical in form, thus revealing the influence of the allegorical method of interpreting Nature and Scripture encouraged in the Church schools. Wyatt, on the other hand, looked at Nature through his own eyes, and sought to express directly the feelings of his own heart. He was a man of many moods and ideas; his compositions include love verses, epigrams, devotional meditations, satires; and in all of these the force and ardour of his thought is sensibly felt. But equally, in all of them, the poet shows himself to be aware of the imperfection of his native language as an instrument of expression, and submits himself with humility to the superiority of the foreign masters whose manner he seeks to reproduce. In consequence of this his actual poetical achievements are of very unequal merit; he often aims at objects which he ought to have avoided, or at effects to which his resources are unequal; he is most successful when his fiery genius can find out a way for itself untrammelled by the precedents of art.

This is particularly the case in those of his love-poems in which he abandons the models of Petrarch and the Italian and French successors of that poet. The groundwork of the style of the Petrarchists was the poetry of the Troubadours, refined and modified by the classical tastes of the Humanists. The genius of the Troubadours being the natural product of the institutions of chivalry, when these decayed the genuine motive of production ceased, and the poet, seeking merely to preserve the outward manner, fell into a style hard, mechanical, and affected. For example, in the sixteenth century and long afterwards, the most quoted of Petrarch's sonnets was the 156th, which is as follows:—

Passa la nave mia colma d' obblio
    Per aspro mar a mezza notte il verno,
    Infra Scilla e Cariddi, ed al governo
    Siede 'l Signor, anzi 'l nemico mio.
A ciascun remo un pensier pronto e rio,
    Che la tempesta, e 'l fin par ch' abbi a scherno.
    La vela rompe un vento umido eterno
    Di sospir, di speranze, e di desio.
Pioggia di lagrimar, nebbia di sdegni,
    Bagna, e rallenta le già stanche sarte;
    Che son d' error con ignoranza attorto.
Celansi i duo miei dolci usati segni;
    Morta fra l' onde è la ragion, e l' arte.
    Tal, ch' incomincio a disperar del porto.★

Now it must be clear to every reader of manly taste that this sonnet deserves no higher praise than that of ingenuity. As soon as the poet has fixed on the idea that his soul is like a ship, of which Love is the pilot, it is easy enough to associate with this central thought a group of subordinate conceits, in which tears are imaged as rain, and sighs as winds; on the other hand, it is almost inevitable that, in endeavouring to work out the comparison, he should use such violence as to liken his thoughts to oarsmen, and should represent the ropes of the vessel as being 'twisted by error and ignorance.' The passion for riddles, always a symptom of declining taste, caused this mechanical performance to be preferred above sonnets in which Petrarch, having selected a really fine thought, elaborates it with simplicity and propriety. The Petrarchists came to

★ See Wyatt's translation on p. 98.

reckon subject as of little importance in poetry; and every one wishing to show his skill aimed at finding resemblances between objects which were to all appearance the most unlike each other in Nature. Giusto de' Conti, for instance, composed a whole volume of sonnets on 'the beautiful hand' of his mistress; and Serafino dell' Aquila treated the subject of Love in a series of epigrams, under the title of *Strambotti* or Conceits, each of which consisted of an abstract thought illustrated by a sensible image, and was expressed within the limits of a stanza in *ottava rima*. So great was the admiration felt for this poet by his contemporaries that his epitaph assures the traveller that he may hold it an honour even to have seen his tomb.*

It is not surprising that the French and English poets who imitated Petrarch should have tried to reproduce those qualities in his sonnets which they found most appreciated by his own countrymen. Mellin de St. Gelays, who made an attempt—ineffectual as it proved—to transplant the sonnet into French literature some few years before Wyatt introduced it into England, was the author of the following lines, in which it will be seen that the manner of Petrarch, as above exemplified, is prosaically copied:—

> Voyant ces monts de veue ainsi lointaine,
> Je les compare à mon long déplaisir:
> Haut est leur chef, et haut est mon désir,
> Leur pied est ferme, et ma foy est certaine.
>
> D'eux maint ruisseau coule et mainte fontaine:
> De mes deux yeux sortent pleurs à loisir;
> De forts souspirs ne me puis dessaissir,
> Et de grands vents leur cime est toute pleine.
>
> Mille troupeaux s'y promènent et paissent;
> Autant d'Amours se couvent et renaissent
> Dedans mon cœur, qui seul est ma pasture.
>
> Ils sont sans fruit mon bien n'est qu'apparence;
> Et d'eux à moy n'a qu'une différence,
> Qu'en eux la neige, en moi la flamme dure.

Of the thirty-one sonnets composed by Wyatt ten are translated more or less closely from Petrarch, one from Mellin de St. Gelays,[1] two

---

* Qui giace Serafin! Partirti or puoi.
Sol d' aver visto il sasso che lo serva,
Assai sei debitore agli occhi tuoi.
  Vita del facundo Poeta Seraphyno Aquilano,
  per Vincentio Calmeta composta, 1505.

[1] Arthur Tilley (*M.L.Q.* V, 1902), discovered the Italian sonnet, possibly by Sannazaro on which St Gelays and Wyatt drew independently.

are indebted to Petrarch, one is constructed out of two of Serafino's *Strambotti*, one from J. A. Romanello,[1] and the remaining nine are apparently the product of original thought. Not one of the series shows any marks of inspiration, they are the work of a man who has been impressed with the beautiful and ingenious form of the sonnet as handled by the Italians, and who seeks to reproduce its effects in a language not yet sufficiently refined for his purpose. The following, which are renderings of the sonnets by Petrarch and Mellin de St. Gelays[2] already cited, may be taken as average examples of his style:—

> My galley, charged with forgetfulness,
>> Thorough sharp seas in winter nights doth pass
>> 'Tween rock and rock; and eke mine enemy alas!
> That is my lord, steereth with cruelness:
> At every oar, a thought in readiness;
>> As though that death were light in such a case.
>> An endless wind doth tear the sail apace
> Of forced sighs, and trusty fearfulness.
> A rain of tears, a cloud of dark disdain,
>> Hath done the wearied cords great hindrance,
>> Wreathed with error and eke with ignorance.
> The stars be hid that led me to this pain;
>> Drowned is reason that should me consort;
> And I remain, despairing of the port.

This is the production of an energetic mind; nevertheless the means employed are inadequate to the end, as may be specially noted in the unsuccessful attempt to render

> A ciascun remo un pensier pronto e rio,
> Che la tempesta e 'l fin par ch' abbi a scherno;

[At each oar a thought bold and guilty, which seems to think scorn alike of the tempest and the goal]

and by the omission of any equivalent for 'arte' in the thirteenth line caused by the necessity of rhyming. On the other hand, Wyatt's strong individuality asserts itself in his alteration of Petrarch's 'i duo miei dolci *usati* segni' [my two sweet familiar stars], into the vehement

> The stars be hid *that led me to this pain.*

[1] The reference is to 'Who so list to hount' (VII). Opinions as to Wyatt's source vary; Petrarch's 'Una candida cerva' is the most likely, but Wyatt might have used Romanello's imitation of Petrarch (*Rhythmorum Vulgarium*, Verona, n.d. Sonnet III).
[2] I.e. Sannazaro.

The translation of Mellin de St. Gelays'[1] sonnet seems to have been occasioned by a tasteless admiration for the French poet's trivial conceits, and is as follows:—

> Like to these unmeasurable mountains
> Is my painful life, the burden of ire;
> For of great height be they, and high is my desire;
> And I of tears, and they be full of fountains.
> Under craggy rocks they have barren plains;
> Hard thoughts in me my woeful mind doth tire.
> Small fruit and many leaves their tops do attire;
> Small effect with great trust in me remains.
> The boisterous winds oft their high boughs do blast;
> Hot sighs from me continually be shed.
> Cattle in them and in me love is fed;
> Immoveable am I, and they are full steadfast.
> Of restless birds, they have the tone and note;
> And I alway plaints that pass through my throat.

The reader will have some difficulty in making up his mind whether more to blame Wyatt for the flat and feeble close of this sonnet, or to commend him for the glimmering of good taste he shows in rejecting the contrast between fire and snow, in which Mellin de St. Gelays' readers doubtless found a fine stroke of poetical art. Wyatt's fondness for the form of the sonnet was probably caused by a certain metaphysical turn of thought that made him select for imitation those compositions of Petrarch which are most distinguished for the excruciating ingenuity of their sentimental logic. In one sonnet he prays his mistress to receive the heart he proffers her; for if, he says, she rejects it, he will disdain to receive back what she has refused: the heart will then no longer be his:—

> If I then it chase, nor it in you can find
> In this exile no manner of comfort;
> Nor live alone, nor where he is called resort,
> He may wander from his natural kind.
> So shall it be great hurt unto us twain,
> And yours the loss, and mine the deadly pain. [XXXII]

In another place he upbraids his tongue because it fails to express his love, his tears because they will not flow when he wishes to 'make his moan', his sighs which are passive when they should be active; he concludes that his look only is left to reveal his heart (XXV). All this is in

[1] I.e. of Sannazaro's.

the traditional vein of the Troubadours. But the manliness which is, after all, Wyatt's distinguishing characteristic, is constantly revolting against the servility enjoined on the male lover by the code of chivalry, and in several sonnets he gives a different turn to the original he is translating. Thus Petrarch in his 61st sonnet says that, though he is not tired of loving, he is tired of hating himself and weeping, and he wishes himself dead, with Laura's name written on his tomb. But Wyatt, while imitating Petrarch's sonnet, says:—

> I will not yet in my grave be burièd,
>   Nor on my tomb your name have fixed fast,
>   As cruel cause that did the spirit soon haste
>   From th' unhappy bones, by great sighs stirrèd.   [IX]

And at another time he protests that he will renounce his mistress in consequence of her injustice. The sonnet in which he proclaims this intention is perhaps his best:—

> My love to scorn, my service to retain,
>   Therein, methought, she used cruelty,
>   Since with good will I lost my liberty,
>   To follow her which causeth all my pain.
> Might never care cause me for to refrain,
>   But only this which is extremity,
>   Giving me nought, alas! nor to agree
>   That as I was her man, I might remain.
> But since that thus ye list to order me,
>   That would have been your servant true and fast,
>   Displease thee not, my dotting days be past;
> And with my loss to leave I must agree.
>   For as there is a certain time to rage,
>   So is there time such madness to assuage.   [CCXXIII]

The idea of justice in love is not common in the poetry of the Troubadours, who enforced the principle that it was the lover's duty to prove his devotion by submitting to his mistress's will. It is, however, the predominant note in Wyatt's love poetry, who insists that long and faithful service deserves a full reward. For the expression of a feeling so ardent and elementary, the sonnet, with its elaborate structure, was not a good vehicle. Wyatt's best poems are written in simple metrical forms, which enable him to pour himself forth with a strength and energy rarely equalled in English poetry. A fine example of this simpler manner remains in the fervent lines beginning 'Forget not yet the tried intent'

[CCIII];* and in the following, which is less known, there is not a superfluous word to diminish the heat of indignation which inspires the movement of the verse:—

> What should I say!
> Since Faith is dead,
> And Truth away
>   From you is fled?
> Should I be led
>   With doubleness?
>   Nay! nay! mistress.
>
> I promised you,
>   And you promised me,
> To be as true
>   As I would be.
> But since I see
>   Your double heart,
>   Farewell my part!
>
> Thought for to take
>   'Tis not my mind;
> But to forsake
>   One so unkind;
> And as I find,
>   So will I trust;
>   Farewell, unjust!
>
> Can ye say nay,
>   But that you said
> That I alway
>   Should be obeyed?
> And thus betrayed
>   Or that I wist!
>   Farewell, unkist! [CCXV]

Here again is an admirable specimen of forcible feeling expressed in the fewest and best words:—

> Is it possible?
> That so high debate,
> So sharp, so sore, and of such rate,
> Should end so soon, and was begun so late?
> Is it possible?
>
> Is it possible?
> So cruel intent,

* They are inserted in *The Golden Treasury*.

So lusty heat, and so soon spent,
From love to hate, and thence for to relent?
Is it possible?

Is it possible?
That any may find
Within one heart so diverse mind,
To change or turn as weather or wind?
Is it possible?

Is it possible?
To spy it in an eye
That turns as oft as chance or die,
The truth whereof can any try?
Is it possible?

Is it possible?
For to turn so oft;
To bring that lowest that was most aloft;
And to fall highest, yet to light soft?
Is it possible?

All is possible!
Whoso list believe,
Trust therefore first, and after preve;
As men wed ladies by license and leave;
All is possible!   [CLXXXIV]

In poems of this kind Wyatt was, no doubt, helped to his form by the circumstance that poetry was not yet divorced from music. Music, as we see from Castiglione's *Courtier*, was a necessary accomplishment for a gentleman. Henry VIII. was passionately fond of it, and almost all Wyatt's love lyrics were composed for the accompaniment of the lute. The dropping of the final *e* in the language, as spoken, enabled the poet to produce extremely musical combinations of words for the purposes of singing, as appears in that most harmonious ballad *The Nut-Brown Maid*, which is certainly a composition not later than the early part of the sixteenth century:—

Yet take good hede, for ever I drede
That ye shall not sustayne
The thornie waies, the deep valleyes,
The snow, the frost, the raine,
The cold, the hete; for, dry or wete,
We must lodge on the plaine,

None other roof us two aboof
But a brake bushe or twayne.

The reader will have observed in all the poems of Wyatt cited above
a weightiness of matter, prevailing over elegance of form, and accordingly ill adapted to modes of composition in which elaborate terseness
or harmony of expression is indispensable. Want of a perfect instrument, as well as errors of imperfect taste, are very visible in Wyatt's
epigrams. In these he does not aim so much at the condensed expression
of a witty thought, as at the invention of an ingenious paradox. His
model is Serafino, five of whose *Strambotti* he has rendered into English;
and whose form—the *ottava rima* stanza—he generally uses, whether he
is expressing a thought of his own, or giving a version of ideas met with
in the course of his reading. Among the many authors to whom he is
indebted for the matter of his epigrams are Josephus, Seneca, Plato, and
Pandulfo Collinutio; and the character of his style may be illustrated by
his version of the following epigram ascribed to Plato:—

χρυσὸν ἀνὴρ εὑρὼν ἔλιπεν βρόχον· αὐτὰρ ὁ χρυσὸν
ὃν λίπεν οὐχ εὑρὼν ἧψεν ὃν εὗρε βρόχον.

It would be impossible to condense more thought into two lines;
indeed, the idea is so closely packed, that it would be unintelligible to
any one who did not know the story on which the epigram is based.
Ausonius, in his Latin version, expanded the couplet into four lines:—

Thesauro invento qui limina mortis inibat
Liquit ovans laqueum quo periturus erat.
At qui quod terræ abdiderat non repperit aurum
Ouem laqueum invenit nexuit et periit.*

Wyatt treats the idea in Serafino's eight-line stanza:—

For shamefast harm of great and hateful need
In deep despair as did a wretch go
With ready cord out of his life to speed,
His stumbling foot did find an hoard, lo!
Of gold I say, when he prepared this deed,
And in exchange he left the cord tho';
He that had hid the gold, and found it not,
Of that he found he shaped his neck a knot.   [CCLVII]

* Ausonius, *Epigrammata* xxii. It may be rendered into English:—

A man, about to hang himself one day,
By chance found gold, and flung his noose away,
The owner came and—each thing has its use—
Finding his gold was gone, employed the noose.

So that while he gives Ausonius' last two lines, almost word for word in his closing couplet, he takes six lines to work up to the point, nor does he even then contrive to tell the story distinctly. On the other hand, where he expresses a sincere feeling of his own, he is often admirably energetic, as is shown by the verses I have already cited, written to Bryan from the Tower [CCXLIV], and by his *Farewell* to the Tagus [XCIV].

The same strength of individual feeling appears in Wyatt's Satires. These are the fruit of his retirement at Allington, and are undoubtedly the most pleasing of all his regular compositions. They express the ardent love of country life natural to an English gentleman conversant with affairs, and all the disdain and indignation proper to a lofty mind familiar with the mean servility prevalent among the creatures of a Court. But even when he is dealing with matters so congenial, Wyatt gets his inspiration from foreign models. He is indebted for the form of his Satire to Luigi Alamanni, one of the few truly noble Italians of the sixteenth century, who were ready to suffer all things in behalf of that ideal of liberty and patriotism which they inherited as the late descendants of republican Rome. After making a vain stand against the restoration of the despotic power of the Medici in Florence, his native city, Alamanni withdrew to France, where he was received by Francis I. with the honour that he deserved. His Satires breathe a fiery indignation against the corruptions of his time, and the following very fine verses may be cited in apt illustration of the continuous tradition cherished by the Italian poets; they show how readily the allusive and metaphorical style of Dante and Petrarch lent itself to the purposes of Satire:—

> Oggi ha d' altr' acqua Roma ed altra sete,
>> Che di Samaria, ed altri pesci prende
>> Che già il buon Pescator, con altra rete.
> Or per altro sentier nel ciel s' ascende
>> Non chi si pente, ma si monda e scarca
>> Chi la mano al pastor con l' oro stende.
> Con più ricco nocchier nuove onde varca,
>> Con le sarte di seta, e d' or la vela,
>> Lunge da Galilea la santa barca.
> D' altro Simon per te s' ordisce tela,
>> Che di chi di Cefas riporta 'l nome,
>> Per quello acceso amor ch' a te si cela.
> Oh! chi vedesse il ver, vedrebbe come
>> Più disnor tu, che 'l tuo Luter Martino,
>> Porti a te stessa, e più gravose some.

Non la Germania, no! ma l'ozio, il vino,
Avarizia, Ambizion, Lussuria, e Gola,
Ti mena al fin, che già veggiam vicino.
Non pur questo dico io, non Francia sola,
Non pur la Spagna, tutta Italia ancora,
Che ti tien d' eresia, di vizi scola.
E chi nol crede, ne domanda ogn' ora
Urbin, Ferrara, l' Orso, e la Colonna,
La Marca, il Romagnuol, ma più chi plora,
Per te servendo, che fu d' altri Donna.*

In his twelfth Satire, Alamanni sets forth the various arts of the
Courtier which he professes himself unequal to acquire; and Wyatt,
in his second Satire [CV][1], has adapted this poem with much spirit and
success to his own circumstances in England. He has also borrowed
Alamanni's *terza rima* as the vehicle for his first and third satires,[2]
in the former [CVI] of which he imitates Horace's Fable of the Town
and Country Mouse, and in the latter [CVII] the Latin poet's Advice
of Tiresias.† The opening 'Of the mean and sure estate' is extremely
picturesque, and shows Wyatt's satirical style at its best:—

My mother's maids, when they did sew and spin,
They sang sometimes a song of the field mouse;
That, for because her livelode was but thin,
Would needs go seek her townish sister's house.
She thought herself endured to much pain;
The stormy blasts her cave so sore did souse,
That when the furrows swimmed with the rain

* Alamanni, *Satire* iii.: 'To-day Rome has other water and thirst for other water than that
of Samaria, and takes with other net than once did the good fisherman, other fish. Now
by another path climbs to heaven, not the penitent; but he who stretches out his hand to
the shepherd with gold is purged and discharged. With a richer pilot, with shrouds of
silk and sails of gold, the holy bark crosses new waves far from Galilee. By thee is woven
the web of Simon, other than the one who takes his name from Cephas, smitten with that
love which is hidden from thine eyes. O he that could see the truth would see that thou
bringest upon thyself more dishonour and a more grievous burden than does that Martin
Luther of thine. 'Tis not Germany, no! but ease, wine, avarice, ambition, luxury, and
gluttony, that are bringing thee to the end which we see to be so near. Nor is it I alone
who say this, nor France alone, nor Spain, but all Italy to boot, which holds thee as the
school of heresy and vice; and he who does not believe this, let him ask at any time Urbino,
Ferrara, Orsino, Colonna, La Marca, Romagna, but most of all her who through thee
weeps in slavery, though she was once the mistress of others.' I presume by the last
words he means Florence.
† Hor. *Sat.* lib. ii. Sats. v. and vi.
[1] Usually printed in modern editions as the first satire.
[2] Second and third in modern editions.

> She must lie cold and wet, in sorry plight;
> And worse than that, bare meat there did remain
> To comfort her, when she her house had dight;
> Sometimes a barley corn, sometimes a bean,
> For which she laboured hard both day and night,
> In harvest time, whilst she might go and glean;
> And when her store was 'stroyed with the flood,
> Then well-away! for she undone was clean.　[CVI]

The moral of the Satire is conveyed in language full of energy, plainly coming straight from the heart of the writer, and extremely significant as the reflection of a man so widely experienced in the ways of the world:—

> Then seek no more out of thyself to find
> The thing that thou hast sought so long before;
> For thou shalt feel it sitting in thy mind,
> Mad if ye list to continue your sore.
> Let present pass, and gape on time to come,
> And deep yourself in travail more and more.
> Henceforth, my Poynz, this shall be all and sum,
> These wretched fools shall have nought else of me:
> But to the great God, and to his high doom,
> None other pain pray I for them to be,
> But when the rage doth lead them from the right,
> That, looking backward, virtue they may see,*
> Even as she is so goodly, fair, and bright;
> And whilst they clasp their lusts in arms across,
> Grant them, good Lord, as thou mayst of thy might,
> To freat inward for losing such a loss.

In this passage we find a vein of sentiment which runs through the works of many of the religious Reformers, and makes a link between that party and the men of the Renaissance. As the first men of letters in mediæval Europe found a metaphysical connection between the doctrines of Christianity and the philosophy of Plato, so their successors, who opposed the corruptions of the scholastic system in the beginning of the sixteenth century, fell back on the works of those classical authors who most largely embodied the morality of the Stoics. Very many of the scholars and philosophers of that age were, in one aspect or another, favourers of the reform movement, and in this way much of the Pagan imagery employed by the Latin and Greek poets came insensibly to be associated with Christian dogma.

* Persius, *Sat.* iii. 88, 'Virtutem videant intabescantque relicta.'

Wyatt had early allied himself with the Lutheran party. Ardent in all his feelings, the spirit of devotion strengthened in him with advancing years, and from his Satires, which have much of the temper of Persius, he passed naturally to another line of composition, in the path which had already been opened by Dante and Alamanni, namely, a rendering of the seven penitential Psalms of David.[1] But here, too, he showed his originality by adopting a method different from that of his predecessors, who had contented themselves with simple translation or rather paraphrase. Wyatt, on the other hand, presents his paraphrase of the psalms themselves in the framework of a narrative, inserting before each psalm a kind of poetical comment of his own, to explain the mood in which David composed it. Very characteristically the idea of this framework is borrowed from the Reformer Beza's *Præfatio Poetica in Davidis Psalmos quos penitentiales vocant*;[2] and there is something extremely suggestive in the mixture of Pagan imagery and genuine Christian sentiment which comes from the combination. Beza begins his preface in the following genuinely classical style:—

> Forte pererratis cælo, terraque, marique,
> Alex Amor sacras Judææ callidus urbes
> Visebat, pharetrâque minas, flammataque gestans
> Tela manu. Jamque hospitium sedemque petebat
> Venturæ nocti; dumque acres undique versat
> Sæpe oculos, dubitatque etiam que sede moretur,
> Tandem ad Bersabes convertit lumina formam.*

This is of course the manner in which Ovid would have treated the subject, but Ovid is not exactly the poet whom we should expect to be associated with a theme dealing with sin and repentance. Still there can be no question of the depth and sincerity of religious feeling by which Wyatt's paraphrase is inspired. It is indeed evident that each original psalm of David is only the channel into which the English poet poured the stream of his own emotion: the ten verses, for example, of which the sixth psalm consists, are expanded in the Paraphrase into 112 lines; and many ideas not expressed by the penitent king are developed out of his thought by the imagination of the paraphrast. The psalm in the

---

* Cited in Nott's *Memoir of Wyatt*, vol. ii, p. cxxxv.

[1] There is no proof positive that Wyatt was a Lutheran, or even that his Psalms were composed after his Satires. Courthope's dating is probably correct: the first satire must follow the publication of Alamanni's Provençal satires in 1532-3, while the Psalms must follow that of Aretino's *Sette Salmi* in 1534.

[2] Since Courthope wrote, the source of the Satires has been discovered by Arundel Esdaile in the Catholic Aretino.

original says: 'Have mercy upon me, O Lord; for I am weak: O Lord, heal me; for my bones are vexed. My soul also is sore vexed: but thou, O Lord, how long? Return, O Lord, deliver my soul: Oh save me for thy mercies' sake. For in death there is no remembrance of thee: in the grave who shall give thee thanks?'[1] Wyatt's version is as follows:—

> I Lord am stray'd. I, sick without recure,
>   Feel all my limbs, that have rebelled, for fear
>   Shake; in despair unless thou me assure.
> My flesh is troubled; my heart doth fear the spear;
>   That dread of death, of death that ever lasts,
>   Threateth of right and draweth near and near.*
> Much more my soul is troubled by the blasts
>   Of these assaults, that come as thick as hail,
>   Of worldly vanity, that temptation casts
> Against the weak bulwark of the flesh frail:
>   Wherein the soul in great perplexity
>   Feeleth the senses with them that assail
> Conspire, corrupt by use and vanity;
>   Whereby the wretch doth to the shadow resort
>   Of hope in thee, in this extremity.
> But thou, O Lord! how long after this sort
>   Forbearest thou to see my misery?
>   Suffer me yet, in hope of some comfort,
> Fear, and not feel that thou forgettest me.
>   Return, O Lord! O Lord! I thee beseech,
>   Unto thy old wonted benignity.
> Reduce, revive my soul; be thou the leche
>   And reconcile the great hatred and strife,
>   That it hath ta'en against the flesh, the wretch
> That stirred hath thy wrath by filthy life.
>   See! how my soul doth freat it to the bones,
>   Inward remorse, so sharp'th it like a knife.   [CVIII, 97–123]

This gives the very essence of the feeling that moved Luther, and lay at the bottom of the Teutonic revolt against the external system of Latin Christianity,[2] the intense consciousness of sin, the 'fearful looking forward to judgment and fiery indignation', the consequent fear of death, the sense of despair, and the overwhelming need of Divine

---

* Nearer and nearer.

1 Courthope refers, of course, to Psalm 6, the first Penitential Psalm.

2 Lines 103–15 are translation of Aretino, and this somewhat undermines Courthope's case for a Lutheran Wyatt. H. A. Mason has indicated, however, borrowings from Zwingli (l. 99) and Campensis (l. 103).

Mercy and Grace. We can understand, from lines so charged with individual feeling, how deep must have been the impression which these paraphrases made on the society of the time.

Changed conditions, and the fluctuations of religious feeling, have rendered the moral qualities of Wyatt's paraphrase less impressive than when it first appeared; while the inexorable hand of time has brought into cruel relief that harshness of expression peculiar to this poet's style, depriving his paraphrase of the popularity which it might have secured if the loftiness and grandeur of its spirit had found an adequate vehicle. Indeed, the fate of most of Wyatt's poetry has been that which must overtake all compositions in which matter prevails over form. He occupies a position in English poetry in some respects almost as important as that of Chaucer. A statesman, a courtier, and a scholar, he thought vigorously and felt ardently in each position that he occupied. As he said forcibly of himself:

> Such hammers work within my head,
> That sound nought else into my ears; [CCIX]

and his native energy forced him abroad in search of moulds more suitable for his thoughts than the seven-line Royal Stanza which had been the favourite instrument of metrical expression in England since the time of Chaucer. But his art was not equal to his imagination. He attempted to naturalize the sonnet; but as I shall show, when considering the poetry of Surrey, he did not understand the secret of its structure. Nor was he much more fortunate in his treatment of the *ottava rima* of the Italians, which, admirably adapted for the peculiar vein of Italian romantic poetry, is certainly not suited to the nature of the epigram.

Of the other iambic metres introduced by Wyatt, the most important was the *terza rima*, and as this in his hands proved an instrument of noble compass and harmony, it seems somewhat strange that it should never have been naturalized in the language. It may be that the English ear, accustomed from early times to the limitation of the stanza, could not reconcile itself to the concatenated harmony of this metre, and preferred, both for long narrative poems, when the stanza was not employed, and for satire, the heroic couplet as used by Chaucer in the Prologue to the *Canterbury Tales*. Wyatt was also the first to combine the Alexandrine with the verse of seven accents and fourteen syllables, a metre which was much in favour during the sixteenth century, though it has since become entirely obsolete. His most successful experiments were undoubtedly his songs written for the

accompaniment of the lute, for here the laws of music kept his thought
within well-defined limits, and, at the same time, gave sufficient scope
to the energy of his genius. I have already given specimens of his short-
metred songs, the majority of which are written to the key-note of
some burden, but it would be unjust to refrain from citing perhaps the
most beautiful and finished of his lyrical compositions, viz. *The Address
to his Lute*:—

> My lute, awake! perform the last
> Labour that thou and I shall waste,
>   And end that I have now begun;
> For when this song is sung and past,
>   My lute, be still, for I have done.
>
> As to be heard where ear is none,
> As lead to grave in marble stone,
>   My song may pierce her heart as soon:
> Should we then sing, or sigh, or moan?
>   No, no, my lute! for I have done.
>
> The rock doth not so cruelly
> Repulse the waves continually,
>   As she may suit and affectión;
> So that I am past remedy;
>   Whereby my lute and I have done.
>
> Proud of the spoil that thou hast got,
> Of simple hearts, thorough Love's shot,
>   By whom, unkind, thou hast them won;
> Think not he hath his bow forgot,
>   Although my lute and I have done.
>
> Vengeance, may fall on thy disdain,
> That makest but game of earnest pain:
>   Trow not alone under the sun
> Unquit to cause thy lover's plain,
>   Although my lute and I have done.
>
> May chance thee lie wither'd and old
> The winter nights that are so cold,
>   Plaining in vain unto the moon:
> Thy wishes then dare not be told:
>   Care then who list! for I have done.
>
> And then may chance thee to repent
> The time that thou hast lost and spent,

To cause thy lover's sigh and swoon:
Then shalt thou know beauty but lent,
   And wish and want as I have done.

Now cease my lute! this is the last
Labour that thou and I shalt waste,
   And ended is that I begun;
Now is this song both sung and past:
   My lute! be still, for I have done.   [LXVI]

Wyatt is a noble figure in English poetry. His strength, his ardour, his manliness, his complete freedom from affectation, make him a type of what is finest in the national character, and there is little exaggeration in the very fine epitaph written on him by his great contemporary, Surrey:—

[Quotes the whole of 3d.]

12. Foxwell on Wyatt

1913

Introduction to *The Poems of Sir Thomas Wiat*, ed. A. K. Foxwell (1913), II, xii–xxii.

Agnes Kate Foxwell took three degrees at the University of London, culminating in D.Litt. (1914). Her teaching career was pursued both in London University and at Cheltenham Ladies' College.

In the art of words, in the domain of poetry, Wiat is by no means the least among those who, in the sixteenth century, sought to express the Beauty of life through Truth.

The upholding of Truth in life, and the continual war waged against falseness, are the two dominant notes in Wiat's poetry. True, in his first bitter experience of the falseness that rides so insolently abroad in the very highway of life, he cries—

> What vaileth trouth? Or by it to take payn?
> To be juste and true: and fle from doublenes?   [II]

And in another rondeau he says—

> Thou hast no faith:
> Eche thing seketh his semblable
> And thou hast thyn of thy condition.   [XIX]

And again—

> Truth is tryed where craft is in ure.   [XLV]

One of the fine expressions of his code of life for honourable manhood is expressed in the somewhat difficult original Sonnet,

> . . . no way man may fynde
> Thy vertue to let: though that frowerdnes
> Of ffortune me holdeth
> . . . .
> Suffice it then that thou be redy there
> At all howres: still under the defence
> Of tyme, trouth, and love, to save thee from offence.   [XXVII]

Again, by contrast, he expresses his allegiance to truth, following the teaching of the *Courtier* to refrain from 'Jestes'—

> To rayle or jest ye know I use it not
> Tho that such cause somtyme in folkes I finde.   [CCXI]

But the finest expression (apart from the Psalms) of his adherence to truth in life is expressed in the following stanza—

> Within my brest I never thought it gain
> Of gentle mynde the fredom for to lose;
> Nor in my hart sanck never such disdain
> To be a forger, faultes for to disclose;
> Nor I can not endure the truth to glose:
> To set a glosse upon an earnest pain;
> Nor I am not in nomber one of those,
> That list to blow retrete to every train.   [CCXLVII]

These verses attest Wiat's actual standard of life, and are the outcome of his convictions.

In connection with this ingrained virtue lies the most sombre experience of his life. He was separated from his wife, with no possibility of reconciliation, as far as he was concerned, since Truth had been shattered; various hints in his poems show how deeply he suffered in this connection—

> Though that with pain I do procure
> For to forgett that ons was pure. [XLV]

The poem—

> What shulde I saye,
> Sins faithe is ded
> And truth awaye
> From you ys fled, [CCXV]

is the cry that proceeds from the deep pain of the heart, and expresses the anguish of lost confidence in one who had been dear to him.

In Wiat is to be found the embodiment of Shakespeare's lines beginning 'To thine own self be true.'

He not only believes in the old saying, 'Know thyself', but his keen power of observation gives him an insight into the characters of others. His faculty of 'avysing' unlocks much to him which is closed to the casual-minded, and gives him a knowledge of life in all its phases. Of the double-faced acquaintance, he says—

> None is worse than is a friendly foo, [XLIX]

and again

> . . . . . .
> Yet knowes it well that in thy bosom crepeth. [XLIX]

In the Satires he ironically writes—

> The friendly ffoo with his dowble face,
> Say he is gentill, and courtois therewithall
>
> . . . . . .
> Say he is rude that cannot lye and fayn
> The Letcher a Lover. [CV, 65–6, 73–4]

And in the same Satire he says to his friend in a tone of intense earnestness—

> My Poynz, I cannot frame me tune to fayne,
> To cloke the trouthe for praise withoute desart. [CV, 19–20]

In the third Satire he strikes deeper. It is not only the want of truth in the world, but the assumption of truth by the false-hearted in an outward show of morality that does most harm. His satiric advice to Brian is to refrain from truth if he wishes to prosper—

> Thou knowst well first, who so can seke to plese
> Shall pourchase frendes where trowght shall but offend
> Ffle therefore trueth, it is boeth welth and ese
> For tho that trouth of every man hath prayse
> Full nere that wynd goeth trouth in great misese.   [CVII, 32–6]

And finally, in the Letter to his Son he implores him to be 'honest'; but, failing honesty, he assures him that 'to seme to be' is the greater sin.

This deeply rooted love of truth has its origin in the fine character of his parents. Sir Henry Wiat carried out in his life Chaucer's description of the 'Knight' who loved—

> Truth and honour, freedom and courtesy.

His mother was a finely intellectual and strong character, managing the estates, rearing her sons, and keeping up a standard of morality within her domain during her husband's frequent absences in the King's service. Wiat, trained under these influences, early learnt the habit of obedience to authority and acquired the love of truth and simple courtesy which distinguished his father. Whole-hearted service to King and country appears in the Epigram 'Tagus fare well'—

> My King my Contry alone for whome I lyve.   [XCIX]

Truth, inbred in Wiat, gives the clue to his attitude towards love and women. Respect and honour for the sex, belief in the equal distribution of moral right and wrong, and in equal punishment and reward for man and woman, is clearly discernible in his writings. And this is the attitude of his day, which in some respects was even more 'modern', as we term it, than our own. Passages in the Utopia of More, the Colloquies of Erasmus, and the *Courtier*, all touch upon the necessity of an equal standard in morality for men and women. For, as nature has decreed that man and woman are the complement of one another, no lasting morality can accrue from unequal burdens.

The women of Wiat's day with whom he came into contact at the Courts of Europe were such as Shakespeare portrays them, intellectual, resourceful, knowing life in all its bearings, and using it for good. Such were Margaret of Navarre, Renée of France, the Duchess of Ferrara, Vittoria Colonna, Catherine of Aragon (to a certain extent), Mary Richmond, the Lady Margaret Howard, and Wiat's mother and sister;

all these women held their own by the force of their intellect, the high standard of their morality, and their personal charm.

Occasionally, indeed, Wiat uses the stock phrase that change pleases a woman's mind; he also says—

> 'Like to like the proverb saieth.' [LIII][1]

Wiat married early, and the domestic trouble which followed later deprived him of the fullness of joy in happy married life, such as Robert and Elizabeth Browning express in some of the finest love lyrics that the world has produced—enthrallingly beautiful because of their truth. Wiat's lyrics are poems of emotion rather than of love, for the deepest feelings expressed are sorrow at parting, bitter grief at loss of confidence. In this respect Wiat strikes an original note in the lyrical poetry of his day. Nothing could be more beautiful in its profound pathos than the song, 'And wylt thow leve me thus' [CLXXXVI].

The dignity of sorrow is expressed in the finely modulated harmony of 'Fforget not yet' [CCIII], and the pain of memory is finely expressed in an original manner in the song, 'When fyrst myn eyes did view and mark'; the note of pathos is intensified in the stanza beginning—

> And when my handes have handled ought
> That thee hath kept in memory. [CCLII]

One little poem, indeed, 'Grudge on who liste' [CCXX], strikes a note of gladness, but it is put in the mouth of a woman, and one wonders whether it were not intended for Mary Richmond. Of all Holbein's portraits, the loveliest in its portrayal of the beauty of youth, combined with strength of character and womanly sweetness, is the portrait of Mary, the child-wife of the King's son, Henry Richmond; a face that fulfilled its promise in the deepened character of later years, and called forth Wiat's single poem on his ideal of womanhood in the Epigram, 'A face that shuld content me' [CXXIII].

In the Petrarchan sonnets Wiat's selection is guided partly by the rules laid down for the perfect courtier in *Il Cortegiano*, and partly by his preference for conceits rather than for descriptions of nature or of the lady. What appears artificial to-day had a special charm to Wiat's contemporaries, the charm of the 'dolce stil nuovo' which had transformed and irradiated Italian verse in the thirteenth century.

The artificiality rests not so much upon the conceit, but in the false

---

[1] Cp. XIX, 4; M. P. Tilley, *A Dictionary of Proverbs in England in the Sixteenth and Seventeenth Centuries* (Ann Arbor, 1950), L 286.

conception of the woman. This struck equally upon the minds of thoughtful people in the sixteenth century; passages in *Il Cortegiano* reflect upon the absurdity of regarding a woman as a monster if she refused to accept attention, and of punishing her with everlasting slander if she yielded to the prayers of the lover. Still more artificial is the belief in the inconstancy of women. The irony of the situation reaches its height in the poems of Donne, who continually affirms inconstancy to be the chief attitude of a woman, while he unblushingly affirms that in him 'Inconstancy hath begot a constant habit.'

The ugliness of passion is clearly distinguished in Wiat's poetry from the love experienced in friendship and in married love. A hard and fast line is drawn between unlawful passion and love. It is clearly expressed in the debate, 'Lo, what it is to love' [LXXXVII], and in the Epigrams 'Cruell desire' [LXXV][1] and 'From thes hye hills'. The intense note of the Psalms, and the fine poem 'If thou wilt myghty be, flee from the rage' [CCLXI], utters the last word in his final expression of the Truth of life that cannot rest in baseness of any sort. He expresses on this side what Blake puts so tersely in the proud utterance of the polished pebble of the brook—

> Love seeketh only self to please
> To bind another to its delight
> Joys in another's loss of ease,
> And builds a Hell in Heaven's despite.

Wiat, however, refuses to name this aspect of passion as love, but significantly calls it 'cruell desire'.

Wiat shares with Browning the gift of looking at different sides of a question. There are sundry pairs of poems, following one another, expressing two different points of view—

Patience, tho I have not [XXXIX]	with	Paciens for my devise [XL],
Full well yt maye be sene [CXCVII]	with	Syns love ys suche [CXCVIII],
Longer to muse [CCXXV]	with	Love doth againe [CXLVIII].

Single poems may be included in this connection, such as 'Most wretched hart' [XCI], and 'Lo, what it is to love' [LXXXVII]. The first poem is a debate on life, contrasting optimism with pessimism; the final word is given to the optimistic point of view. The best poem representing two points of view is the dialogue 'It burneth yet' [CCLV].

---

1 This poem, 'Desire, alas, my master and my foe' [LXXV], is in Foxwell's mind: it does in fact open 'Cruell desire' in the Devonshire version.

Its supreme beauty lies in the tensity of restrained emotion that throbs through every line. But the greatness of the poem lies in Wiat's portrayal. The 'Lady' is the comprehension of the tenderness and sympathy and unselfishness that true love awakens in the woman.

Wiat's power to see different sides brings with it that optimism that Browning possesses. Though of all men Wiat knew the sorrows of life, he never falters in truth—

> Never dreamed though right were worsted wrong would triumph.
> Held we fall to rise, are baffled to fight better.
> Sleep to wake.

The strength and power of Wiat's verse lies in the terza rima. Here, with variety of cæsura and overflow, he allows his thought to flow, hardly hampered by rhyme, which just serves for accent and rhythm. Here we find many personal touches. In the Satires are references to his home, to animal life, and to the simple pursuits of a country life. In the Psalms certain reminiscences of his own life run between the lines. For example, the joy of the prisoner who escapes his enemy's ward, the simile of the 'seman in his jeoperte', who—

> By soden light perceyvid hath the port, [CVIII, 269]

And of the horse—

> I lo for myn errour
> Ame plongid up, as horse out of the myre,
> With strok of spurr, such is thy hand on me. [CVIII, 333-5]

Such allusions are vivid recollections of his own experiences. To take one example, he writes, December 1539, from Amboys, 'The Emperor having set off for Loches, I followed, with much ado, on *plough horse* in the deepe and foule way. . . .'

There are magnificent passages in the Psalms that soar up in their divine wonder and faith, rising at times to the pure flame of joy of the mystic, whose mind discovers the vision of the eternal beauty of goodness in ecstatic vision (cf. Seventh Prologue). The Jehovah is a Presence with the power of a God and the attributes of a father.

> Within thy lok thus rede I my comfort . . .
> Myn Iye shall tak the charge to be thy guyde.—Ps. xxxii. [CVIII, 271, 275]

In the Psalms Wiat expresses all the radiance of joy which has been denied to him in earthly love.[1]

---

[1] See below, p. 166, for Tillyard's more sceptical view.

The following verses might have been written by Blake, where joy, the radiance of emotion, proceeding from the belief in a reality of Divine goodness, is incorporated with the Divine Being as Joy personified—

> Suche Joy as he that skapis his enmys ward
> With losid bondes, hath in his libertie,
> Such Joy, my Joy, thou hast to me prepard.   [CVIII, 265-7]

Wiat's life and work is a song of harmony. The 'music of the spheres' is here. It is a vindication of what man can become with lofty aim and set purpose. Faults he has, including those to which an impulsive, hottempered, generous nature is prone. In later years a profound calm and impartial manner of viewing life succeeded to the impulsiveness of his early manhood, while the love of truth grew and became centred in a sympathy with humanity which burns with intense radiance through the Psalms.

Wiat's life is the practice of his views. He had many friends; the devotion of John Leland, one of the greatest men of his day in learning and achievement, and the love and respect that Surrey, self-centred and proud to a fault, bore him, are the greatest witnesses. The men and women who gathered round him during the three happy years at Court; Cromwell's affection and the King's partiality for him all attest the worth of his character.

His reputation for scholarship outlived him, and he was to his generation the 'chief lantern of light'. Puttenham, who prides himself upon writing verse in the reign of Edward VI, constantly draws examples from Wiat's verse in the *Arte of Poesie*, evidently writing from a personal knowledge of the great reputation that outlived him. Gascoigne, Turberville, and the poets who wrote in the long couplet from 1540 to the Elizabethan age, were well-meaning but dull imitators of a moral view that in Wiat is set off by a rare vitality and a charming style.

In the early Elizabethan sonnets phrase after phrase may be traced to Wiat. In Daniel and Drayton the influence is strong; and in Shakespeare various passages are derived from Wiat's fine lines in the Satires.

Such a passage as that beginning, 'All tho thy head were howpt with gold', [CVI, 77], anticipates the famous speech on ceremony in *Henry V*.

In verse Wiat has influenced poetry down to the present day. The Elizabethans took from him the sonnet, the poets of the seventeenth century used his octave, the eighteenth preferred the couplet of which his poem, 'Speke thou and spede' [CCLXX], is a perfect example, and in the nineteenth century Shelley was the first to write in terza-rima in the same free style that characterizes Wiat's use of this form, contrary to the Italian rule.

Lastly, the wealth and variety of his lyrical forms and his power to interpret the harmony of language in musical refrains, has gained for him no mean reputation amongst lyrical poets.

Wiat is a poet for all time because he interprets life, in the stress and emotion of the mind; and fearlessly proclaims the high purpose in life which he so strongly believes in himself. His presentment of life is neither mawkish nor bitter, neither over-passionate nor over-severe. He shows by his own convincing faith, by his own rectitude of life, that truth is to be found, that good exists. 'All is possyble' [CLXXIV, 30] for those who believe in truth, for they are endowed with the divine gift of clear vision.

Henry Howard, who loved Wiat as a man, and respected and honoured him as a great master of verse, wrote the following lines, which represent Wiat's personality and ring true. The friend, writing the character of the man who placed 'truth above all the rest' had perforce to be true to that friend by drawing his character truthfully.

[Quotes 3d above]

13. Berdan on Wyatt

1920

John M. Berdan, *Early Tudor Poetry* (New York, 1920), pp. 447–53, 468–87.

Berdan (1873–1949) was a noted scholar and teacher in American universities.

(a) Definite as is the text and definite as are the facts of his life, difficulty arises when we try to put two and two together; unhappily they do not make four, but x!* Given a poet with such opportunities, the natural expectation would be that his verse would show signs of foreign influence. And as he spent approximately four years at Calais,—a place, at least in the case of Lord Berners, favorable to literary composition,— two assumptions seem plausible; (1) that a certain amount of his work was done there, and (2) that the work done there would be that in which the foreign influence appears most strongly. Unfortunately, however plausible, these are only suppositions. During this time Clément Marot had become recognized as the dominant French poet. Although his first collected volume, *L'Adolescence Clémentine* was not published until 1532, the poems certainly had circulated before, and even had been printed.† Again the natural supposition would be that in the works of Wyatt would be found traces of Clément Marot.

Such traces would be shown either in form or in content, or in both. Wyatt's poems are indexed under the headings rondeaux, sonnets,

* This is illustrated by the different dates assigned to individual poems by Professor Simonds and Miss Foxwell. The latter believes that the poems in the Egerton MS. are in chronological order of composition. Then by making certain poems refer to definite events it is possible to give 'approximate' dates for the entire set. But apparently the order is casual, since later Wyatt himself sorted them into groups. If he had to take the trouble to arrange them chronologically in the first place, why did he re-arrange them?

† Marot's *Préface de L'Adolescence Clémentine*: Ie ne sçay (mes treschers Freres) qui ma'a plus incité à mettre ces miennes petites Ieunesses en lumiere, ou voz continuelles prieres, ou le desplaisir que i'ay eu d'en ouyr crier & publier par les rues vne grande partie toute incorrecte, mal imprimée, & plus au prouffit du Libraire qu'à l'honneur e l'Autheur.

epigrams, satires, the Psalms, and miscellaneous poems. So far as merely the form is concerned, the sonnets, satires and psalms may be rejected, leaving French influence to be shown in the rondeaux, epigrams and miscellaneous pieces. Of the total, two hundred and five poems, only nine are in the rondeau form. Six have the conventional rime-scheme aabba, aabR, aabbaR, although two of these have octosyllabic lines. The rime-scheme of the fourth is aabba bbaR aabbaR; of the fifth, aabba bbaR bbaabR; and of the eighth, aabbcR ccbR aabbaR. In other words, of the small number of rondeaux over half the number do not follow the type selected by Marot! Of the thirty-one epigrams all but six are in the ottava rima. Of the six, two are in the rime-royal, and the remaining four seem rather curious experiments in riming. The only feature in the miscellaneous section suggestive of the French is the use of the refrain,—a feature that is not necessarily French at all. As many of them were written to be sung, the origin of the refrain is obvious. For, the form alone considered, French influence must be regarded as curiously slight. Some there undoubtedly is, but the surprising fact is that there is not more.

When it comes to discussing the content of the poems, the question is exceedingly difficult. It was the fashion of the age in France and Italy, as well as in England, to write occasional verses to be given to ladies. As the conditions that called them forth were similar in all three countries, the poems themselves are very similar. It was a social convention without deep feeling. The age of chivalry had passed, but there yet remained the literary tradition of the cruel lady and the longing lover. There is little more emotion in these trifles than in the verses for St Valentine's Day; it was good form to have a bleeding heart. But as the same condition prevailed in all the courts, extensive reading in the literatures is sure to produce analogies. Wyatt, Marot and the Italian Serafino have short poems in which the heart after separation accompanies the loved one.* Certain phrases in Wyatt's are suggestive of either of the other two. The poems differ in that in both the French and Italian it is the lady that has the lover's heart, whereas in the Wyatt the condition is reversed. It is quite possible, therefore, that further research

---

* Foxwell 2, 18: The refrain and setting, however, is influenced by C. Marot's Rondeau, 'S'il est ainsy.' This Rondeau was first printed by M. Jannet from the MS. FF. 2335, f. 65. This would seem to settle the question as a poem Marot himself rejected would probably not be copied by Wyatt, were it not that the same rondeau, in a better text, was printed in 1731 edition, 5, 262, and there attributed to Jean Marot! [There can be no doubt that the French rondeau is the source of Wyatt's 'Yf it be so', and that it is by Jean, not Clément, Marot.]

may unearth others more alike. The resemblances between Wyatt's poems and those of Marot are all of this type, occasional similarity in the treatment of conventional subjects.

This may, perhaps, be worth further illustration. One of Marot's celebrated *vers de société* is his étrenne *A Anne*:*

> Ce nouvel an pour estrenes vous donne
> Mon cueur blessé d'une nouvelle playe,
> Contrainct y suis, Amour ainsi L'ordonne,
> En qui un cas bien contraire j'essaye:
> Car ce cueur là, c'est ma richesse vraye:
> Le demeurant n'est rien ou je me fonde;
> Et fault donner le meilleur bien que j'aye
> Si j'ay vouloir d'estre riche en ce monde.

The charm of this little New Year's present is clearly due to its brevity; in eight lines the compliment is turned. With this compare the analogous poem by Wyatt.

> To seke eche where, where man doeth lyve,
>   The See, the Land: the Rocke, the Clyve,
>   Ffraunce, Spayne, and Inde and every where:
> Is none a greater gift to gyve
>   Lesse sett by oft, and is so lyeff and dere,
>   Dare I well say than that I gyve to yere.
>
> I cannot gyve browches nor ringes,
>   Thes Goldsmithes work and goodly thinges
>   Piery nor perle, oryente and clere;
> But for all that is no man bringes
>   Lesser Juell unto his Lady dere
>   Dare I well say then that I gyve to yere.
>
> Nor I seke not to fetche it farr,
>   Worse is it not tho it be narr,
>   And as it is, it doeth appere
> Uncontrefaict, mistrust to barr;
>   Lest hole and pure withouten pere
>   Dare I well say the gyft I gyve to yere
>
> To the therefore the same retain
>   The like of the to have again
>   Ffraunce would I gyve if myn it were

*Lenglet du Fresnoy on the doubtful possibility that Anne refers to the Duchesse d'Alençon, dates it 1528. [Wyatt's probable source is Serafino's 'Donar non ti poss'io' and his other strambotti on the same theme.]

> Is none alyve in whome doeth rayne
> Lesser disdaine; frely, therefore, to here
> Dare I well gyve I say my hert to yere. [LXXXV]

To place these two poems in juxtaposition is cruel to Wyatt. The conceit is the same, but Marot's graceful eight lines are paralleled by twenty-four with a refrain, composed entirely of monosyllables, that is grammatically clumsy. Fortunately the conceit is so obvious that it is not necessary to infer that Wyatt was familiar with the Marot, for, if the Frenchman were the master, it must be confessed that he had a poor pupil.* French influence, as represented by the effect of Marot upon Wyatt, is thus unexpectedly slight.

More definite traces may be found in the connection between Wyatt and Melin de Saint-Gelais. Although older than Clément Marot, Saint-Gelais survived him fourteen years and maintained 'la veille tradition gauloise' against the Pléiade. Marot thus apostrophizes him:

> O Sainct Gelais, créature gentile,
> Dont le scaçvoir, dont l'esprit, dont le stile,
> Et dont le tout rend la France honorée, . . .†

The verses that Marot greets so enthusiastically lack both the depth and the brilliance of his own. They are light, rather clever, and sometimes rather broad, *vers de société*. And as he is without Marot's Huguenot inclinations, they probably better reflect the gay court of the time. Saint-Gelais is the typical courtier. As he was continually connected with the court, Wyatt in his various embassies in all probability knew him personally. There are three poems in which the resemblance is striking. A sonnet, 'Like to these unmesurable montayns' [XXXIII], an epigram, 'Thenmy of liff, decayer of all kynde' [LXIV], and one in the section of miscellaneous poems, 'Madame withouten many wordes' [XXXIV]. Of these three the question of the sonnet is the important one, for reasons that do not concern the English. In the *Epitre au lecteur*, prefixed to Du Bellay's *Olive*, occurs the phrasing:

estant la sonnet d' Italien deuenu François, comme je croy, par Mellin de Sainct gelais . . .

At the time when these words were written Saint-Gelais had published only one edition, the 1547, and in that there was not but one sonnet, the

---

* It is only fair to Wyatt to append Miss Foxwell's comment. In her opinion Wyatt 'has not come short of the original'. 'This is the best instance among the lyrics of Wiat's masterly handling of material, in stamping his own individuality upon it.' 2, 117–118.
† Jannet's ed. 1, 211.

one in question. Consequently the inference was made, not unnaturally, that this particular sonnet was the first sonnet to be written in French.* Then the dating followed, 1536, because in that year Saint-Gelais was in view of the Alps! It is tenuous reasoning that justifies the oft-repeated statement, that the sonnet made its appearance in France in 1536. But this chain of reasoning was overthrown by the discovery of Mr S. Waddington† that the Saint-Gelais sonnet was a translation of one attributed to Sannazaro.‡ As the three sonnets, the Italian, French and English are so very much alike, there is no doubt of translation. It is interesting to note that the general tendency was to infer that the order was, as I have given it, Italian, French and English. This was assumed really without much question. We are so familiar with English dependence upon the French in the eighteenth century, and even in the Elizabethan, that in the early Tudor period, given a resemblance between a French and English poem, we automatically assume that the English is a translation from the French. In this case it is clearly not true, because the English is more like the Italian than is the French. The next position is that the two writers translated from the Italian independently. Even this seems to me untrue.§ The single sonnet from Sannazaro, translated by both authors, is doubtfully attributed to him, and, as such, appears in only four of the ten editions previous to 1547; certain expressions in the French seem more like the English than like the Italian; the riming in the French follows the English, not the Italian; and the French terminates in a couplet, the conventional English ending. Any one of these by itself might be accidental, but the cumulative effect is interesting. The solution cannot be proved; it is merely a question which hypothesis is preferable. Surely the assumption is more probable that Saint-Gelais knew Wyatt's sonnet than that two men working independently chanced upon the same author, chanced upon one sonnet only, chanced upon the same sonnet, chanced upon a sonnet that appears in but few editions, and chanced upon the same renderings. But this assumption is 'startling' not for itself, but for what it implies. And the first implication

---

* Modern scholarship has shown that Marot published sonnets much earlier.

† *Athenaeum*, July 11, 1891.

‡ Without knowledge of this note, subsequently Mr Arthur Tilley, Professor Kastner and myself each discovered the same fact independently. [It does indeed appear that both derive independently from the Italian.]

§ This is the subject of a controversy between Professor Kastner and myself *Modern Language Notes*, February, 1908; Professor Kastner objected in *Modern Language Review*, April 1908; I replied in *Mod. Lang. Review*, January, 1909; as my article was sent to him in proof, he replied in the same number; I responded in *Mod. Lang. Notes*, January, 1910; to my knowledge there has been no reply to this last.

is that for poems of the early Tudor period one should be very careful of speaking of French 'sources'. This is applicable to the two other pieces 'borrowed' from Saint-Gelais. The first of these is an epigram, the point of which is that the arrow of death striking the arrow of love already in his heart only makes him love the more [LXIV].* It is noticeable that the form Wyatt here employs is the ottava rima. Under the circumstances it seems probable that the original is an unknown Italian poem; further than that it is impossible to go. The other consists of three quatrains:†

> Madame withouten many wordes
> Ons, I am sure, ye will or no;
> And if ye will, then leve your bordes
> And use your wit, and shew it so:
> And with a beck ye shall me call;
> And if of oon that burneth alwaye
> Ye have any pitie at all,
> Aunswer him faire with ye or nay.
> If it be ye, I shalbe fayne:
> If it be nay, frendes as before;
> Ye shall an othr man obtain
> And I myn owne and youres no more.

The similarity between this and Saint-Gelais' *S'amour vous a donne au cueur en gage* is so marked as, I think, to preclude independent working. The question then arises whether both are taken from a common source, or whether the one is translated from the other. It does not seem to come from the Italian,[1] as the attitude assumed by the lover is quite different from the conventional Italian one. And it is not, presumably, due to Wyatt, since the French version is the more polished. Moreover the tone is characteristic of Saint-Gelais, the lightness, the cleverness and the antithesis at the climax:

> Un autre aurez et moy ne pouvant estre
> Servant de vous, de moi je seray maistre.

In this case it seems safe to assume that Saint-Gelais is the master and Wyatt the disciple.

(b) Wyatt's poems then, may be divided into his short pieces, his satires, and his psalms, probably written for the most part in that order. In his

* Identified first by Emil Koeppel, *Anglia*, 13, 77.
† Foxwell's ed. 1, 83. Identified first by Miss Foxwell.
[1] The discovery that Wyatt's poem is a translation of one by the Italian Dragonetto Bonifacio undermines Berdan's point here.

manuscript these short pieces are grouped according to the form, rondeaux, sonnets, epigrams, and miscellaneous poems. Even in the first group, where purely French influence might be expected, the subject-matter of the whole of the first rondeau is taken from Petrarch, and the first five lines of the seventh.* He seems to have had the notion that in some way the rondeau was a possible equivalent for the Italian madrigal.¹ In the first he makes an attempt to render his author in so far as the form allows; in the second, the Italian merely gives him his start. Apparently the transformation was unsatisfactory. Perhaps for that reason he translates the sonnets in the sonnet form. And he translates them incredibly literally. Anyone who has ever written sonnets will remember the difficulty in handling the form; anyone who has ever tried to translate a sonnet will appreciate the *tour de force* of the following rendition. It is almost word for word. In order to illustrate this, I shall break the first sonnet into pieces and interpose the two versions.†

> Cesare, poi che'l traditor d'Egitto
>   Li fece il don de l'onorata testa,
>   Celando l'allegrezza manifesta,
>   Pianse per gli occhi fuor, si comme è scritto;

> Cesar, when that the traytor of Egipt,
>   With thonorable hed did him present,
>   Covering his gladnes, did represent
>   Playnt with his teres owteward, as it is writt: [III, 1–4]

> Et Anibâl, quando a l'imperio afflitto
>   Vide farsi fortuna si molesta,
>   Rise fra gente lagrimosa e mesta,
>   Per isfogare il suo acerbo despitto.

> And Hannyball, eke, when fortune him shitt
>   Clene from his reign, and from all his intent
>   Laught to his folke, whom sorrowe did torment,
>   His cruel dispite for to disgorge and qwit.   [III, 5–8]

> E cosi avèn che l'animo ciascuna
>   Sua passion sotto 'l contrario manto
>   Ricopre co'la vista or chiara or bruna;

* In Foxwell's *Study*, 76–78 the original discoverers of all of Wyatt are carefully listed. To this table the reader is referred.
† I am using the Scherillo text of Petrarch, the modern edition most carefully following Cod. 3195 Vatican.
¹ This is perfectly possible. Alternatively, an as yet undiscovered French rondeau intervenes between, say, Petrarch's madrigal 'Or vedi amor' and Wyatt's 'Behold, love' [I].

So chaunceth it oft, that every passion
  The mind hideth, by color contrary,
  With fayned visage, now sad, now mery: [III, 9–11]

Però, s'alcuna volta io rido o canto,
  Fàcciol perch'l non ho se non quest'una
  Via da celare il mio angoscioso pianto.

Whereby if I laught, any tyme or season,
  It is: for bicause I have nother way
  To cloke my care, but under sport and play.   [III, 12–14]

Clearly there is no question here of vague influence, or even of imitation. It is not only translation, but surprisingly accurate translation. But of the thirty-two sonnets eighteen are practically of this character. And of the eighteen, all but one, the Sannazaro already discussed, are taken from Petrarch. And there are two more where the idea may have come from an Italian source. So far as the sonnet is concerned, there can be no question that Wyatt went to Italy.

Of these sonnets there are two usually quoted for their autobiographic value. The first is a version of the CCLXIX Sonnet of Petrarch. As this is an extreme case, even at the risk of inevitable boredom, it is better to quote it entire.

Rotta è l'alta colonna e'l verde lauro
  Che facean ombra al mio stanco pensero;
  Perduto ho quel che ritrovar non spero
  Dal borea a l'autro, o dal mar indo al mauro.

The pillar pearishd is whearto I lent:
  The strongest staye of myne unquyet mynde;
  The lyke of it no man agayne can fynde,
  From East to West, still seking thoughe he went.
                                            [CCXXXVI, 1–4]

Tolto m'hai, Morte, il mio doppio tesauro
  Che mi fea viver lieto e gire altero;
  E ristorar nol pò terra nè impero,
  Nè gemma oriental, nè forza d'auro.

To myne unhappe! for happe away hath rent
  Of all my joye, the verye bark and rynde;
  And I (alas) by chaunce am thus assynde
  Dearlye to moorne till death do it relent.   [CCXXXVI, 5–8]

Ma se consentimento è di destino
  Che posso io più se no'aver l'alma trista,
  Umidi gli occhi sempre e'l viso chino?

But syns that thus it is by destenye,
  What can I more but have a wofull hart,
  My penne in playnt, my voyce in wofull crye,   [CCXXXVI,
                                                            9–11]

Oh nostra vita ch'e si bella in vista,
  Com'perde agevolmente in un matino
  Quel che'n molti anni a gran pena s'acquista!

My mynde in woe, my bodye full of smart.
  And I my self, my self alwayes to hate
  Till dreadfull death, do ease my dolefull state.   [CCXXXVI,
                                                            12–14]

There is practically no doubt that the Petrarchan sonnet was written on the events of 1348, when the Cardinal Giovanni Colonna died, and also Laura. The first line, therefore, opens with a pun. There is no doubt, also, that Wyatt knew this, since all the early commentators carefully explain the allusions. It will be noticed that this is not an exact translation, that all allusions to the laurel and the double treasure are omitted, and the last half of the sextet differs radically. The question then arises whether this sonnet was not written in commemoration of the fall of Cromwell, July 28, 1540. This is almost invariably answered in the affirmative. The general opinion may be illustrated by the note appended by Miss Foxwell:

Ll. 12–14 are original, and though less poetical than Petrarch's conclusion express Wiat's sincere feeling, and show also that he had a definite purpose in writing this Sonnet. It is evidently late, and the sentiment expressed fits in with Cromwell's fall in 1540.

Since he had in no way been responsible for Cromwell's fate, it is hard to understand why he should hate himself; since Cromwell had been his protector, 'whose minion he was', there was every reason for anxiety concerning his own future and his own safety. Under the circumstances if all that he could do was the frigid sonnet with its lame and impotent conclusion,—its perishing pillars and the bark and rind of joy—one cannot have a high estimation of his poetic ability. If, on the other hand, it be considered a prentice piece,—that in the sextet, for instance, he was caught by the rime 'destiny' and did the best he could,—its presumable early date would excuse its lack of either art or feeling. Much the same line of reasoning applies to the other:

    Who so list to hount: I know where is an hynde,
    But, as for me: helas, I may no more.

The vayne travail hath werid me so sore,
I ame of theim, that farthest cometh behinde
Yet, may I by no means, my weried mynde
Drawe from the Der; but as she fleeth afore
Faynting I folowe. I leve of therefore:
Sins in a nett I seke to hold the wynde.
Who list her hount: I put him oute of dowbte:
As well as I: may spend his tyme in vain.
And graven with Diamonds in letters plain:
There is written, her faier neck rounde abowte:
Noli me tangere for Cæsara I ame
And wylde for to hold: though I seme tame. [VII]

To the modern reader the allegory seems clear; the last two lines can
refer only to Anne Boleyn and the King. But, as Nott pointed out a
hundred years ago Wyatt's sonnet is only a re-working of a sonnet by
Petrarch.* Allegorizing the lady as a milk-white hind was usual,† and
the phrase *Noli me tangere quia Caesaris sum* was a proverb. Romanello,
also, has a sonnet in which, like Wyatt's, both ideas are combined.‡
And the interpretation of the Petrarch sonnet by Wyatt's Italian contemporaries is only that Laura is married.§ But if that be the idea Wyatt
is trying to convey, it surely would not apply to Anne, unless it were
written after 1532. On the other hand, if the *Caesaris sum* refers only to
the Julian laws of adultery, as the Italian commentators aver, the Wyatt
may have been written to any married woman at any time, or it may
again be merely an effort at translation. The safer position, surely, is to
assume in Wyatt's work no autobiographical value until that value is
proved.

But not only are Wyatt's sonnets for the most part translations,
imitations and adaptations of Petrarch, those chosen have proven the
least permanent in the *Rime*. Part of Petrarch's inheritance from the
Provençal troubadours was the purely intellectual type of poem wherein a metaphor is first selected and then pursued to its last ramification.
For this no poetic feeling is required; the brain is scourged to think out
the analogies. And it is this type that Wyatt preferred. This was pointed
out, long ago, by Warton, in a passage that has never been bettered.[1]

* Sonnet CXC.
† Cf. Boccaccio's *Decamerone* IV, 6.
‡ Romanello's Sonnets are published together with *La Bella Mano* of Giusto de'Conti, ed.
by Mazzuchelli, Verona, 1753.
§ Petrarca, ed. Leonardo, 1533.
[1] See No. 8, pp. 42-3.

It was from the capricious and over-strained invention of the Italian poets, that Wyat was taught to torture the passion of love by prolix and intricate comparisons, and unnatural allusions. At one time his love is a galley steered by cruelty through stormy seas and dangerous rocks; the sails torn by the blast of tempestuous sighs, and the cordage consumed by incessant showers of tears; a cloud of grief envelopes the stars, reason is drowned, and the haven is at a distance. At another, it is a Spring trickling from the summit of the Alps, which gathering force in its fall, at length overflows all the plain beneath. Sometimes it is a gun, which being overcharged, expands the flame within itself, and bursts in pieces. Sometimes it is like a prodigious mountain, which is perpetually weeping in copious fountains, and sending forth sighs from its forests; which bears more leaves than fruits; which breeds wild-beasts, the proper emblems of rage, and harbours birds that are always singing. In another of his sonnets, he says, that all nature sympathises with his passion. The woods resound his elegies, the rivers stop their course to hear him complain, and the grass weeps in dew. These thoughts are common and fantastic.

Of course it is at once obvious that such poems are more easily imitated. When once the original conception,—such as the lover, as hunger, chasing the loved one, as deer, who is unapproachable because another's, —is adopted, language is no bar; like a geometrical problem it may be expressed as easily in English as in Italian, and it cannot be said to have lost in the transference. Owing to the difficulty of the sonnet form certain modifications are almost inevitable, but such modifications neither detract from the poem, nor add to the originality of the poet. Such translation is a game of solitaire, played primarily for amusement, a contest between the writer and the language. For such a purpose poems expressing delicate shades of poetic feeling are too difficult; they defy translation. Perforce the writer must choose such pieces as can be transferred from one language to another. And the ornamentation will consist in balance and antithesis,

> Pace non trovo, e non ho da far guerra
> I fynde no peace and all my warr is done.

Poetry of this sort abounds in the quattrocento writers, each of whom, the center of his own particular little circle, adapted Petrarch to his own particular needs. They followed him, to be sure, but at a respectful distance. As a group they impress the reader as a serious set of men elaborately grinding out complicated conceits. Yet to speak of them as a group is a mistake; there was little communication between them. The similar literary characteristics are due to similar literary demands in the various courts, demands for short complimentary poems, poems to be set to music, light love lyrics, etc., etc. And as Petrarch's work offers models for all such composition, naturally they all accepted him as master. Probably the most popular of these writers was Serafino De'Ciminelli, called from his birthplace Aquila, Aquilano.* During his short life (1466–1500), in contrast to most of the other writers, he stayed for some time at each of the various courts, Naples, Rome, Ferrara, Mantua, Milan, Venice,—almost all the literary centers, in fact, with the exception of Florence. Consequently these peregrinations gave him a vogue the length and breadth of Italy. During his life he was too much occupied in composition to publish,† but immediately after his death, beginning with 1502, the press poured forth edition after edition, so that before Wyatt's arrival in Italy twenty-one editions had already appeared. I do not think it is difficult to understand the cause of his popularity. He has a distinct vein of sweetness and a lyric quality that make some of his verses charming. It is quite comprehensible, to a certain degree, what his friend Vincentio Calmeta‡ says of him:

Nel recitare de'soi poemi era tanto ardente e con tanto giuditio le parole con la musica consertava che l'animo de li asscoltanti o dotti, o mediocri, o plebei, o donne equalmente commoveva.

He sang, quite literally sang, of the passing of youth and the flight of time, of lady's love and knight's despair,—most musical, most melancholy.

The criticism of his work is given acutely by Il Pistoia in the sonnet just quoted:

Serafin *solo* per la lingua è grato.

Unfortunately it is true, that Serafino pleases by the words alone, that there is no thought behind them. His love poems sound hollow, because they are empty. Fortunately this is not inductive; we are told so. Calmeta naïvely remarks:

* The early editions always call him Seraphino; in modern indices he is listed as Aquilano; and sometimes he appears as De'Ciminelli. It may save confusion if it be realized that these are all one and the same poet.
† The only modern edition is *Le Rime di Serafino De'Ciminelli dall' Aquila* by Mario Menghini, *Collezione di Opere Inedite o Rare*, Bologna, 1896. Unfortunately only the first volume, containing the sonnets, eclogues and epistles, appeared. Of the early editions I have used the 1508, 1539 (not listed in Vaganey), 1540 and 1550.
‡ This life was published in 1504 in a collection celebrating his praises. It is fortunately, given in full by Menghini, as the lives prefixed to the early editions are merely condensations of this, and refer the reader to it.

Non ebbe in soi poemì alcuno particolare amore per oggietto, perché in ogni
loco dove se trovava faceva piú presto innamoramento che pigliare casa a pisone.

Nor does the reader feel this limited only to his love poems. Behind
all the words there seems so little feeling. There is such a small quantity
of thought to such a deal of words. They need the music to make us
forget how little is said, to justify the constant repetition, to eke out the
sense by the sound.

When Serafino's immense popularity is considered, it was inevitable
that Wyatt should imitate him. Not only were the sonnets set to music,
but from Chariteo (according to Calmeta) he learned the strambotto, an
eight lined verse in *ottava rima*,—the form in which he achieved his
greatest celebrity. These differ from the sonnet in that the restricted form
allows even less space for the development of the idea, and the termina-
tion in a couplet necessarily gives an epigrammatic close. In some cases
Wyatt translates very carefully:*

> Ogni pungente e venenosa spina
> se vede a qualche tempo esser fiorita,
> crudel veneno posto in medicina
> tal uolta torna lhom da morte uita
> el foco che ogni cosa arde e ruina
> spesso resana vna mortal ferita
> cosi spero el mio mal me sia salute
> chogni cosa che noce ha pur uirtute.

> Venemus thornes that ar so sharp and kene,
> Sometyme ber flowers fayre and fresh of hue:
> Poyson offtyme is put in medecene,
> And causith helth in man for to renue;
> Ffire that purgith allthing that is unclene,
> May hele and hurt: and if thes bene true,
> I trust somtyme my harme may be my helth:
> Syns evry wo is joynid with some welth.   [LXXVI]

In other cases only the idea, or some significant phrases, are taken.
Wyatt's 'Epigrams' show the country of their birth by both content and
form. As has been said before, of the thirty-one epigrams all but six are
in the *ottava rima*. It may be granted at once that all these have not been
traced to their sources and that many so-called sources are extremely
doubtful, yet enough that can be positively shown to be translation has

---

* The text is from the 1508. Wyatt's indebtedness has been largely studied by Koeppel.
The same poem, however, is assigned by Carducci to Poliziano (*Rime* 1912, 606).

been found to justify the generalization that here also Wyatt's main function was to introduce Italian methods to sixteenth century England.

If we may for the moment postpone the discussion of the miscellaneous group and turn at once to the Satires, a new figure is introduced upon the scene in the person of Luigi Alamanni.* In both life and character he forms a striking contrast to the graceful superficial Serafino. Born of a noble Florentine family, he was educated in the refinements of the time, surrounded by classic monuments of both art and letters. In particular he belonged to the group meeting at the home of Bernardo Rucellai, or rather in the shade of the Orti Oricellari,—a group of which Macchiavelli was a member and Trissino an honored guest,—in which the literary discussions recalled memories of the earlier brilliant circle of Lorenzo. The contrast between these two literary circles shows the development of the Renaissance spirit. Whereas the first was primarily interested in classic culture per se, Alamanni and his friends were primarily interested in bringing Italian culture to the classic levels. This ideal assumed suddenly a practical shape when in 1522, following the examples of Harmodus and Aristogiton, they entered the plot to restore the liberties of Florence by the assassination of Giulio de'Medici. Unhappily the Cardinal, when the plot was betrayed to him, was unable to appreciate the beauty of classical precedent, and Alamanni escaped into exile with a price upon his head. Until the middle of 1527 he lived a life of enforced leisure, indefinite waiting, and postponed hopes. In the spring of 1527 he was at Lyons, the French gate to Italy, and in all probability he was there, when Sir John Russell, with Wyatt in his train, passed through. And apparently by that time he had written his satires, which were first published in his *Opere Toscane* 1532–1533. On the expulsion of the Medici in 1527 he returned to Florence, but shortly, on their return, he is again driven into life-long exile and becomes a pensioner of the French Court.

The events of this varied and exciting life find their poetical expression in poems that are always dignified, if somewhat ponderous. Serafino was predominantly a poet, but a poet without much to say; Alamanni has no lack of subject matter, but not very much poetical afflatus. His early training had taught him the value of classical restraint, and restraint of any kind was the last lesson he needed to learn. He takes himself so seriously! As he writes, one feels him wondering how the Orti Oricellari will like this verse, and how he may justify it. The inevitable result is

* Cf. *Luigi Alamanni*, par Henri Hauvette, Paris, 1903. To M. Hauvette I am indebted for all the facts of the life.

negative; the absence of faults is balanced by an absence of virtues,—the type of work so distressing to critics, wherein all rules are carefully preserved, no blemishes to be condemned, and yet without the impression of the personality to vitalize it. Of all forms of writing where such a negative becomes a positive, the chief is surely the verse-letter. Here a minor writer may be excellent merely by being himself. Consequently Italian literature of the period is flooded by such compositions, call them satires, letters, *capitoli*, what you will, wherein the end sought is amusement. The one thing necessary is lightness of touch. Unhappily that is the qualification that Alamanni did not possess. His satires lack both the grace of Horace, and the sting of Juvenal. They are perfectly good and perfectly commonplace.

Also unhappily it is Alamanni that Wyatt chose for his model in satire. Again the simpler method will be that of quotation.*

> Questo fa che'l mio regnio, e'l mio thesoro
> Son gli'nchiostri & le carte, & piu ch'altroue
> Hoggi in Prouenza uolentier dimoro.
> Qui non ho alcun, che mi domandi doue
> Mi stia, ne uada, & non mi sforza alcuno
> À gir pe'l mondo quando agghiaccia & pioue.
> Quando e'gli è'l ciel seren, quando e gli è bruno
> Son quel medesmo, & non mi prendo affanno,
> Colmo di pace, & di timor digiuno.
> Non sono in Francia à sentir beffe & danno
> S'io non conosco i uin, s'io non so bene
> Qual uiuanda è miglior di tutto l'anno,
> Non nella Hispagnia oue studiar conuiene
> Piu che nell'esser poi nel ben parere,
> Oue frode, & menzognia il seggio tiene,
> Non in Germania oue'l mangiare e'l bere
> M'habbia à tor l'intelletto, & darlo in preda
> Al senso, in guisa di seluagge fere.
> Non sono in Roma, oue chi'n Christo creda,
> Et non sappia falsar, ne far ueneni
> Conuien ch'à has casa sospirando rieda.
> Sono in Prouenza. . . .

> This maketh me at home to hounte and to hawke,
> And in fowle weder at my booke to sitt;
> In frost and snowe then with my bow to stawke;
> No man doeth mark where so I ride or goo;

* The text is taken from the 1542 edition of the *Opere Toscane*. Satire X.

In lusty lees at libertie I walke;
And of these newes I fele nor wele nor woo,
Sauf that a clogg doeth hang yet at my hele.
No force for that; for it is ordered so,
That I may lepe boeth hedge and dike full well.
I ame not now in Ffraunce to judge the wyne
With saffry sauce the delicates to fele.
Nor yet in Spaigne where oon must him inclyne
Rather then to be outewerdly to seme;
I meddill not with wittes than be so fyne.
Nor Fflaunders chiere letteth not my sight to deme
Of black and white, nor taketh my wit awaye
With bestlynes; they beestes do so esteme.
Nor I ame not where Christe is geven in pray
For mony, poison and traison at Rome,—
A commune practise used nyght and daie.
But here I ame in Kent and Christendome, . . .   [CV, 80–100]

This is a fair illustration of Wyatt's procedure. In the first place he keeps the meter exactly.* The difficulty of the terza rima in English, owing to the scarcity of riming words, is of course due to the triple rime. In Wyatt's attempt to render the meter, the sense of the original is apt to be lost, the value of the phrase usually goes, and sometimes his lines make no sense at all. Inevitably with so difficult a rime-scheme there is dilution. Part of the dilution may be due to a desire to adapt the original to his own individual conditions. Thus it begins,

> Myn owne John Poynz,   [CV]

and runs in occasionally local allusions, such as that to Kent in the passage quoted. Of these the most interesting is the substitution for classical reference in the two lines,

> Praise Syr Thopas for a nobyll tale,
> And skorne the story that the knyght told . . .   [CV, 50–1]

While such deception is not in accordance with modern ethics, in the sixteenth century property rights in poems were not regarded. Such

---

* Saintsbury (*Hist. of Prosody*, 1, 311) as quoted by Miss Foxwell (*Study*, 89) comments: 'the best name for the metre of the remarkable poems . . . is probably interlaced heroic couplets' . . . In a note he adds: 'or they may be classed as simply *terza rima*, unskillfully written, but Wyatt has not got the *terza* movement at all, indeed quatrains suggest themselves and quintets and almost everything.' This remarkable pronouncement must be due to a limiting of the name *terza rima* to the Dantesque manner; but Wyatt's model is the *terza rima* of the cinquecento!

additions were made for a personal application, or, as in the case of Barclay, for a moral purpose. The difficulty here is to distinguish between additional matter put in for the sake of the meter and that put in to give a more intimate tone. This difficulty is enhanced by the fact that the Alamanni original is insincere; written at a time when he was moving heaven and earth to please Francis Ier, platitudes on the wretchedness of court life strongly suggest the fable of the fox and the grapes. And it cannot be said that the facts of Wyatt's life as we know them indicate that he lived on a superior plane, untouched by the baser motives of the common courtier. His intimacy with Sir Francis Bryan scarcely argues for a lonely moral isolation. The two other satires follow Horace, but it must be granted that they follow at a respectful distance,—at such a distance that one is tempted to assume an unknown intermediary, which *more suo* Wyatt has adapted.* But whatever may have been the procedure, these satires form an instructive contrast to the first three of Barclay.† The vigour of the early writer, due to his use of the concrete instance, has been lost in elegant generality. On the other hand, the somewhat amorphous couplets of Barclay have been replaced by the elaborate terza rima. What has been lost in force has been gained in form.

Petrarch, Serafino, and Alamanni,—for, although Wyatt imitates others occasionally, these are his chief sources,—form a curious group without much in common; the final touch is to find that he has copied his version of the Penitential Psalms from Pietro Aretino.‡ Aretino is one of the most interesting figures of the Italian Renaissance, because in the midst of sham and convention he dared to be himself. Preëminently he is a realist. Son of a shoemaker, hanger-on of the Papal Court, follower of Giovanni de la Banda Nera, soldier of fortune at Venice, at no period of his active life did he have leisure to learn from books. The world was his school. Although some of his work—and of course it is that that is the best known and most often associated with his name!—is outside the pale of polite conversation, the vitality of his writing, which gave him honor and riches in his own day, has remained.§ After 1530, the

---

* In the Third Satire [usually presented as the Second in modern editions], which contains the fable of the town mouse and the country visitor, curiously enough the latter mouse is apparently French. [Cp. line 54.] But this is not conclusive. It looks very much as though Wyatt had reversed the process used in the rondeaux and put French content into an Italian form.

† Lengthy illustrations are given from Barclay's satires, pp. 238-242.

‡ Miss Foxwell attributes this discovery to Mr. Arundell Esdaile of the British Museum.

§ There is no modern edition of the works of Aretino and there is no writer more mis-

year in which the Doge finally succeeded in obtaining his pardon from the Pope, Aretino began composing religious works from motives of policy. The contrast between his life of open, unashamed, boastful licentiousness and these books of a sickly, pious sentimentalism is too extreme; it combines the flaunting of vice and the smirking of hypocrisy. The modern reader, as he turns the pages of the *Humanitd di Cristo*, is too conscious of the painted faces of the harlots grinning over his shoulder, not to experience a sensation of almost physical repugnance. The literary manner is no more pleasing. It consists in taking the scriptural narrative, or the life of a saint, and retelling it with incredible dilution. In 1534, in this way he produced *I sette Salmi de la penitentia di David*, a wordy prose version of the Psalms, joined together by prologues which give a stage setting. This much may be said in behalf of this production. Any rendition of the Bible into the vulgar tongue, especially if it were uncontaminated by Lutheranism, was a novelty, and the Psalms themselves are so fine that even Aretino cannot completely ruin them. As the public is apt to confuse art and morality, perhaps it is not surprising that the book proved popular; there were three Italian editions and one French translation before Wyatt's death.* Evidently Wyatt is to be numbered among the admirers of this curious production. He copies the framework of the prologues, translates some of the prologues, and parts of the Psalms themselves. As in the case of his version of Alamanni's satire, he makes no pretence at representing his author faithfully, and, it is interesting to note, it is the early part of the work that shows the most indebtedness. Later he follows the Vulgate.† In any case, his main indebtedness to Aretino lies in his conceiving the work from a standpoint purely literary. It is this that differentiates his production

---

* In 1741 Mazzuchelli thus comments: Di tutte l'Opere in prosa che scrisse l'Aretino, questra sopra i Salmi si può riputar la migliore, non già perche diasi da noi fede a quel Predicator Bolognese riferito dallo stesso Aretino, il quale predicando in Venezia, *che vuol vedere*, disse, *in la penitentia David, leggali, e vedrallo*; ma per testimonio anche del Crescimbeni, il quale le chiama *degni d'esser letti, e ammirati*. *La Vita di Pietro Aretino*, Padova, 1741, 218.

† Miss Foxwell tries to show that he is indebted to the Psalter of 1530, because he probably composed them while travelling and the Great Bible would have been cumbersome. Apparently she forgets that Wyatt was brought up on the Vulgate. Moreover the Italian *nottulo*, the *nycticoxax* of the *Vulgate*, while it does mean 'bat' also means *owl*. Wyatt's *owl*, therefore, does not signify anything.

---

understood. For a mass of misinformation the reader is referred to the article in the *Encyclopedia Britannica*. For a clear and brief summary of his literary position, cf. Arturo Graf, *Attraverso il Cinquecento*.

from the Psalms of Coverdale, or Sternhold, or Clément Marot. Those were written to be sung. As they were sung, the tendency was to replace the authorized hymns of the Church by them. Moreover, this was the intention of the heretical authors. But there is no such purpose as this in Wyatt. His Psalms were written to be read. The composition is a single unit, where the prologues give the scenery for the dramatic monologues. It is dramatic, therefore, and not lyric, in conception. This is also shown by the fact that whereas the prologues are in the ottava rima, a lyric measure, the psalms themselves are in the terza rima, a purely narrative measure.

To discuss the Psalms from this literary point of view is almost impossible for the modern English reader. The superbly beautiful phrasing of the *Authorized Version* is so familiar that the addition of rime seems cheap and the dilution impertinent. But this necessarily renders him unfair to Wyatt, for the majority of the readers of his age thought of the Psalms in terms of Latin. Any English version was still tentative. Yet it must be granted that the meter chosen was unfortunate. Terza rima is so difficult in English that he is forced to expand the simple lines of the Vulgate. Although naturally the work is better in proportion as there is less Aretino and more Vulgate, even at the best it seems diffuse. For example, the two lines of the Fiftieth Psalm (the Fifty-first in English) read:

> Asperges me hyssopo, et mundabor;
> lavabis me, et super nivem dealbabor. [verse, 7]

Wyatt's version runs:

> And as the Juyz to hele the liepre sore,
> With hysope clense,—clense me, and I ame clene;
> Thou shalt me wash, and more then snow therfore
> I shall be whight,—how foule my faut have bene. [CV, 469-72]

Surely no one can maintain that Wyatt has improved the *Authorized Version*:

Purge me with hyssop, and I shall be clean; wash me, and I shall be whiter than snow.

The meter has forced him, not only to unnecessary additions, but also to an awkward inverted order. And Aretino is not responsible here.

Among the Italian authors Wyatt not only chose poor models, but he also selected poor examples of their work.* The question naturally arises, why were these particular poems chosen, when the best of the cinquecento was open to him. The answer to this question is clear from the previous analysis. The one characteristic common to all of Wyatt's translations is that the appeal in them is to the mind, rather than to the heart. The emotional sonnets of Petrarch are passed by in favor of those in which a conceit is carefully worked out; the musical strains of Serafino are ignored to translate an antithesis; the moralization of Alamanni and the sentimentality of Aretino are chosen for intellectual reasons. Each work, whether sonnet or strambotto, whether psalm or satire, is in itself a clearly defined unit. The strambotto is not an undeveloped sonnet, but, from the beginning, the author had a clear perception of exactly what he wished to accomplish; nor is the sonnet by chance a sonnet, but it was originally conceived as a sonnet. However trite this may seem to us, only a glance is needed at the works of his contemporaries to realize that it was a revolutionary conception. There is no place here for poems written 'to eschew ydelnes,' works that are accretions of years brought together because of a common topic, such as Skelton, or Hawes, or Barclay, or Heywood. Wyatt's works are on a different plane of literary art.

This is his great contribution to literature. It is for this reason that the Elizabethans recognized in him the beginning of English poetry, why Puttenham calls him a 'lantern of light'. And it was perceived even in his own time. Immediately after his death in 1542 Leland, the antiquary, published a volume of Latin elegies in his honor.† In most of them the worthy antiquary is particularly interested in doing full justice to his own classical learning, so that the result is platitudinous. But in them one can see how one man at least judged him. In one of them Wyatt is held comparable to Dante and Petrarch in the vulgar tongue. There are two others which give exactly the fact here stated.

> Anglica lingua fuit rudis & sine nomine rhythmus
> Nunc limam agnoscit docte Viate tuam.

> Nobilitas dedicit te præceptore Britanna
> Carmina per varios scribere posse modos.

* Miss Foxwell (*The Poems*, 2, *Introduction*, vi), tells us: 'At Venice, amongst other great statesmen, he met Navagero and Baldassare Castiglione, the two men whose influence was most felt among other nations.' Consequently he came under the influence of 'the grand' Navagero, Castiglione whose 'own married life was ideally happy', and Trissino. While of course it is possible that he met these men on his Italian journey, just as it is possible that he met an indefinite number of others, as a matter of fact there is no proof that he did.

† *Naeniae in mortem Thomae Viati equitis incomparabilis, Londini 1542.*

That expresses precisely Wyatt's function. In an age, when art in its narrow sense had been lost, in his work the English language did find again the art of omission, did recognize his file, and did learn to write songs in various clearly differentiated forms.

For such a purpose as this, obviously, the content of the individual poems is a secondary matter. Whether or not they are autobiographical, whether or not he did love Anne Boleyn, whether or not they are translations, whether or not they express his real convictions,—none of these is particularly important. The important thing is that in his work the early Tudor found examples of a large variety of verse forms, coldly but carefully worked out.* It must be granted that a poet whose primary interest is in form, rather than in content, is not great. Poetic technique, clever phrase, witty conceit go a little way, but only a little way. On the other hand, the great emotions that have aroused poets from the beginning are not present in Wyatt's work. The nature in his poems is of the lion-and-tiger sort drawn from books; beauty apparently makes little appeal; and his love serves merely as the occasion to make far-fetched comparisons. This lack of emotion is apparently one of the reasons why critics call him 'virile!' His better poems are observations of the life around him. In them he has mastered the medium, he carries the structure easily, and at the same time is definite and concrete.

> They fle from me, that sometyme did me seke [XXXVII]

suggests an actual occasion, or the epigram written to Bryan from prison [CCLXIV]. But the most successful are those written to be sung. Such poems as *My Lute awake!* [LXVI] *Fforget not yet the tryde entent*, [CCIV], or *Blame not my lute* [CCV], have maintained their place in all anthologies. They deserve all the praise that has been lavished upon them. The union of strength and grace makes a rare and felicitous

---

* Miss Foxwell tries to show that Wyatt deduced the principles of his versification from the Pynson *Chaucer* of 1526. (*Study*, Chapter VI.) 'Wyatt deliberately and conscientiously studied Chaucer with a view of carrying on his method of work, and made his exercise in versification parallel with his introduction of the Petrarchan Sonnet.' From that he made rules of versification. 'The rules collected from the above include the chief rules of Wiat's versification, such as the slurring of vowels, . . . weak syllables ending in vowel-likes (*i.e.* n, r. l, n), and slurring of verbal ending "-eth" in the body of the verse; the absence of weak stress after the cæsura, and before the strong stress of the second foot; the cæsura after the third syllable as in "pàlmèrs", and the occasional variety of an octosyllabic line. (*The Poems*, Appendix D.) In regard to this there are two comments: (a) these 'rules' are subjective in that they depend upon the way in which the line is read; (b) Wyatt's versification, like that of his contemporaries, including the Pynson *Chaucer*, was affected by the principles of the Medieval Latin. In other words, it is unnecessary to discuss Pynson, since Wyatt's versification is that of his age.

combination. But in spite of these, and the six or eight more like them, the proposition remains true that for his age Wyatt's value lay, not in the few pieces where the fire of his passion has amalgamated the content and the form into one perfect whole, but in the many others which may not unjustly be called experiments in stanza-forms. Not only is the rondeau, the sonnet, the terza rima, and the ottava rima to be found, he made experiments also with the monorime, the Medieval Latin types of simple triplets with refrains, of quatrains of different combinations of length of line and different rime-schemes, of quatrains with codas, with French forms in the *douzaine* and *treizaine*, and finally with poulter's meter. There are even two attempts at what will be later the Eliza-bethan sonnet. With the exception of the heroic couplet and of blank verse,—two very important exceptions,—most of the stanzas to be used during the century are there. Of course with our ignorance of what the other writers were doing, it is uncritical to assume that all these novelties were first imported by Wyatt,—an assumption that would make him one of the greatest verse-technicians in the history of the language,—but they prove that the minds of the men in the circle to which Wyatt belonged were seriously occupied in studying the forms of verse.

That Wyatt was a leader in this circle seems probable, not only from Puttenham's statement, but also from the number of manuscripts that have been preserved containing his poems. That he was the founder of a 'school' we have no grounds for believing. The variety of his experi-ments seems to argue that he was still feeling his way, and the imitative nature of them does not suggest a dominating personality.* He was a fearless diplomat and an accomplished courtier, although apparently quick-tempered. His nature seems to have been grave and sweet, meditating over moral issues.† And his poems bear out this judgment. Tottel's phrase 'the weightinesse of the depewitted sir Thomas Wyat the elders verse' is sound criticism; but that he 'reft Chaucer the glory of his wit' is Surrey's exaggeration. The preceding line, however, that he 'taught what might be said in ryme' explains the contemporary

---

* Miss Foxwell's comment [op. cit., II, p. 20; and see No. 12, p. 118] '*Wiat's life and work* is a song of harmony. The "music of the spheres" is here. It is a vindication of what man can become with lofty aim and set purpose', proves rather her sympathetic imagination than her critical ability. Flugel's summary, (Neuenglisches Lesebuch, Halle 1895, Band 1, 376–382), is a careful statement of the case.

† Two letters written by Wyatt while in Spain to his son have been preserved. As they partake of the nature of sermons, one wonders in what mood the son, anxious for news of his father, received these improving epistles.

admiration. If this be true, the assumption may be plausible that such songs as Henry's *Pastyme with good companye,* Gray's *The hunte is vp,* Cornysshe's lyrics, etc., etc., represent the work done in the first quarter of the century. Later, George Boleyn, Lord Vaux, Henry Morley, Heywood, Anthony Lee, etc. composed after foreign models. This would explain Tottel's apology 'If parphappes some mislike the statelinesse of stile remoued from the rude skill of common eares' . . . But this is merely an hypothesis. The authors are really little more than names! Of George Boleyn, a volume of whose *rhythmos elegantissimos* is listed by Bale, one song alone remains and his authorship of that is doubtful. To judge of Lord Thomas Vaux' 'maruelous facillitie',* two short pieces are given us. *Tottel's Miscellany,* as we are told in the Preface gives us those poems 'which the ungentle horders up of such treasure haue heretofore enuid thee.' But the ungentle horders have done their work! Whatever may have been the 'treasures,' they are now lost. Of the group Wyatt alone survives. And if, from his work we may posit conditions and characteristics belonging to the work that is gone, we must recognize that these men consciously followed Italian precedent.

* Puttenham, *op. cit.,* 247.

14. Tillyard on Wyatt

1929

Introduction to *The Poetry of Sir Thomas Wyatt. A Selection and a Study*, by E. M. W. Tillyard (1929), pp. 12, 13–25, 26–50.

Tillyard (1889–1962) was an eminent writer and teacher of English literature, ending his career as Master of Jesus College, Cambridge.

(a) Of the poets of the English Renaissance, Wyatt, Surrey and Sidney, by their lives and character, seem to approach nearest the contemporary ideal of the scholar-courtier. In Wyatt's character there was that balance of antithetical qualities that seemed to mark the type: genius for action and refined scholarship; impetuosity and the restraint (sometimes) of gentle manners; versatility and fidelity—and above all high ambitions and modesty, for Leland in his *Elegies*[1] on one page compares him to the high-soaring eagle and on the next records that he never grew proud by worldly success and the splendour of the court. But if Wyatt approached an ideal common to the western countries of Europe he is yet most transparently English. He was no Italianate Englishman; his familiarity with foreign ways and tongues implied no surrender of nationality. His general feeling about Spain is very much that of a modern English tourist in the same country who discovers a 'mistake' in the change given him by a grave, middle-aged shopkeeper. Honesty, straightforwardness, even bluntness, those were the qualities he prized highest, for all his exotic culture: 'Wisdom, Gentlenes, Soberness, desire to do good, Friendliness to get the love of many, and Truth above all the rest,'[2] are the virtues he recommends to his son. There is irony in these words if it is remembered that this very son was to pay the penalty of death for treason to his sovereign.

[1] See No. 1.
[2] Wyatt, *Collected Poems* (1949), p. 245.

143

(b) Wyatt in his poetry plainly combines two elements—the native and the foreign. He was the heir of an English lyrical tradition; he also let the Renaissance into English verse. But it is not easy to mark the limits. Through exotic ideas in exotic measures he will sound a personal or national note; or, conversely, he will sing the most artificially Italianate love-longings in lyric measures inherited from mediaeval England. For instance, in translating Alamanni's *terza rima*, a metre never before used in English, he can adapt sufficiently to cry with a patriotic enthusiasm that has a curiously modern tone:

> But here I am in Kent and Christendom   [CVI, 100]

while the Petrarchian sentiments of

> If willingly I suffer woe,
> If from the fire me list not go,
> If then I burn, to plain me so
>   What may it avail me?   [LV, III]

are set to a measure common to many of the English carols of the fifteenth century:

> Mary is quene of alle thinge,
> And her sone a lovely kinge.
> God graunt us alle good endinge!
>   *Regnat Dei gracia.*

To set limits, then, is difficult, but it is easy to note the different literary traditions by which Wyatt was affected.

In many of Wyatt's lyrics there is no breach with the English mediæval tradition. He may choose Italian themes; some of his lyrics may be mere exercises: but lyric spontaneity and the intimate connection of words and tune are inherited not from Italy but from England. The simplicity of

> I promised you,
>   And you promised me,
> To be as true
>   As I would be   [CCXV]

carries on the tradition of

> I sing of a maiden
>   That is makeles,
> King of all Kinges,
>   To her sone sche ches;

and these short lines, so suggestive of music,

> No tiger's heart
> Is so pervert,
> Without desert
>   To wreak his ire;
> And you me kill
> For my good will;
> Lo, how I spill
>   For my desire!   [LI]

though conveying an Italian conceit, carry on the tradition of the song-
books of the early sixteenth century.

The note of lyric spontaneity, entering English about the end of the
thirteenth century with the Cuckoo Song and with 'Bytuene Mersh ant
Averil' and the other poems of the Leominster Manuscript, was never
forgotten in the intervening centuries. It appears in some of the carols
of the fifteenth century, and that it had not been lost in the generation
before Wyatt is shown by such a poem as 'Western wind, when will
thou blow?'

The close connection of words with tune, found in several of
Wyatt's lyrics, was derived partly from Wyatt's own musical skill but
largely (as Sir E. K. Chambers has pointed out) from the revival of
English music that occurred at the court of Henry VI and is associated
with the name of John Dunstable. Although the full impetus of this
musical revival slackened after Dunstable's death, the interest of the
English court in music did not perish, and is reflected in the song-books
of the time of Henry VII and Henry VIII. The words in these song-
books are rarely of much value, but what is so striking about most of
them is their dependence on music or even their subservience to it. The
following lines, for instance (in spite of the topical reference), scarcely
exist but for the tune to which they are set:

> Above all thing
> Now let us sing
>   Both day and night.
> Adieu morning;
> A bud is springing,
> Adieu, now let us sing,
> A bud is springing
>   Of the red rose and the white.

Similarly several of Wyatt's lyrics almost force the suggestion of a tune on the reader, for instance 'Perdie, I said it not' [CLVIII], 'All heavy minds' [LXXXIV] and 'If with complaint' [CCVIII]; Wyatt's invocations to his lute are by no means fictitious.

But Wyatt's debt to the early Tudor song-books does not end with these two lyrical qualities: he frankly writes in their manner, though of course he writes better. The following two verses from the song-books sound very much like Wyatt in his least inspired moments:

> Methink truly
> Bounden am I,
> And that greatly,
>   To be content,
> Seeing plainly
> Fortune doth wry
> All contrary
>   From my entent—

and

> Oft time for death forsooth I call
> In release of my great smart,
> For death is end and principal
> Of all the sorrows within my heart.
> A pain it is hence to depart;
>   Yet my life it is so grievous
>   That death is pleasure and nothing noyous.

Such are the English lyrical traditions to which Wyatt was open; what use he made of them and what he added, will be discussed later.

The effect of the non-lyrical poetry with which Wyatt grew up was very different. Professor Saintsbury, in an illuminating interchapter of his *History of Prosody*, points out that the changes of pronunciation that took place in the fifteenth century had entirely opposite effects on different classes of metrical forms. In the light metres they suggested unthought-of subtleties of rhythm without destroying the underlying pattern of a short line. But in the heavy metres they worked havoc, and in particular resolved the five-foot iambic line of Chaucer to chaos. And so it happens that while the English lyric tradition did Wyatt a service, the tradition of other English verse, which was written mostly in a heavy metre, was worse than useless to him: facts that readily explain the ease and mastery of some of Wyatt's verses, the stiffness and puerility of others.

The regular iambic line is a thing so much taken for granted as a corollary of the English tongue that it is hard to conceive a time when men speaking more or less modern English could have no perception of it. The language of Hawes and Barclay is not so very different from ours of to-day, but their sense of rhythm appears simply barbaric. Most ordinary English verse is constructed on the background of a certain fixed pattern. The lines

> How sweet the moonlight sleeps upon this bank

and

> O monstrous act! Villany, villany, villany!

are as different as they can be except in that the pattern behind them is the same. But when the verse departs too far from the pattern, the sense of regularity on which metre depends is lost and a kind of prose has resulted, as in the work of some of the Jacobean dramatists. The following lines, quickly read, are only with difficulty recognizable for blank verse:

> What excellence of nature's this! Have you
> So perfectly forgiv'n already as to
> Consider me a loss? I doubt which sex
> I shall be happier in. Climates of friendship
> Are not less pleasant, 'cause they are less scorching,
> Than those of love; and under them we'll live:
> Such precious links of that we'll tie our souls
> Together with, that the chains of the other
> Shall be gross fetters to it.

In Hawes and Barclay, too, there is no unifying pattern. If you read one line in a certain way, you will probably find that the next or the next but one cannot be read in that way; and in fact that the only way to read these people's verses is to gabble them breathlessly with the hopeful intention of lighting on four main accents a line. This passage from Barclay's *Ship of Fools* exemplifies the kind of verse that Wyatt was perforce accustomed to:

> But moste I marueyll of other folys blynde
> Which in dyuers scyencis ar fast laborynge
> Both days and nyght with all theyr herte and mynde,
> But of gramer knowe they lytyll or no thynge,
> Which is the grounde of all lyberall cunnynge;
> Yet many ar besy in logyke and in lawe,
> Whan all theyr gramer is skarsly worth a strawe.

Even the earliest of Wyatt's rondeaus and sonnets are metrically better than this, but the existence of such writing must have made him initially less critical and more tolerant of harshness. The opening of this sonnet, for instance, is hopelessly rough:

> Each man me telleth I change most my devise;
> And on my faith, me think it goode reason,
> To change propose like after the season;
> For in every case, to keep still one guise
> Is meet for them that would be taken wise. [X]

Whether Hawes and Barclay were more than a general influence is uncertain. It is possible that the immediate model of such lines of Wyatt as have just been quoted was Chaucer. Wyatt knew Chaucer well, for he imitates him frequently in word and phrase; but like his contemporaries, he must have read him without taking into account the final e's that must be pronounced. Chaucer in Pynson's edition, published in 1526 when Wyatt was beginning to write, has a close metrical resemblance to Wyatt's first efforts in the heavier metres.

From Skelton Wyatt is as far separated as Skelton is from Barclay and Hawes. In one sonnet[1] and in an occasional verse of his lyrics he seems to imitate him; but his lyric achievements and his painful and halting experiments are alike utterly alien from Skelton's fine, headlong, masterful clatter.

Wyatt's roughness can easily be misunderstood by those who forget that there are two kinds of roughness: the unconscious and the deliberate; the barbaric and the cultured; the roughness of Barclay and the roughness of Donne. In Barclay the roughness is no part of the sense; in Donne it is the very stamp of his passion: shift the accent as we will in Barclay's verse, we get no recognizable rhythm; shift it in a verse of Donne that at first sight appears rough, and we get a recognizable, distinctive and highly expressive rhythm. Barclay's couplet

> But of gramer knowe they lytyll or no thynge,
> Which is the grounde of all lyberall cunnynge.

is reducible to no rhythm. At first sight the line of Donne,

> If thou beest borne to strange sights,

the first line of the second stanza of 'Goe, and catch a falling starre', seems harsh and out of keeping with the obvious rhythm of the opening line of the poem; but by accenting the words *thou, borne* and *strange*

1 Tillyard refers to 'I abide and abide' (CCXXVII).

148

sights we not only get a rhythm conformable to that of 'Goe, and catch
a falling star', but find that the emphasis thrown on *strange sights* (words
that have to be long drawn out in pronunciation) is itself singularly
expressive of the surprise that strange sights might be expected to cause.
The difficulty in Wyatt's poetry is that both kinds of roughness occur.
The quotation given above from 'Each man me telleth I change most
my desire' is an example of meaningless roughness, but in the line

> It was no dream; I lay broad waking,

from 'They flee from me that sometime did me seek' [XXXVII] there
is a deliberate irregularity of rhythm. The strong stresses on *láy broád
wáking* create a profound feeling of wonder. It is because this subtle type
of metrical irregularity has been confused with experimental clumsiness
that Wyatt has sometimes been under-estimated. This confusion is the
easier because in most poets (in Shakespeare, for instance) the line of
development is from an obvious regularity to a more subtle irregularity: the transition from a gross to a refined irregularity is less easy to
detect.

In speaking of foreign literatures I shall mention only the immediate influences. What the song-books of the first years of the sixteenth
century, from which he got his lyric tradition, owed to French or to
mediæval Latin verse lies outside the scope of these remarks.

The most powerful foreign influence Wyatt underwent was the
Italian. Further, it is likely that what really stimulated him was less the
specific example of Petrarch than the vigorous belief current in Italy
when he visited it, and to a lesser degree in France too, that it was an act
of patriotism as well as a desirable accomplishment in a courtier, to
write verse in one's native tongue. It was a belief that inspired Ariosto,
the Pléiade and Spenser, and that it was a ruling principle of Wyatt's
experiments can be guessed from the way his contemporaries praised
him. Leland, the King's Antiquary, himself famous for his Latin verses,
wrote in his elegies on Wyatt's death:

> Anglica lingua fuit rudis et sine nomine rhythmus;
> Nunc limam agnoscit, docte Viate, tuam—[1]

and again

> Nobilitas didicit te praeceptore Britanna
> Carmina per varios scribere posse modos.[2]

[1] See No. 2f.
[2] See No. 2g.

Surrey, in his fine elegy beginning 'Wyatt resteth here' speaks of Wyatt's 'lively brain',

> . . . where that some work of fame
> Was daily wrought *to turn to Britain's gain*.[1]

If it was patriotic to write well in the English tongue, it was doubly patriotic to write in an Italian or French form, to show that an English poet could compete with the foreigner on his own ground. Hence the injudicious admiration of Wyatt's contemporaries for the sonnets and the Penitential Psalms. By the sonnets he matched himself with Petrarch and his imitators, by the Psalms with Marot and Aretino.

But whatever was Wyatt's motive for imitating the Italians, and even though their example is most clearly seen in some of his worst poems, he benefited by his contact with Italy. It was probably the stimulus he felt from that contact, the impulse to take literature seriously, to take pains (even with a trifle) that enabled him to transform a trivial lyric tradition into something more vital.

Of the Italian poets it was Petrarch whom Wyatt copied most freely. From Petrarch he derived the sonnet and certain conventional sentiments, which, once introduced into English love poetry, formed its staple subject-matter, with certain interruptions and revolts, for about a century and a half. Despair, not fruition, is the lot of the Petrarchian lover: 'Fair is my love and cruel as she's fair' is his burden. It is a mistake, however, to see Petrarch in every phrase uttered by the despairing lover. Petrarch developed the mediæval *amour courtois*, which had been expressed in English verse on and off for two centuries before Wyatt wrote and of which Chaucer could supply him with examples:

> Your yen two wol slee me sodenly,
> I may the beaute of hem not sustene.

Whatever the novelty and importance of Petrarch's sonnets, the Petrarchian themes, so eagerly seized on in the sixteenth century, soon became stale; and Wyatt's making use of them has no bearing on his worth as a poet. Nevertheless there is one important implication in his Petrarchising: to Petrarchise was the fashion of the cultured, and by adopting the fashion Wyatt implied that he was acquainted with the humanistic ideas of the Renaissance.

Other Italian models were Serafino, Alamanni and Pietro Aretino. From Serafino he derived a second impulse to write conceitedly and the

---

[1] See No. 3d.

ottava rima, his second metrical importation, used in the epigrams. From Alamanni he derived the *terza rima* and used it in his Satires; from Aretino's prose Penitential Psalms he derived his own version of the Psalms.

Wyatt undoubtedly knew the poems of his French contemporaries, Marot and Mellin de Saint-Gelais, as he adapted half a dozen of their poems. He wrote rondeaus, a French form, and he may have been encouraged by his French contemporaries to try to trifle gracefully and to use a refrain frequently and now and again an elaborate stanza form.

There is little classical influence. The only classical poet to whom Wyatt owed anything appreciable was Horace. He is indebted to Horace in his Second and Third Satires, and in one or two of his lyrics he seems to have had odes of Horace in his mind. Sir Arthur Quiller-Couch compares Wyatt's 'They flee from me' [XXXVII] with 'Vixi puellis nuper idoneus' and puts it at the head of English imitations of Horace. In 'My lute awake!' [LXVI] one is reminded of *Odes*, I, 25. Another poem where the debt to Horace may be detected is that strange but beautiful lyric beginning 'What rage is this?' [CI]. The sentiment is Petrarchian, but I cannot help thinking that Wyatt is here searching for an English metrical equivalent of Horace's sapphics:

> What rage is this? What furour of what kind?
> What power, what plague doth weary thus my mind?
> Within my bones to rankle is assigned
> What poison, pleasant sweet?

Wyatt's manuscript corrections confirm what should be obvious, namely that this poem was very carefully executed. In every verse the last syllable of the fourth, unrhymed, line is made phonetically as different as possible from the rhyme-word of the three preceding lines, with the result that it creates an arresting contrast, Wyatt was, I believe, attempting to create a contrast similar to that existing between the fourth and the first three lines of a Sapphic stanza.

(c) In neither the rondeau, the sonnet, nor the eight-lined epigram was Wyatt really at home: he wrote in these forms as a schoolboy hammers out elegiacs or alcaics. The rondeau, a difficult form, requires an exquisite and artful ease; the English sonnet must be monumental ('A sonnet is a moment's monument', says Rossetti); and the epigram must be both polished and pointed. Wyatt's rondeaus are anything but exquisite and easy: the intolerable metrical jolt that he had inherited from Barclay and Pynson's Chaucer makes them grotesque and uncouth. There is something really ludicrous in hearing Petrarch's genteel conceits 'run like a brewer's cart upon the stones, hobbling'. Speaking of his heart Wyatt opens a rondeau thus:

> Help me to seek, for I lost it there;
> And if that ye have found it, ye that be here,
> And seek to convey it secretly,
> Handle it soft and tenderly;
> Or else it will plain and then appear.
> But rather restore it mannerly,
> Since that I do ask it thus honestly,
> For to lose it it sitteth me too near.
> Help me to seek. [XVII]

The poem should have been a finished trifle, but a pupil in the art of walking a tight-rope, fearing every moment that he will fall, cannot be expected to achieve the easy smile of the adept. Only once in the rondeaus does Wyatt leave off writing English verses and create poetry, namely in the last lines of 'What no, perdie!' [XLV]. Addressing his false love he says:

> Though that with pain I do procure
> For to forget that once was pure,
> Within my heart shall still that thing,
> Unstable unsure and wavering,
> Be in my mind without recure?
> What no, perdie!

Like the rondeaus, the sonnets are experimental, but they extend over a longer period of time and ultimately approach nearer perfection. Wyatt did, in fact, write one or two tolerable sonnets. Technically, he almost invented the Shakespearean form. His 'Such is the course' [CCL] consists of three quatrains and a couplet, agreeing with the Shakespearean form except for there being allowed but two rhyme-sounds in the first twelve lines. All Surrey did more was to write some of his sonnets with the full Shakespearean liberty of rhyme. The credit of evolving the Shakespearean form is thus almost entirely due to Wyatt. Of the thirty-one sonnets, twenty may be criticized in the same way as the rondeaus. They are early works, laboriously experimental, often very rough, interspersed with an occasional line of poetry. Wyatt seems, and very tactfully, to have chosen the most conceited sonnets of Petrarch to imitate. Here is an example of what Wyatt at his worst can make of a Petrarchian conceit. He is addressing Love, the god, and writes:

What webs he hath wrought well he perceiveth;
Whereby with himself on love he plaineth,
That spurreth with fire and bridilleth with ice.
Thus is it in such extremity brought,
In frozen though now, and now it standeth in flame.   [XXIX]

The best, as well as the best known, of the immature sonnets is 'My galley charged with forgetfulness' [XXVIII], which, though crude in part, contains some poetry and in particular the line

The stars be hid that led me to this pain.

Occasionally too we get lines that might come from the early sonnets of Shakespeare, for instance:

But armed sighs my way do stop anon
Twixt hope and dread lacking my liberty,   [LVI]

or

And yours the loss and mine the deadly pain.   [XII]

How laborious was the progress from metrical disorder to order may be seen from the curious sonnet, 'I abide and abide' [CCXXVII], in which Wyatt indulges with obvious glee in the old, bad, Skeltonic rattle.

I abide and abide and tarry the tide,
And with abiding speed well ye may!
Thus do I abide I wot alway
Nother obtaining nor yet denied.

It shows us Wyatt playing truant from the hard school in which he had set himself to learn, and is a far better poem than any of the early sonnets, for it has life and they have not. And then, perhaps after an interval of years, Wyatt surprises us by showing that he has learnt his lesson, that he can write a sonnet in a recognizable rhythm and intelligently constructed. Once having learnt his lesson, he appears to write few more sonnets, and those few, though never without merit, show little sign of being his natural expression. A sonnet to please must be either exquisite or grand. Wyatt could at times be exquisite in the lyric measures of which he was a master, but the effort of writing sonnets was always too great to allow exquisiteness. Of grandeur he was never a master: he can be powerful or poignant, but not grand. The sonnet was not his proper medium.

The epigrams are poems of eight, very rarely of seven, lines, those of eight being in *ottava rima*. Most of them are trifles addressed to some lady. Wyatt writes, for instance, that his cruel mistress imagining her embroidery to be his heart, takes delight in stabbing it with her needle. Seeking pardon for having stolen a kiss, he reminds her that her revenge is easy: she has but to kiss him again to hale his heart clean from his breast and kill him. Wyatt is supposed to have composed epigrams of this sort during the years he was at court, and to have made something of a reputation by writing them. If this be true, we can only conclude that for lack of better the court of Henry VIII was easily pleased. The courtly epigrams are not in general as rough in rhythm as the early sonnets, but they lack the necessary elegance. Wyatt makes a poor show when he competes with Austin Dobson. Again we get isolated patches of felicity. In the epigram

> From these high hills as when a spring doth fall,
> It trilleth down with still and subtle course,   [XCV]

the second line has a surprising and seemingly unpremeditated beauty about it. This poetical surprise, which often appears in the songs, is one of the chief delights in Wyatt's poetry.

But not all the epigrams are courtly trifles. Nothing is plainer than that Wyatt had a serious disposition and that the mood to trifle was but fitful. Several of the epigrams are thoughtful, sometimes moral, in tone and translate his own experiences and feelings into earnest verse. 'Tagus, farewell' [XCIV] is an eloquent expression of his eagerness to see home; 'Within my breast' [CCXLVII] is a sincere and sober state-ment of his love of truth and hatred of crooked ways; 'Lux, my fair falcon' [CCXLI] is a bitter complaint of the faithlessness of his friends, presumably before his last imprisonment, and contains the fine ending

> But ye my birds, I swear by all your bells,
> Ye be my friends and so be but few else;

'Sighs are my food' [CCXLIV] is a passionate cry of pain from his prison. The last is also an excellent example of expressive and inten-tional irregularity of metre. We could ill spare these personal epigrams.

Not all Wyatt's songs are good. Some of those written in the heavier measures are uncouth; some are dull and flat. But in most, at least a spark of fire is evident, and the positively good are sufficient in number to be treated as representative of what Wyatt was really fit for, not as mere exceptions. What follows is meant to apply to the better songs alone.

'The deeper accents of emotion, with much else that is of the soul of literature,' says Sir E. K. Chambers, 'come back with Wyatt'. These words state an essential truth about Wyatt: there are few of his better poems that do not convince us that we are listening to the words of an eager passionate man. Even when he is trivial he is emphatic; his triviality is that of a serious man who thinks it worth while to trifle well, not of one whose levity is constitutional. Take, for instance, the first two lines of the first poem of this anthology, one of the less serious poems picturing the lover who has doubt of the good faith of his mistress:

> It may be good, like it who list,
> But I do doubt; who can me blame?

This is not great or very serious art, but there is matter in it and as much seriousness as is in place. The poet might so easily have surrendered himself to making his theme the excuse for a pretty tune; but he means what he says, he has grappled with his subject, has made his subject the real theme of, not the excuse for, his rhythm. The broken movement of the lines, the natural emphasis on the words *may* and *doubt*, carry conviction. The doubting lover has for the moment lived in the poet's imagination. Or take a more exquisite and more trivial poem:

> With serving still
> This have I won,
> For my goodwill
> To be undone.
>
> And for redress
> Of all my pain,
> Disdainfulness
> I have again;
>
> And for reward
> Of all my smart,
> Lo, thus unheard
> I must depart!
>
> Therefore all ye
> That after shall
> By fortune be,
> As I am, thrall,
>
> Example take
> What I have won,
> Thus for her sake
> To be undone!   [CLXXIV]

The subject of this is not serious: the imagined lover is not dangerously in love; there is no hint of a 'wonder and a wild desire'. Yet how vividly the poet has imagined the situation! The lover, snubbed and left alone by his saucy mistress, soliloquizes indignantly. The emphasis on THIS *have I won*, on *disdainfulness* occupying the whole of a line, on THUS *for her sake*, makes us feel that a real lover is speaking just after the girl has bounced out of the room. The essence of the poem is drama not a Petrarchian convention.

But Wyatt can be more serious without losing his power of being vivid and dramatic. In 'Madame, withouten many words' [XXXIV] the lover's plea, though short, is earnest and eloquent. More moving but still dramatic are the love-litany of 'Forget not yet' [CCIII], and the delicately passionate pleading of 'And wilt thou leave me thus?' [CLXXXVI]. Equally strong passion is found in his songs of farewell to a faithless mistress, 'Spite hath no power' [CCXIX], 'My lute awake!' [CCV], 'Blame not my lute' [LXXI] and 'In eternum'.

> Farewell, unknown, for though thou break
>   My strings in spite with great disdain,
> Yet I have found out for thy sake
>   Strings for to string my lute again.
> And if perchance this silly rhyme
> Do make thee blush at any time,
>   Blame not my lute.   [CCV]

And again (from 'My lute awake!'):

> Vengeance shall fall on thy disdain
> That makest but game on earnest pain;
>   Think not alone under the sun
> Unquit to cause thy lovers plain,
>   Although my lute and I have done.
>
> Perchance thee lie withered and old
> The winter nights that are so cold,
>   Plaining in vain unto the moon;
> Thy wishes then dare not be told;
>   Care then who list, for I have done.   [LXVI]

In these two verses Wyatt rises to a height of passion that he never quite reaches again.

In illustrating the 'deeper accents of emotion' I have called attention to the touch of drama, not only because of its intrinsic importance, but because it marks Wyatt off from most writers of love lyrics and espe-

cially from those of the Middle Ages. Critics are wrong when they
state that Wyatt introduced the personal note into the English lyric, for
it is plainly present in the mediæval lyric also.

> Foweles in the frith,
> And fisses in the flod.
> And I mon waxe wod;
> Mulch sorwe I walke with
> For best of bon and blood:

this cannot be called impersonal, nor can

> Icham for wowing al forwake,
> Wery so water in wore;
> Lest eny reve me my make
> Ichabbe y-yerned yore:

nor

> She hath left me here alone,
> All alone, as unknown,
> Who sometime did me lead with herself,
> And me loved as her own.

It is not the personal but the dramatic element that marks the passages I have quoted from Wyatt off from these. Somehow the receptive
faculties of Wyatt's consciousness are more numerous and more varied:
he is alive to more diverse impressions and more impressions simul-
taneously. The poem from which the last quotation was taken, 'As ye
came from the holy land of Walsingham', has a certain kind of beauty,
an unearthliness, that it would be difficult to parallel; it is a poem that
could very ill be spared: but it is confined; the spirit, if prisoned long in
the atmosphere of that poem, would languish. There is absent the lively
contact of mind with mind. But in the best poems of Wyatt there is
freedom, movement, life.

Other writers of lyric, too, will offer the same contrast with Wyatt.
Take Surrey, for instance. In his best lyric, 'When raging love', the con-
struction, the masterly way in which the comparison is worked out,
excite our admiration; but there is no more drama, no more sense of the
here and now, than in most of the lyrics of Matthew Arnold. And the
vivid picture in 'O happy dames' of the lonely wife, who tells how

> I stand the bitter night
> In my window where I may see
> Before the winds how the clouds flee

is but the exception that proves the rule. Nor did the Elizabethans in general make their lyrics any more dramatic than Surrey did his. Exceptions spring to the mind at once, but they *are* exceptions. In general, the untrue love to whom adieu is bidden, the nymph whom the swain bids live with him and be his love, the lady in whose face there was a garden of roses and lilies, Laura with the rosy cheeks, and the rest of the company, are shadowy creatures addressed by equally shadowy lovers. All is beautiful, but remotely or vaguely circumstantiated. It was Donne who carried on the movement that Wyatt had begun, and let the Elizabethan drama he loved into the Elizabethan lyric he despised. I would not for a moment suggest a close comparison between Wyatt and Donne. The dramatic element appears in only a part of Wyatt's lyrics and it is rarely allowed to encroach on their fitness as songs: reality, the urgency of the present hour, possess most of Donne's love lyrics, none of which are suitable to sing. It would be better to say that Wyatt is often nearer to Donne than to Campion or Fletcher. Where Wyatt and Donne most resemble each other is in their power of emphasizing crucial words.

> Make me a mandrake, so I may groane here,
> Or a stone fountaine weeping out my yeare

says Donne in *Twicknam Garden*, with powerful emphasis on *groane* and *weeping*.

> But all is turned thorough my gentleness
> Into a strange fashion of forsaking

says Wyatt in 'They flee from me' [XXXVII], and succeeds in getting the stress on *strange* well enough.

But though the touch of drama may mark Wyatt off so clearly from his predecessors and contemporaries, it is not found everywhere in his best songs. More frequently it is the melody and the free and varied lyrical movement that holds us. In this Wyatt is the first of the Elizabethans. If any one of the songs illustrates the gift of melody best it is 'What should I say?' [CCXV]

> What should I say?
> Since faith is dead,
> And truth away
> From you is fled,
> Should I be led
> With doubleness?
> Nay, nay, mistress!

In the extracts quoted before, melody was there, but not so dominantly as in these lines, which look forward to such a masterpiece as 'Fain would I change that note'. Another song of great melodic beauty is 'All heavy minds' [LXXXIV]: these lines, for instance—

> Where is my thought?
>   Where wanders my desire?
> Where may the thing be sought
>   That I required?
>
> Light in the wind
>   Doth flee all my delight;
> Where truth and faithful mind
>   Are put to flight.
>
> Who shall me give
>   Feathered wings for to flee,
> The thing that doth me grieve
>   That I may see?

Here again it is the music we heed. There is indeed emotion present; but it is the poet's exultation in the rhythms he creates, or some nameless feeling expressible only by music, not the emotion that arises from the immediate intense preoccupation with an action. It is worth while to give more examples and from little-known songs, for Wyatt's power over the music of words has not been praised enough. Here is a beautiful beginning (suggesting a minor key), to the level of which the rest of the poem does not keep up;

> Now all of change
>   Must be my song,
>   And from my bond now must I break,
> Since she so strange
>   Unto my wrong
>   Doth stop her ears to hear me speak.
>
> Yet none doth know
>   As well as she
>   My grief which can have no restraint;
> That fain would follow
>   Now needs must flee
>   For fault of ear unto my plain. [CCXXVI]

Another beautiful beginning, whose quality is this time sustained to the end, is:

> What death is worse than this,
>   When my delight,
> My weal, my joy, my bliss,
>   Is from my sight?
>   Both day and night
> My life, alas, I miss.   [LXIII]

Often in generally mediocre lyrics passages of melodic beauty will occur, for instance:

> But fancy is so frail
>   And flitting still so fast,
> That faith may not prevail
>   To help me first nor last.
>
> For fancy at his lust
>   Doth rule all but by guess;
> Whereto should I then trust
>   In truth or stedfastness?   [XLIII]

and

> It lasteth not that stands by change:
> Fancy doth change; fortune is frail.   [CXCII]

The above passages are all well fitted to be set to music: others suggest that Wyatt had music in his mind when he wrote, as do so many of Campion's songs. The swiftness of

> Your looks so often cast,
>   Your eyes so friendly rolled,
> Your sight fixed so fast,
>   Always one to behold   [CXXXVII]

is peculiarly suggestive of a tune, as is

> My hope, alas, hath me abused,
>   And vain rejoicing hath me fed;
> Lust and joy have me refused,   [LXII]

where one can imagine the musical stress on *lust*. And the varied cadence of 'If in the world' [LXXXIX] suggests very plainly a shifting cadence of the music.

The quotations given illustrate sufficiently the variety of metre in which Wyatt wrote, and, more important, the variety of movement. If there is monotony in Wyatt's worst, there is variety in his best. Wyatt's songs vary between speed and slowness, between a staccato and a sustained rhythm, in a way that proves a high mastery of his medium. You cannot say that 'With serving still' [CLXXIV] and 'In eternum' are rhythmical tautology, or that the rattle of

> Perdie, I said it not,
>   Nor never thought to do:
> As well as I ye wot
>   I have no power thereto   [CLVIII]

remotely resembles the swell and fall of

> If with complaint the pain might be expresst
>   That inwardly doth cause me sigh and groan,
> Your hard heart and your cruel breast
> Should sigh and plain for my unrest;
>   And though it were of stone
> Yet should remorse cause it relent and moan.   [CCVIII]

The notion that Wyatt was a mere experimenter is by such lines as the last reduced to absurdity.

In several of the extracts quoted a peculiar quality of Wyatt's verse was evident: an extreme simplicity of language and an almost conversational cadence. Wordsworth might well have quoted some of Wyatt to illustrate his theory of poetic diction. And just as Pope can simply talk and at the same time produce impeccable couplets, so Wyatt will write words, simple and the least removed in their order from prose, which are charged with a delicate lyric fragrance.

> Can ye say nay
>   But you said
> That I alway
>   Should be obeyed?   [CCXV]

or

> Alas, my dear,
>   Have I deserved so,
> That no help may appear
>   Of all my woe?   [LXXXIV]

or

> She wept and wrung her hands withal;
>   The tears fell in my neck;
> She turned her face and let it fall;
>   Scarcely therewith could speak.
>   Alas the while!   [XXXVIII]

No one till Suckling can converse so easily in a lyric.

What gives a special vitality to some of Wyatt's poems is a certain unexpectedness. The very monotony of much of what he wrote gives anything out of the ordinary a peculiar force, enhancing the surprise of passages or poems already surprising in themselves. For instance, the lines quoted from 'My lute awake!' [LXVI] about his mistress, grown old, complaining to the moon on the cold winter nights (borrowed though the sentiment may be) startle like some rare flower among the ordinary daisies and buttercups of a meadow. We cannot help being struck, amid the conventional lamentations of the lover, by the simple realism of

> The clothes that on the bed do lie
> Always methink they lie awry,   [CLXXXIII]

or by the surprising novelty of rhythm in

> Process of time worketh such wonder
>   That water, which is of kind so soft,
> Doth pierce the marble stone asunder
>   By little drops falling from aloft.
>
> And yet an heart that seems so tender
>   Receiveth no drop of the stilling tears,
> That alway still cause me to render
>   The vain plaint that sounds not in her ears.   [LXXXII]

Gutta cavat lapidem; the sentiment is not startlingly original: but the rhythm—what a strange mixture of *The Vision of Piers the Plowman* and *Irish Melodies*! Of all Wyatt's poems the most surprising, as different from one another as from the rest of what he wrote, are 'They flee from me' [XXXVII] 'In eternum' [LXXI] and 'What rage is this?' [CI]. All three give one the feeling of having had their birth spontaneously in some unexplored region of Wyatt's brain. Even if sources were discovered (which they have not been), it is unlikely that they would do anything to explain the strangeness of these poems, which are simply another illustration of the habit poets have of writing the unexpected: *The Phœnix and the Turtle, Sir Eustace Grey, In the Garden at Swainston.*

Even a slight touch of feeling, of drama, of realism or of the strange in Wyatt's poems stirs us in a peculiar and even disproportionate way; and for the same reason that any kind of immature art has a peculiar

power. Any art which is in the stage of working out a technique is apt
to leave the emotions to take care of themselves, with the result that
when feeling does creep in, it is expressed with a purity and an absence
of self-consciousness impossible of attainment in more sophisticated
ages. The idea that art is primarily concerned with expressing feeling is
comparatively new. Longinus knew it, some critics of the eighteenth
century voiced it, but it was not generally accepted in England till after
Wordsworth's preface to *The Lyrical Ballads*. Be the idea true or not,
for the sake of artistic creation it had better never have been stressed;
for the simple reason that when artists think that art should primarily
express feeling they are inclined to force their own feelings unnaturally.
The makers of the Delphic Charioteer or of the Ludovisi Throne would
have been puzzled at the idea that they were expressing their feelings;
they thought they were making copies of nature: but deep feeling they
did express and in a singularly pure and unsentimental way. Similarly
Malory is first concerned with his story and his picture of chivalry; with
the result that the touches of feeling have an effect quite out of proportion to the feeling's apparent intensity.

And so it is with Wyatt. His professed object was to experiment
with the English tongue, to civilize it, to raise its powers to those of its
neighbours; but in experimenting he could not help expressing now and
again his own feelings. And this expression by its very unpremedi-
tatedness is more precious than its bulk or depth would appear to
warrant.

Wyatt's Satires have been overpraised as literature because of their
subject-matter. If we are interested in Wyatt we cannot but enjoy the
account he gives of his own life at home while he was banished from
court; but we need not therefore be persuaded that poetically the
account can compare with his best songs. The truth is that all three
Satires are experimental, written in a metre of which he was not master
and through which one feels he was struggling towards something—he
does not quite know what. They have many good points and contain
poetical and interesting passages, but as a whole they fail.

The Satires were probably written about the year 1536, after Wyatt
had been dismissed from the court and placed for a spell under the
supervision of his father at Allington Castle. Like a sensible man, he
made the best of his exile, praised the country and railed at the court,
till he was once more summoned to serve the King. There is no reason
to doubt either the sincerity of what he said or his pleasure in getting
back to the life he had just abused.

Haec ubi locutus faenerator Alfius,
  iam iam futurus rusticus,
Omnem redegit Idibus pecuniam,
  quaerit Kalendis ponere.

In the history of English literature Wyatt's Satires are important as the first example of *terza rima* in the language. He derived the metre from Alamanni, whose Tenth Satire he more or less translated into his own First Satire. I cannot agree with Wyatt's editor[1] that he uses the metre with any success. The essence of the metre is that the tercets should be kept mainly intact. An occasional run-on from one tercet to another may give a pleasing variety, but constantly to run on destroys the metre's character, tending to split it up into quatrains and isolated lines or groups. Wyatt constantly breaks the tercet, thus turning a strong, hard and severe measure into something incoherent and smudgy. When he is translating Alamanni at the beginning of the First Satire he sticks fairly closely to his metrical model, but even during this fairly close adherence he writes in a way that violates the metre's function.

> But true it is that I have always meant
> Less to esteem them than the common sort,
> Of outward things that judge in their intent
>
> Without regard what doth inward resort.
> I grant some time that of glory the fire
> Doth touch my heart; me list not to report
>
> Blame by honour and honour to desire.   [CV, 10–16]

Wyatt breaks up three tercets in these lines, which translate two unbroken tercets of the Italian original. After some forty lines of the First and in the other two Satires, Wyatt runs on very frequently and in fact seems to be trying to turn *terza rima* into a free, flowing measure. He is trying to do what Spenser in *Colin Clout* did with more success to the decasyllabic quatrain. But neither metre was destined to compete with the couplet as a metre with flow suppleness and impetus. It is, however, remarkable what impetus Wyatt *can* give to the metre for a few lines when he is really moved.

> Alas! my Poynz, how men do seek the best
> And find the worst, by error as they stray!
> And no marvail, when sight is so opprest

[1] A. K. Foxwell.

And blind the guide. Anon out of way
Goeth guide and all in seeking quiet life.
O wretched minds! there is no gold that may

Grant that ye seek, no war, no peace, no strife.
No, no, although thy head were hoopt with gold,
Sergeant with mace, hawbert, sword, nor knife

Cannot repulse the care that follow should.   [CVI, 70–9]

The quality of this passage depends entirely on the rhythm and not at
all on the rhymes (or at least not on the arrangement of the rhymes in
the scheme of the *terza rima*). Ignore the rhymes and you get a piece of
blank verse unequalled till the rise of Elizabethan drama. Such athletic
movement was only reached again from the side of monotonous regularity: Wyatt worked differently, stirring his uncouthness to life by
sheer force of feeling.

But there are few passages in the Satires so good. In general the
movement is halting, not free; we feel like saying not *sufflaminandus erat*
but the opposite, take the brakes off. The desire for movement is there,
but it is rarely fulfilled. Wyatt has, however, advanced on the early
sonnets. Certain licences, later abandoned, he does indeed allow himself. The second line of the First Satire, for instance, has only nine
syllables:

The cause why that homeward I me draw. [CV,2]

Such lines are frequent, but usually they can be fitted into the measure
easily and were doubtless written deliberately and not through mere
bungling. The line just quoted, with *cause* strongly, and *why* fairly
strongly, accented, runs tolerably. Sometimes even, a line, apparently
rough, will yield an expressive emphasis.

I cannot speak and look like a saint   [CV, 31]

is not promising at first reading, but read it

Í / cannót/ speák/ and loók/ like a saínt/

and you feel the man means what he says. Now out of the early sonnets
no amount of juggling will get harmony or an expressive emphasis;
but in the Satires Wyatt seems usually to know what he is at and to have
reached a marked stage beyond Hawes and Barclay.

Finally, it would be unfair to leave the Satires without mentioning
the air of unaffected self-expression that for all their faults lends them a
certain charm. It is impossible not to enjoy Wyatt's account of himself

'stalking' with his bow in frosty weather or sitting at his book when the weather is foul, telling us that he picked up the fable of the town mouse and the country mouse from his 'mother's maids when they did sew or spin', or thanking God he is in 'Kent and Christendom' with the heartiness of a 'Georgian' poet thanking God he is in the finest land in the world, the County of Sussex.

Miss Foxwell writes that 'the Psalms deserve more recognition. The Satires have been justly praised, but they are fine translations from a worthy model. The Psalms show more originality . . . they claim a higher, or at least as high a place, as the Satires'. And again: 'All the best qualities in Wiat are found in the Psalms: a wealth of language, vigorous and clear thought, rising to fine moral expression. . . . He touches at times the mystical vision which to Blake was the only domain of poetry and the only reality of life.'[1] With the best will to see good in Wyatt's verse, I can only disagree entirely. It is quite possible that the *Psalms* are an effusion of real piety. They were written after Wyatt's return from Spain, whence he sent his two letters of moral exhortation to his son. It seems likely that he frequently turned his thoughts to God in the last years of his life and perhaps felt penitent for his not altogether exemplary youth.[2] But piety does not necessarily cause poetry, and judged as poetry Wyatt's *Psalms* are academic exercises, penitential not merely in matter, but to those whose task it is to read them. The prologues are in heavy *ottava rima*, the actual psalms in *terza rima*, showing no improvement on that of the Satires. There is an occasional flicker of inspiration, as in the opening of the first prologue:

> Love to give law unto his subject hearts
> Stood in the eyes of Barsabe the bright;

but the general effect is dull and heavy. It cannot be said that Wyatt's last work shows any signs of a brilliant development cut off by early death.

The remarks in this section are intended to introduce the best of Wyatt's poems, not to perform the more ambitious task of giving an account of his character. To do that one would have to take into account all that remains of his prose and what we know of him from his contemporaries. But I would have it remembered that the best of Wyatt's

[1] Cp. pp. 116–18 above in which Foxwell gushes about the Psalms, and compares a passage from them to Blake's poetry.
[2] Tillyard does not explain how Wyatt, who died a natural and sudden death in 1542, should *know* that he was 'in the last years of his life'.

lyrics are glimpses into a character remarkable for depth and richness. The very fact that they are but glimpses helps to explain their power: there is so much behind them. Through them we are privileged to get an inkling of a nature whom, if he were living now, we should be eager and proud to know. We can never know him as his contemporaries did, and Surrey's epitaph on him, 'Wyatt resteth here', which commemorates him as a man rather than as a poet, can hardly fail to remain of criticism the most illuminating.

15. Extract from unsigned review of Tillyard's edition of Wyatt's poems

The Times Literary Supplement (19 September 1929), 709

Writers of histories of English literature and kindred works are obliged to take notice of Sir Thomas Wyatt. In the history of English poetry and of English prosody he must be assigned his very important place as a reformer and an adventurer. Students must learn about the anarchy into which rhythms and metres had fallen, and how first Wyatt and then Surrey, learning mainly from Italian and a little from French, took firm hold on the broken rhythms of the fifteenth century and sternly and rather laboriously imposed order. Wyatt's sonnets must be held up for view, because the strict and rigid form of the sonnet helped, as it has been said, almost automatically to produce order; and his rondeaus come in for a share of the same sort of attention. And Wyatt's work as a reformer of English verse is so interesting to watch in progress as well as so great in scope and so fruitful in result that no wonder what Mr. Tillyard calls his 'text-book glory' has diverted attention from his work as poet. In Mr. Tillyard's own book of Wyatt . . . it is the poetry that comes first. Says Mr. Tillyard:—

My choice of poems has been ruled by intrinsic merit rather than by historical importance. Few of the sonnets are included; and it may be remarked that for the sake of his reputation, Wyatt had better not have imported the sonnet into

England, for by so doing he purchased a text book glory at the price of advertising the class of poems that does his poetical powers least credit.

It is not clearly thought nor perfectly expressed; but it reminds one that Sir Arthur Quiller-Couch, an old lover of Wyatt's poetry and an old enemy of all sorts of pedantry, has a Chair of English Literature in the university where Mr. Tillyard is Reader in the same school. His comment as a whole is not so slapdash as the sentence quoted suggests. Indeed, he sometimes gets a voice of thin-lipped frigidity which makes him seem like a schoolmaster who has 'set' Wyatt as a 'subject' and is now correcting the papers; and one or two of his comments seem to be addressed to a class of elementary school children. But his book does well that which we believe it to be the first to do—offer a selection of the best of Wyatt's poetry to readers who like poetry and are not 'getting up' anything in particular. It is in their interest, also, that Mr. Tillyard has adopted modern spelling. Those who have read Wyatt before in Miss Foxwell's edition, which was the first to establish and reproduce the precise text, in many cases from Wyatt's own handwriting, will feel the modern spelling to be rather flat and meagre.

> At the threshold her sely fote did tripp,
> And ere she myght recover it again,
> The traytor Catt had caught her by the hipp—

That is much more thrilling than a silly foot and a mere traitor cat which caught her by a hip. Alteration into modern spelling also has its dangers. One of them is shown very clearly by the transcriber for the American anthology who in one line of a sonnet by Wyatt puts 'hour' where the 'owre' of the manuscript answers to 'remo' in the sonnet by Petrarch which Wyatt was Englishing, and means not 'hour' but 'oar'. Other dangers are pretty frequently exposed in Mr. Tillyard's generally careful modernization (one of several misprints, by the way, occurs in this same sonnet—'drowned in reason' for 'drowned is reason'). He is pretty often compelled to leave the old form, either for rhyme or metre; and sometimes he does not leave it, and sometimes he leaves it where his reason for doing so is not clear. He prints, for instance, again in this sonnet, 'a cloud of derk disdain', where 'dark' would do just as well; and—to go back to our traytor Catt—he prints 'sharp ears' where 'erys' would at least help a little to oil the wheels of the line. Still, there are bound to be slips in so delicate a task as this alteration of old spelling (and with it of old sounds) into modern; and it must be admitted that Wyatt, as printed in Foxwell, is more forbidding than

Wyatt as printed in Tillyard or in Hebel and Hudson.[1]

The reader of Mr. Tillyard's admirably chosen examples of Wyatt will almost wholly miss tasting for himself (though he will read about it in the Introduction) one feature of Wyatt which attracts some minds as strongly as it repels others. He will miss it also in some of the poems printed by the American editors because, in spite of knowing their Foxwell, they have chosen to go for their text to Tottel's Miscellany, the famous—but very dangerous—'Songes and Sonnettes.' In Tottel the ruggedness of Wyatt—and with the ruggedness went a very great deal else—was smoothed away by a hand or hands that were not Wyatt's; and the result is like a new machine-wrought thing compared with an old hand-wrought. The feature referred to is the mystery of Wyatt; and the mystery of Wyatt is simply whether he knew what he was doing or whether he did not. Let us take the octave of one of his sonnets as an example. As printed in Foxwell (except that, to save trouble, we too will put it into modern spelling) it goes:—

> I find no peace and all my war is done,
>   I fear and hope, I burn and freeze like ice,
>   I fly above the wind, yet can I not arise
> And nought I have and all the world I season.
> That loseth nor locketh holdeth me in prison,
>   And holdeth me not, yet can I scape nowise,
>   Nor letteth me live nor die at my devise;
> And yet of death it giveth me occasion.   [XXVI]

The first impression is that the poet does not know what he is doing. To get lines one and four and five and eight to rhyme, one must come down with a bang on the last syllable of 'season', and that means somehow cramming together the four words before it. In line five, in order to get the stress on the last syllable of 'prison' the poet must be allowed to make the third-persons-singular disyllables or trisyllables just as he pleases and without warning, and in the last line there must be a good deal of eliding in the last three words. Read the lines in the natural way and the only possible conclusion seems to be that the poet has no ear at all. But he wrote that third line:—'I fly above the wind, yet can I not arise'; and nothing so beautiful, so fundamentally one in word and meaning, could possibly have been written by accident; it is the work of a master. This is the mystery of Wyatt. At one moment he is the

[1] J. W. Hebel and H. H. Hudson were amongst the compilers of the anthology *Tudor Poetry and Prose* (New York, 1953).

equal of the greatest in his command of rhythm and metre; at another he seems to be laboriously counting syllables on his fingers—and getting them wrong sometimes—and at a third he is, like some of his predecessors, floundering about for a foothold on stresses that may happen anywhere in the bog. It is more than an academic question. The doubt interferes with the reader's enjoyment of the poetry. A well-known sonnet of Petrarch, which Surrey also translated, has in Wyatt's version this for its first line:—'The longe love that in my thought doeth harbar.'[IV] The modern reader earnestly wants to make 'longe' a single syllable worth (if the scansion may for convenience be reckoned in these terms) the long syllable of the first iamb and the short syllable of the second. But some believe that Wyatt meant the final letter to be sounded. And then again, if the rhymes are to go right, 'harbar' must be all by itself the final foot, and that means that Wyatt was counting syllables again, and 'longe' must be only the last syllable in the first foot. No wonder the editor of Tottel worked his mischief, and was afraid of recognizing, when he saw it, a stroke of metrical mastery. Mr. Tillyard worthily enjoys a great line in one of Wyatt's most beautiful poems: 'It was no dream; I lay broad waking.' Tottel funked it and made it: 'It was no dreame: for I lay broade awakyng.' But Wyatt was quite capable of trying the timorously correct higher than they could bear. There is one case in which even Mr. Tillyard may be accused by some of letting the poet's deliberate daring escape his notice:

> Sighs are my food, drink are my tears
> Clink of fetters such music would crave
> Stink and close air away my life wears;
> Innocency is all the hope I have.
> Rain, wind or weather I judge by mine ears.
> Malice assaulted that righteousness should have.
> Sure I am, Brian, this wound shall heal again,
> But yet, alas, the scar shall still remain. [CCXLIV]

Mr. Tillyard's comment is:—

The measure is plainly (and intentionally) mixed; the first three lines are anapaestic; the fourth iambic; the fifth anapaestic again; the last three iambic, of which the last of all is perfectly regular. The impression given is that of unbearable grief gradually mastered.

The poem is one of Wyatt's Epigrams, and in only one other of these short poems (a gay little riddle) does he use any measure except the iambic. Any triple foot, anapaestic or dactylic, has a tendency to suggest jauntiness and happiness rather than unbearable grief; and such sudden changes as Mr. Tillyard's reading of the poem would entail might seem to some unbearably lacking in the dignity of a proud man's sorrow. Wyatt was then, after years of labour, at the height of his poetic mastery, since the epigram was written during his imprisonment in 1541, the year before his death. Is it not possible that he stretched his mastery as far as ever it would go? In other words, is it not possible that there is no, so to speak, three-time in the poem at all? Then the first line would fall into four bars of four beats each 'sighs' and 'drink' filling each two beats and 'food' and 'tears' filling each a whole bar. If this could be granted, the rest of the poem falls pretty easily into four-time, especially when 'music' and 'air' are seen in the original spellings, 'musycke' and 'ayer.' The editor of Tottel evidently did not suspect anapaests, since he laboured to make every line scan in iambics. But it is true that he was a poor judge.

Some slight glance at the mystery of Wyatt will help the reader to the full enjoyment of the feast that Mr. Tillyard has spread before him, because it will draw attention to the deliberate, technical, as we should say now professional, labour by which this English gentleman, courtier and Ambassador worked a revolution in English poetry and—for the moment still more important—perfected the instrument for his own poetic genius. He went early to France; he spent much time in Italy. And from France and Italy he learned ideas for poetry and technical details about poetry. They, and all his labour on them, might have done him and England but little service but for two other very valuable elements—his own remarkable mind for one, and the English tradition of poetry for the other. Wyatt was a laborious worker at poetical technique—so much is plain whatever the solution of the mystery may be. But he was also a poet, a thinker and a man of unusual independence. Setting aside his more obvious exercises in verse and in translation, chips from the workshop which Mr. Tillyard is right to leave alone, Wyatt sad and sorry, Wyatt angry, Wyatt happy, Wyatt even rollicking, has had an extraordinary faculty for convincing his reader, that he means what he says. He came first, it is true, upon ideas, conceits, images and so forth, which have lost all their freshness and all but the air of being 'the right thing' before the poetry of the English Renaissance, wisely and generously gathered up by Mr. Hebel and Mr. Hudson, has run its course. But, as he finds his feet, Wyatt cares less and less to leave anything exactly as he finds it, and he will take an idea from one of his Italians or his French and make it anew and different for himself.

From these high hills as when a spring doth fall,
It trilleth down with still and subtle course;
Of this and that it gathers aye and shall,
Till it have just off flowed the stream and force;
Then at the foot it rageth over all;
So fareth love when he hath ta'en a source,
His rein is rage, resistance 'vaileth none;
The first eschew is remedy alone.   [XCV]

In Ariosto, from whom Wyatt took his idea, the stream peters out till a child and a woman can walk over it dryfoot. Wyatt had something else to say, and Mr. Tillyard's note helps the reader to see how aptly he says it.

16. C. S. Lewis on Wyatt

1954

C. S. Lewis, *English Literature in the Sixteenth Century Excluding Drama* (Oxford, 1954), pp. 222–30.

Lewis (1898–1963), noted for his distinguished contributions to English literary studies, theology and fiction, was eminent as a Fellow and Tutor of Magdalen College, Oxford, and ended his career as Professor of Medieval and Renaissance Studies at Cambridge.

The 'new company of courtly makers' who came up, says Puttenham, at 'the latter end' of Henry VIII's reign are usually, and rightly, taken to constitute a decisive novelty in the history of our literature. Yet they too had their precursors. During the later Middle Ages in England the lyric had suffered less than any other form. The tune of the shorter line, as anyone can see by comparing Lydgate's *Reason and Sensuality* with his *Troy Book*, had never been so completely lost as that of the deca-syllable; and in the lyric, which was nearly always written to be sung, it was still further supported and disciplined by the music. In the late fifteenth and early sixteenth centuries we were a very musical nation. The art flourished at the courts of Henry VI and Henry VIII, the names of Dunstable, Fairfax, and Cornish are still remembered by the his-torians of music, and Erasmus complimented us on our skill. Most, perhaps all, the lyric poetry of that age is to be regarded as words for music; hence purely literary judgement on it may be as unfair as the study-criticisms we make about plays we never saw acted.

The stanzas used by this poetry are mainly derived from those of rhyming Latin. The rhyme schemes are never very complex, the macaronic is often used, refrains are common. Short lines or (what is the same thing to the ear) lines with internal rhymes are favourites. The language is very plain. There is little aureation, few metaphors, no stylized syntax, and none of the sensuous imagery loved by the Eliza-bethans. One reason for this plainness is that we are reading songs; rich-ness and deliciousness would be supplied by the air and the lute and are therefore not wanted in the words. When they are read merely as poems it produces results which were probably unforeseen by the authors. It makes some pieces seem flat and dull; others, admirably fresh and ingenuous. But those which make dull poems need not have made dull songs. One that I had thought very dry and colourless came danc-ing into life as soon as a learned pupil (Mr. Norman Bradshaw) played me the air on his recorder.

The best specimens of early Tudor lyric have long since won their place in our anthologies. The 'Nut Brown Maid' may be a little too long, but it has no other fault. 'Who shall have my fair lady' is alive with chuckling gaiety. 'He bare him up he bare him down' contrives, in homeliest language, to sound like news from another world. 'My lady went to Canterbury' is among the best nonsense poems in the language. The quatrain 'Western Wind' need fear no rival in the Greek Anthology. There is almost everything in it—weather, distance, longing, passion, and sober home-felt reality. Many poets (not con-temptible) have said less in far longer pieces.

All that is best in Sir Thomas Wyatt (1503–42) is rooted in this poetry, such poetry as the song books have preserved. But he cannot be regarded simply as the last of the early Tudor lyrists. He modified the tradition by several new borrowings and added something of his own.

He is, for one thing, the first of our Italianate poets, though this element in his work may not have quite that importance which the older critics claimed for it. In the first place, to translate Petrarch was not necessarily to introduce a new note into English poetry; it depended on the poems you chose and on the quality of your rendering. Thus Wyatt's 'Myne olde dere enmy my froward maister' [VIII] is in fact a version of Petrarch's canzone *Quel antiquo mio dolce*; but the canzone (an erotic allegory in the *Rose* tradition) is so medieval, and Wyatt's version in stumbling rhyme royal is so like the rhyme royal of Hawes or Skelton, that if the original had been lost and Wyatt were not known to be the author, no one would dream of classifying the poem as anything but late medieval. It is not a bad poem, but it is written by a medieval Wyatt, who appears again in the poem 'Like as the bird' [CCXLVI] (which is bad) and in the translation from Boethius 'If thou wilt mighty be' [CCLXI], which is good though not very lucid. And some medieval habits hang about him elsewhere; tags like *without any fable* and *if Livy doth not lie*, and doggerel that reminds us of Heywood. And, secondly, even where the thing translated might be expected to impinge on English poetry as a novelty, the translation may be so bad that the impact is muffled: some of Wyatt's sonnets from the Italian are so. No later sonneteer could learn anything from lines like

> Yet this trust I have of full great aperaunce
> Since that decept is aye retourneable
> Of very force it is aggreable
> And therewithal be done the recompense.   [XVI]

The rhyme scheme may be that of the sonnet: the poetics are those of Barclay. To be sure, Wyatt wrote better sonnets than this: the gap between his worst and best in this kind shows both the difficulties he faced and the fine perseverance with which he overcame them. Witness the liquid movement of

> Vnstable dreme according to the place
> Be stedfast ons; or else at leist be true:
> By tasted sweetenes make me not to rue
> The sudden losse of thy false fayned grace.   [LXXIX]

But it is not in these rare anticipations of the Elizabethan sonnet that Wyatt's true importance lies. Knowledge of the Italians, both directly and through their French disciples, was to be so common in the Golden period that its poets had no need of such scanty help as Wyatt's sonnets could give them. The Elizabethan sonnet might not have been very different if Wyatt had never lived.

His real place in the evolution of English poetry (as distinct from his intrinsic value, his place of honour among English poets) is really an unfortunate one. His own lyric gift he did not bequeath to most of his successors; he did bequeath to them, by his worst poems, the terrible poulter's measure* and the flat, plodding style which almost inevitably goes with it. His 'Song of Iopas' [CIV] and 'Complaint of the Absence of his Love' [XCVIII]† proved a ruinous legacy. The latter, incidentally, shows how ambiguous the expression 'Italian influence' may be. It is a translation of Petrarch's *Si è debile il filo*; but not one drop, not one breath, of the Petrarchan quality has gone into it. The thudding verbiage of

> Thes new kyndes of plesurs wherein most men reioyse
> To me they do redowble still off stormye syghes the voyce,

raises a wonder why the man who thought Petrarch could be translated so, also thought Petrarch worth translating. Historically considered, Wyatt is not the father of the Golden, but of the Drab, Age.

His metre has lately become a controversial subject. A majority of his lines scan according to the principles which governed English verse from Spenser to the Edwardians: a fairly large minority do not. The regular lines occur chiefly, not exclusively, in his lyrics: the irregular, chiefly, not exclusively, in what look like decasyllabic poems. The older critics took it for granted that the irregular lines were due to the blundering of a prentice poet who had not yet learned how to scan. Some modern critics find in them extreme, and deliberate, subtleties of rhythm. One critic thinks that this holds for some of the irregular lines, but that others are mere blundering. In favour of the modern view is the fact that some of the irregular lines give great pleasure to our ear. Most of us like the reading of the Egerton MS.

> Into a straunge fasshion of forsaking   [XXXVII]

better than Tottel's

> Into a bitter fashion of forsaking.

This, I allow, favours the modern view; but everything else is against it. We have seen that Wyatt is often on a level with Barclay. We have seen that, at the other end of the scale, in his poulter's, he ticks out regular metre with the ruthless accuracy of a metronome. Both phases

---

* A couplet consisting of an Alexandrine followed by a Fourteener.
† Sometimes called 'In Spayne'.

are what we should expect in a man who was escaping from the late medieval swamp; first, his floundering, and then, after conversion, a painful regularity. That both extremes should be absent from his lyrics is again what we should expect, for the lyrical music had never been lost. It is immensely improbable *a priori* that the same man at one period of his career should have gone on, beyond the regularity, to the subtlest departures from it. It is immensely improbable that such departures could have had for him or for his contemporaries the beauty they have for a modern. To us the variation is beautiful because we hear it against the background of the imagined norm: when the norm itself was a novelty to Wyatt (and a mystery to most of his hearers) the particular beauty which we feel could hardly have existed. Nothing, it seems, could incline us to the modern view except our reluctance to believe that melody can come by chance; and I am not sure whether it is a rational reluctance. Fortunately the question, though important for our verdict on Wyatt, is of no importance for the general history of our poetry. Even if Wyatt had such a subtle scheme as has been supposed, the secret of it had been lost before Tottel printed him, and had no influence on later poets.

Wyatt's work as a translator or adapter was not confined to sonnets and epigrams. His longer attempts are of very unequal merit. The *Penitential Psalms* are based on a prose version by Pietro Aretino set in a narrative framework, with help from Ioannes Campensis and from Zwinglius. The pictures of David entering the cave and of the sunbeam falling upon him are striking. The two opening lines of the Prologue,

> Love to gyue law vnto his subiect hertes
> Stode in the iyes of Barsabe the bryght,   [CVIII, 1–2]

show Wyatt in one of his rare Elizabethan moments. But the work as a whole is flat and sometimes cacophonous. Much better are the *Satires* based on Horace and Alamanni. From the latter he borrows *terza rima*. The excessive enjambment between the tercets which makes Wyatt's satires read almost like blank verse is not wholly due to the original; by comparing Alamanni's tenth satire with Wyatt's second we find that Alamanni has thirty-four stopped tercets out of a total of thirty-six, Wyatt twenty-four out of a total of thirty-four. It is more an imitation (in the eighteenth-century manner) than a version: as Juvenal's *graeculus esuriens* became Johnson's 'fasting monsieur', so Alamanni's *Provenza* becomes Wyatt's 'Kent'. Alamanni mentions winter to exult in the fact that, being now no courtier, he need not go out *quando agghiaccia e piove*; Wyatt sees in winter a chance of going out with a bow. The whole thing has a pleasantly English, country-house, atmosphere and reads like an original [CV]. The foreign model has here been thoroughly assimilated. In another piece the story of the town and country mouse is told with considerable spirit [CVI].

But Wyatt's permanent value is to be found in his lyrics. They are not, except in a very few places, precursors of the Elizabethan lyric. A single line such as 'The erth hath wept to here my heavines' [XXII] or a whole poem like 'The answer that ye made to me my dere' [XC] may look forward; but essentially Wyatt is doing work of a different kind. His language is usually as plain as that of his English lyric predecessors; to a taste formed on the decorated tradition which runs through English poetry from Spenser to Tennyson it may even sound sub-poetical. The point can be brought out by comparing his refrains with those of other poets. From others we get refrains like Αἴλινον αἴλινον εἰπέ, τὸ δ'εὖ νικάτω,* and *cras amet qui numquam amavit quique amavit cras amet†* and *Mais où sont les neiges d'antan?* or 'Sweet Thames run softly till I end my song', or 'Put on perfection and a woman's name', or 'With hey-ho, the wind and the rain'. But Wyatt makes refrains out of words like 'Ye old mule', 'Spite of thy hap, hap hath well happ'd', 'Disdain me not', 'Therefore take heed', 'It is impossible'. Clearly, we are not dealing with an incantatory or evocative poet. We are in fact dealing with a Drab poet—provided we remember always that 'Drab' is not a pejorative term. All Wyatt's weaknesses, and nearly all his strength, are connected with his unadorned style. When he is bad, he is flat, or even null. And when he is good he is hardly one of the irresistible poets. He has no splendours that dazzle you and no enchantments that disarm criticism. It is almost as though he said 'If you don't want to like me, you need not'. In order to appreciate Wyatt you must read with great attention and do your fair share of the work. He is not necessarily the worse on that account.

Here is a specimen of what I take to be bad Wyatt (though not Wyatt at his absolute worst)

> For cause yourself do wink
>   Ye iudge all other blinde;
> And secret it you think
>   Which euery man doth finde.
> In wast oft spend ye winde

* 'Say alas alas, but let the good prevail.'
† 'Let him love tomorrow who never loved, and let him who loved love tomorrow.'

> Yourself in loue to quit;
> For agues of that kinde
> Will show who hath the fit.   [CXXXVII]

The thought and emotion are those of the dreariest wrangle, and the expression differs from that of prose only by being a little less flexible and lively. Compare with this,

> I promiside you
> And you promisid me,
> To be as true
> As I wolde bee.   [CCXV]

It is, in one way, divided only by a hair's breadth from the previous example. It is no more adorned and certainly no more elevated. But the creaking inversions are gone; the rhythm exactly underlines an intonation that would occur in real speech; and yet the rhythm pleases. It is characteristic of Wyatt that his bad pieces are very like his worst. He is a miniaturist; one false stroke mars the work.

It is possible to cull from Wyatt, as from other poets, phrases or lines which remain beautiful when torn from their context. Dr. Tillyard has analysed with great accuracy the various ways in which the stanza 'Perchance thee lie withered and old' [LXVI] surpasses its Horatian counterpart (I do not say its Horatian original, for that would be hard to prove). Everyone remembers 'With naked fote stalking in my chambre' [XXXVII] and

> for sodenly me thowght
> My hart was torne owte of hys place.   [CXCIII]

and again

> But yet, alas, that loke all sowle
> That I do clayme of right to haue.   [XCIII]

But such things do not necessarily come in the best pieces; it is not on them that Wyatt's success depends. It depends much more on the degree to which he has been able to give a whole poem a shape. His danger is that of being unprogressive, of writing poems that stop rather than end, poems that do not carry in themselves the reason for their length or for the order in which the stanzas come. Such are 'Farewell the heart' [XI] (or *rayn*) and 'I see that chance' [CCLVI]. Each stanza might occur in a good lyric, but you cannot make a poem by simply stringing half a dozen such stanzas together. I think Wyatt himself was aware of the problem. In 'Marvel no more' [LII] he seems to have realized by the end of the third stanza that something must be done to make a capital for the column he was building and to have attempted to supply it by some verbal wit on the word 'chance'. In 'Disdain me not' [CCLXVI] the return to the original refrain in the last stanza was probably made for the same reason. But these are his unsuccessful pieces. In 'My Lute Awake' [LXVI] the whole poem is, as it were, an ending, but it turns from this into another idea at the fifth stanza and then resumes the main theme with an air of great finality in the eighth. 'Perdie, I said it not' [CLVIII] similarly offers a new twist (a counter-attack) in the fifth, and after it a real conclusion. 'What rage is this' [CI], in a stanza admirably suited to the purpose, hurls line after line at us in a sullen monotony of passion for four stanzas and then rises to a curse. *In eternum* [LXXI] is subtler. The refrain is given a slightly different meaning at each repetition. The last two lines do not in my opinion mean that he has found a new mistress. They mean that another thought, the thought of eternity, now occupies him; he is doing his palinode, 'Leave me, oh love that reachest but to dust.'

Except for the form of the rondeau (and he did not make much of that) Wyatt's debt to French poetry is small. If one tried to reduce his lyrics under a recipe, one would have to say 'Petrarchan attitudes expressed in the traditional form of the Tudor lyric'. But this would be most misleading. In a sense the Petrarchan matter is all there, the ice and fire, the implacable beauty. But when Wyatt handles them they all become different. Nothing could be more alien to him than the devout *Frauendienst*, and the drugged or tranced melancholy of the *Rime*. (Readers who do not know Italian will, by the way, learn much more of that strange, great work from Synge's prose version than from all the Elizabethans and all the Pléiade put together.) His poems are full of resentment. Except in one short, pleasant trifle about fingers [LXXXVI], he does not praise ladies. He never goes out of himself: how badly his mistress has treated him, how well he deserves to be treated, how much more fortunate he has been with other women, how sorry she will be some day—such are his recurrent themes. Hence when we read him in bulk, some of us find in him an atmosphere which is from the first oppressive and finally suffocating. Poor Wyatt seems to be always in love with women he dislikes. My sympathy deserts my own sex: I feel how very disagreeable it must be for a woman to have a lover like Wyatt. But I know this reaction to be unjust; it comes from using the songs as they were not meant to be used. Look at them again:

My days decaies, my grefe doeth gro
The cause thereof is in this place. [CCIX]

This was not intended to be read. It has little meaning until it is sung in a room with many ladies present. The whole scene comes before us. The poet did not write for those who would sit down to *The Poetical Works of Wyatt*. We are having a little music after supper. In that atmosphere all the confessional or autobiographical tone of the songs falls away; and all the cumulative effect too. The song is still passionate: but the passion is distanced and generalized by being sung. We may hear another of Sir Thomas's inventions another night; but we are not going to have ten or twenty on end. Each will be judged by itself; they will never build up into the composite picture which the modern student gets from the printed page. So taken, his best pieces are very remarkable work indeed. They reach an intensity, and sometimes a dramatic quality which the English lyric had hardly even attempted before. And they do this with great economy, never going beyond the resources of Drab poetry, using little sensuous imagery and no poetic diction. For those who like their poetry lean and sinewy and a little sad, he is a capital poet. His fame is in the ascendant.

Bibliography

There have been no books or articles focused on criticism of Wyatt, but readers might find the following of use in determining extremes of recent criticism of him.

MASON, H. A., *Humanism and the Early Tudor Court* (1959).

SMITH, HALLETT, 'The Art of Sir Thomas Wyatt', *Huntington Library Quarterly* IX (1946), pp. 323–55.

Index

The index is divided into three sections. I. General Index, listing only works of literature and criticism; biographical matter is omitted. (For example, Henry VIII is listed as a poet but not as king.) Major criticism of Wyatt appears in bold print, minor in italic, and general references in roman. II. Discussions of Wyatt's works. Since references to Wyatt's works appear on almost every page, only major references to the various categories of his works are given. III. Comparisons of Wyatt with other authors.

I. GENERAL INDEX

II. DISCUSSIONS OF MAJOR GROUPS OF WYATT'S WORKS

III. COMPARISONS WITH WYATT

THE CRITICAL HERITAGE SERIES

GENERAL EDITOR: B. C. SOUTHAM

Volumes published and forthcoming

Continued